CONTEXTS

Series Editor:

Steven Matthews
Oxford Brookes University, UK

Other titles in the series

RENAISSANCE DRAMA

ANDREW McRAE

School of English, University of Exeter, UK

A member of the Hodder Headline Group
LONDON
Distributed in the United States of America by
Oxford University Press Inc., New York

For my students

First published in Great Britain in 2003 by
Arnold, a member of the Hodder Headline Group,
338 Euston Road, London NW1 3BH

http://www.arnoldpublishers.com

Distributed in the United States of America by
Oxford University Press Inc.,
198 Madison Avenue, New York, NY10016

The advice and information in this book are believed to be true and
accurate at the date of going to press, but neither the author nor the publisher
can accept any legal responsibility or liability for any errors or omissions.

British Library Cataloguing in Publication Data
A catalogue record for this book is available from the British Library

Library of Congress Cataloging-in-Publication Data
A catalog record for this book is available from the Library of Congress

ISBN 0 340 76346 9 (hb)
ISBN 0 340 76347 7 (pb)

1 2 3 4 5 6 7 8 9 10

Typeset in 10 on 13 pt Sabon by Phoenix Photosetting, Chatham, Kent
Printed and bound in Great Britain by MPG Books Ltd, Bodmin, Cornwall

What do you think about this book? Or any other Arnold title?
Please send your comments to feedback.arnold@hodder.co.uk

Contents

Series editor's preface

The plural in the title of this series, *Contexts*, is intentional. Literature, while it emerges from, and responds to, historical, social and cultural moments, also to a large extent establishes its own contexts, through the particular inflection it puts upon its ostensible 'materials', themes, and preoccupations. Therefore, rather than offering a traditional 'major works/ historical background' parallel discussion, each *Contexts* volume takes its instigation from the ways in which literary texts have defined their areas of reference, and in which they are in active dialogue with key cultural ideas and events of their time. What aspects of a period most concerned writers? What effect upon literary form have various social and cultural trends had? How have different texts responded to single historical events? How do different texts, ultimately, 'speak back' to their period?

Historical background is made readily available in each volume, but is always closely integrated within discussion of literary texts. As such, the narrative woven around each literary historical period in the individual volumes follows no uniform pattern, but reflects their particular authors' sense of the ways in which the contexts of their period establish themselves – generically, thematically, or involving debates about language, gender, religion or social change, for example. While each volume provides detailed discussion of its period's most studied literary works, it also asks informed questions about the canon and periodization itself. Each volume also contains a timeline, full bibliography, and several contemporary literary, cultural, or historical documents which provide material for further reflection and discussion.

Steven Matthews

Acknowledgements

Writing this book has given me the opportunity to review my experiences of teaching Renaissance drama at four different universities over the past 10 years. Throughout that period, I have confronted the challenge of bringing to the classroom truly interdisciplinary approaches. Colleagues at all those universities have helped me to refine those approaches: through agreement and disagreement, suggestions and debate. From the University of Sydney, I am grateful especially to Tony Miller and G. A. Wilkes; from the University of New South Wales, Mary Chan; from the University of Leeds, Martin Butler and Paul Hammond; and at the University of Exeter, Karen Edwards, Nick McDowell and Philip Schwyzer. I am also grateful to the many excellent students I have had the good fortune to teach over these years, and for the countless seminar discussions that have prompted me to rethink my ideas about particular texts.

Throughout the period of writing (which was condensed into rather less than 10 years) I have incurred further debts. I owe thanks to my Renaissance colleagues at Exeter, and also to the series editor, Steven Matthews, who all read the manuscript and offered useful comments. Domestically, I am grateful to Karen Edwards and Anthony Fothergill, who each provided generous hospitality at an unstable time. From afar, my mother was a constant source of support. And Jane Whittle – a real historian – did her spectacular best to keep me relatively sane.

Andrew McRae

A note on texts

Renaissance plays survive in a variety of different forms, and as a result the texts we read can vary considerably from one edition to another. In this book, I have chosen to quote, where possible, from two reliable volumes which will often be used by students. All references to Shakespeare's plays are from *The Norton Shakespeare*, ed. Stephen Greenblatt *et al.* (New York and London, 1997). References to many plays by other authors are taken from *English Renaissance Drama: A Norton Anthology*, ed. David Bevington *et al.* (New York and London, 2002). To avoid cluttering the pages of the book, I have not footnoted the editions I have used for plays that are not published in either of these two anthologies. Instead, these are listed at the end, in the bibliography of dramatic texts.

There are seven extracts from non-dramatic texts, printed as 'Documents' at the end of the volume. I have selected one document to correspond with the concerns of each chapter, and in the course of the book I will discuss each piece at the appropriate time. It is hoped that readers will use the documents as a way of further exploring the cultural contexts of Renaissance drama.

In quotations from non-dramatic texts (in the 'Documents' section and also within the chapters), spelling and punctuation have been modernized.

Introduction

Renaissance drama in context

'Renaissance' means 'rebirth'. We use the term specifically to refer to the great cultural revival that was ignited in Italy in the fourteenth century, swept subsequently across the European continent, and transformed England in the sixteenth and seventeenth centuries. As the word suggests, in this period a range of artists and writers looked afresh at the cultural achievements of Greek and Roman civilization, and sought to revitalize their own cultures in the light of these classical models. But when we turn to study 'Renaissance drama', this narrative can be misleading, because it focuses attention exclusively on a sphere of high culture. In other words, it invites us to examine relationships between literary works produced at very different historical moments, and suggests that great writers are best studied in relation to a trans-historical canon of great writing. What we know as Renaissance drama, though, was also very much a product of its own time. It is embedded in a period that historians describe as 'early modern': a period between the medieval and modern eras, and therefore a period of considerable upheaval, as the outlines of the modern world began to take shape. And this was not merely a matter of tangible change – say, in the size of the population, or the wealth of the nation – but also a matter of shifts in attitudes and values. People at this time were reassessing pre-existent ideas about matters from politics to sexuality, religion to subjectivity.

Reading Renaissance drama in context involves being aware of these processes, which consistently inform the plays staged in English theatres. But it equally involves appreciating that historical developments that may seem relatively straightforward in retrospect were not necessarily so clear to people at the time. For example, while the Reformation of the sixteenth century radically transformed the English Church, the actual shape of Protestant religious practice and doctrine was a matter of constant dispute. Or, to take another example, by the end of the seventeenth century the structures of royal absolutism had disintegrated, and been replaced by a political system that would form the foundation of the modern English state. But in the early decades of the century, as the nation stumbled towards the pivotal civil wars of the 1640s, few people could even have imagined the revolutions ahead. Instead, what we find throughout the period are countless examples of people using the intellectual resources available to them, in an effort to make sense of their world. These people were often highly intelligent – and include some of the greatest minds of all time – but their ways of thinking and their ways of transferring their thoughts into language were markedly different from our own.

The Renaissance theatre was established within this context, and the plays performed at this time consistently engage with contemporary concerns. Importantly, this was a two-way process. Dramatists not only wrote about what they saw around them, they also offered their audiences new ways of understanding their circumstances. In this respect, as recent literary critics have argued, literature emerges as an 'agent in constructing a culture's sense of reality'.[1] It performs this function not necessarily by presenting coherent arguments, in the manner of a philosophical tract, but more by bringing into conflict on the stage a range of different attitudes and ideas. And it does so specifically through the use of language, which is so vital to the way in which any culture understands itself. In the Renaissance theatres, then, hundreds of new plays staged vital contemporary debates, as they represented characters in conflict and societies in turmoil. Crucially, they brought into conjunction different ideologies and discourses: that is, different structures of thought, and different ways of encoding thought in language. We might think, for example, of the way in which Juliet and her father clash so violently in *Romeo and Juliet*. Each has an utterly different attitude towards gender and sexuality, and each employs an entirely different language to express their attitudes.

As we will see in Chapter 1, the growth of Renaissance drama was dependent upon commercial innovations, as various entrepreneurs built theatres and employed playwrights and players. In this respect, the drama was bound to the city of London, which grew rapidly throughout the early modern period. The plays were written for London audiences – which were remarkably diverse in terms of gender and social degree – and many of them are explicitly concerned with the life of that city. While orthodox theories of social order were strictly hierarchical (as we shall see further in Chapter 4), plays might therefore examine tensions between different groups, and bring elite and popular perspectives into conjunction. We will also have cause to consider the other main cultural site in England: the court. In theory, the presence of the court was dependent on the whereabouts of the monarch; in practice, the English court was most commonly located just along the river from the city, at Whitehall. Some plays were written for performance at court, while many others are set at court and consider the experience and behaviour of courtiers and rulers. In Chapter 6 we will look closely at the significance of the court, and examine the ways in which court-based plays interrogate practices and discourses of power. Throughout the book, though, we will regularly have cause to consider the ways in which dramatists represent the experience of a social and political elite to a popular audience.

The period of Renaissance drama is relatively easy to define. Although we will occasionally explore some works from the middle decades of the sixteenth century, we will mainly focus on plays written for London's commercial theatres, which were first established at the end of the 1570s. The theatres flourished throughout the following decades, before being closed in 1642 by the new puritan government. Although some drama was performed throughout the 1640s and 1650s, and although the theatres were successfully reopened on the restoration of the monarchy in 1660, it is common to see 1642 as the end of a cultural era. Over a period of roughly 65 years, therefore, the body of plays we know as 'Renaissance drama' took shape. Obviously there were many important literary and historical developments and innovations throughout this period; however, in this book we will approach Renaissance drama thematically rather than chronologically. That is, we will mainly be concerned with analysing debates within the period, rather than trying to trace particular narratives of change across the period. This is not so much a linear narrative as an exploration of a complex culture and its remarkable texts.

The book's structure is determined by the most important issues and changes of these years, and as such it follows the many historicist critics who have investigated texts and their contexts in recent years. The first chapter will discuss the material and cultural conditions of the commercial theatres. The second chapter will consider the ways in which drama engages with debates concerning the very nature of human identity. The third chapter will turn to issues of desire and domestic life, working with a wealth of texts that stage struggles over questions of love and marriage. The fourth chapter will examine conflicting discourses of social order, and will look in particular at the cultural significance of London and the representation of those on the margins of society. The fifth chapter will examine issues of religion, which was such a fundamental aspect of life at this time, though also a cause of great controversy and conflict. The sixth chapter will focus on the court, as a way of investigating changing political ideas. And the seventh chapter will explore the ways in which dramatists engaged with debates over racial difference and colonialism, in an age of New World exploration and settlement. Throughout, a general discussion will be interspersed with more concentrated discussions of key plays, in a manner intended to illuminate both texts and contexts. Given the scope of the field, the discussion here could never be exhaustive or definitive; hopefully, however, it will be informative and stimulating.

Note

1   Jean E. Howard, 'The New Historicism in Renaissance Studies', *English Literary Renaissance*, 16 (1986), 25.

1

Playhouses and players: the conditions of Renaissance drama

On 31 October 1614, in London's Hope Theatre before the first performance of Ben Jonson's play *Bartholomew Fair*, the audience was read a contract. According to this mock-legal document, the spectators promise 'to remain in the places their money or friends have put them in, with patience, for the space of two hours and an half', while the author undertakes to present 'a new, sufficient play', which will be 'merry, and as full of noise as sport'. The document also grants the audience the right to judge the play:

> It is further agreed that every person here have his or their free will of censure, to like or dislike at their own charge, the author having now departed with his right. It shall be lawful for any man to judge his six-penn'orth, his twelvepenn'orth, so to his eighteenpence, two shillings, half a crown, to the value of his place, provided always his place get not above his wit. And if he pay for half a dozen, he may censure for all them too, so that he will undertake that they shall be silent.
>
> (Induction, ll. 77–82, 85–93)

The statement reflects on an institution which had been in existence less than 40 years. The public theatres of Renaissance England flourished between 1576 and 1642, and in these decades hundreds of thousands of people attended plays, while numerous playwrights and players turned the 'play' into a means of livelihood. Jonson's satire is designed to disarm the audience; he in fact loathes the idea that powers of judgement might be bound to a capacity to pay.[1] Nevertheless, his contract invites us to consider the implications – not only for authors and audiences, but also for the plays themselves – of a commercial theatre.

The theatre remained at this time a highly controversial institution. The extract from Philip Stubbes's *Anatomy of Abuses* printed at the end of this book (pp. 145–7) indicates some of the reasons why many people opposed the theatres, and we will have cause throughout the book to return to these arguments. By the time that Jonson wrote *Bartholomew Fair*, hundreds of plays had been produced for the London theatres, in a truly extraordinary outburst of literary activity. Yet many critics continued to associate plays with ungodly deception, and playhouses with all manner of vice. Such arguments would shadow the theatres through to 1642, when the collapse of royal authority on the eve of the English Civil War gave puritan forces the opportunity to close them down. Consequently, in this opening chapter it will be worth considering the physical, social, economic and cultural conditions of the Renaissance stage. Following the lead offered by Jonson, and attending also to the anxieties voiced by Stubbes, we will examine the ways in which the simple idea of enclosing space for the purposes of theatrical performances produced a radically new form of literature. As we shall see, what we now recognize comfortably as 'Renaissance drama' was, at the time it was written, an unstable and contested form, bound to the demands of one of the greatest entertainment markets in Western history.

1.1 Origins and authority

Jonson's anxiety that mere paying spectators might claim a right to judge the work of playwrights highlights important questions concerning the relation between theatre and authority. For whom, we might ask, does an author write? Who has the right to assess a playwright's work? And how might a playwright establish a status as an artist rather than a mere artisan? Jonson, more than any of his contemporaries, felt compromised by the idea of writing for a popular market, and throughout his career he sought ways of elevating the status of his work. In 1616 he attracted derision when he published his plays in a volume of his *Works*; 'plays', his critics pointed out, could hardly be 'works'. More importantly, he sought to associate himself with the authority of the king, creating for himself the identity of a poet-laureate at a time before that institution had officially been created.[2] Although he was more audacious in this respect than his peers, Jonson was by no means alone in seeking approval and patronage from the court. Many plays were performed at court, and some were doubtless written with such performance in mind; the very title of *Twelfth Night*, for example, suggests a context of courtly festivity. Such texts occupy an evidently privileged position, since they at least appear to have been authorized by the central source of power in the land.

Even in the commercial playhouses, the patronage of the nation's royalty and nobility remained vital. The support of successive monarchs protected the theatre from its powerful enemies, while any active theatre company was required by law 'to be authorised by one noble or two judicial dignitaries of the realm'.[3] Shakespeare's company, for example, was initially the Lord Chamberlain's Men, and in the reign of James I became the King's Men. This structure represents the state's effort to incorporate the theatre into a model of courtly patronage. In theory, the company was representing the patron, and an audience might assume that such a company's plays would be shaped in the interests of that patron. Hence the patronage of the king suggests that the king approves of the company's work, and that he lends it in turn the weight of his authority. Yet this model was at times little more than a convenient fiction, since commercial success was increasingly becoming more important to a company than aristocratic patronage. For all his elitism, Jonson was undeniably dependent on those people paying their pennies for the right to watch his plays. Consequently, as Louis Montrose argues, we should perceive the Renaissance theatre as being sustained by 'an unstable mixture of two theoretically distinct modes of cultural production: one, hierarchical and deferential, based upon traditional relations of patronage and clientage; the other, fluid and competitive, based upon market relations'.[4]

The evident contradictions between these two modes, though an ongoing source of anxiety to many people, created opportunities for the emergence of new types of playwrights and plays. This point should not be exaggerated: notably, women were entirely excluded from the business of theatrical production, and those few plays written by female authors in this period are examples of 'closet drama', designed for private readings and amateur performances.[5] Nonetheless, most of the leading playwrights of the period were men from middling social origins, who would have found it impossible to establish themselves as poets among the social elite at court. Crucially, unlike aristocratic writers, these men aimed to support themselves through writing. At the court of Elizabeth, Sir Philip Sidney was a classic example of the courtier-poet, for whom poetry was an 'unelected vocation', into which he 'slipped' in his 'idlest times'; by comparison, in the Renaissance theatre few men had the luxury of such choice and leisure.[6] Shakespeare, for instance, was the son of a provincial merchant, and he might never have written at all if the London playhouses had not provided him with an outlet for his creativity. Jonson was apprenticed by his stepfather as a bricklayer before he managed to gain a foothold in the theatre.

The financial rewards of authorship were in accord with the humble origins of the playwrights. Economic and legal structures designed to ensure that authors receive a fair reward for their work – such as modern laws of copyright – did not exist at this time, in part because the very notion of literature as a marketable commodity was so radically new. Writers instead sold scripts to theatre companies, and at that moment lost all financial interest in their work. Significantly, Shakespeare's considerable wealth came not from his writing but rather from his shrewd decision to take a financial stake in his company and its principal theatre, the Globe. Perhaps more typical of the playwright's life was the experience of Thomas Dekker, who received a mere £3 for writing *The Shoemaker's Holiday*, at a time when an annual income of £9 would put a Londoner on the poverty-line. Three plays a year is a lot to demand of any writer; not surprisingly, Dekker, for all his admirable industry, spent time in prison for debt. Dekker's career also demonstrates the way in which writing for the stage was frequently treated as a kind of literary hack-work. While we now valorize plays written by particular authors, Dekker's work consisted mainly of indistinguishable contributions to multi-authored texts, most of which are now lost.

In some cases the theatre also offered opportunities for more radical and disaffected writers, who would have been unable to establish themselves within more conservative patronage structures. The latter decades of Elizabeth's rule, in particular, are notable for the phenomenon of educated and intelligent young men being drawn to London, but frustrated in their hopes for advancement within the existing structures of state and Church. Such men were responsible for a flurry of vitriolic verse satire in the 1590s, and for new forms of witty and urbane prose pamphlets. Those drawn specifically to the theatre included Christopher Marlowe, whose plays written in the years before his early and violent death in 1593 helped to shape the very nature of Renaissance drama. Marlowe was educated at Cambridge, but subsequently gravitated towards the world of aspiring writers and disgruntled intellectuals in London. Throughout his short career he was profoundly sceptical of prevailing structures of authority, and acutely aware of the ways in which codes of ideology and morality were fashioned in the interests of power. Accordingly, as we shall see in subsequent chapters, Marlowe's heroes set themselves in various ways against authority, and his plays tend to destabilize orthodox practices of religion, morality and sexuality.

Such challenges to authority were underlined by the very nature of theatrical performance. Recent literary and cultural historians have demonstrated the extent to which authority itself in the Renaissance depended upon forms of spectacle. The monarch and courtiers sustained their power in part through elaborate public displays: from the highly choreographed 'progresses' that Elizabeth undertook throughout her realm, to the daily dramas of competitive social interaction at court. Similarly, the law relied on exemplary spectacles of punishment, the governors of London celebrated their rule in annual processions through the streets, while the Church retained its traditional commitment to clerical vestments and elaborate ceremonies. Power, one might say, had to be seen to be believed. Many defenders of the theatre argued that it could be incorporated into these theatrical conventions – so that, for example, the theatrical representation of a monarch might serve to teach people the importance of obedience. Other contemporary commentators, however, worried about the theatre's representation of vice and insurrection; as Stubbes comments, 'if you will learn to rebel against princes . . . you need to go to no other school' (see p. 146). The crucial point is that, within the marketplace created by the Renaissance theatres, the authority and interests of the paying public were at least as influential as those of the monarch. In Jean Howard's words: 'Theatricality, now institutionalised and commodified, had become an object of cultural contestation.'[7]

We might consider some of the implications of Renaissance drama's institutional context by turning to Shakespeare's *A Midsummer Night's Dream*. Like so many Elizabethan comedies, *A Midsummer Night's Dream* presents a narrative of order at court being re-established after an initial breakdown in relations between the generations. Here, the courtier Egeus unreasonably demands the right to determine his daughter's choice of husband, even though she has arranged for herself a perfectly appropriate match. After a night of magical disorder in the forest, the duke, Theseus, endorses the original choices of the youths, and in so doing he at once silences the claims of oppressive patriarchy and incorporates the forces of youthful desire into his realm. Meanwhile, in the play's sub-plot a group of artisans rehearses an unintentionally comic play, which in *A Midsummer Night's Dream*'s final act they will perform before the united court. A conservative reading of Shakespeare's play, therefore, might interpret this play-within-a-play as a representation of the subordination of theatre to authority. Theseus and his courtiers complacently mock the theatrical efforts of Bottom and his mates, and the duke eventually rewards them because – unlike the players in *Hamlet* – they appear to offer absolutely no challenge to his values or power. Such an interpretation accords with popular (though unsubstantiated) theories that Shakespeare wrote the play for an aristocratic wedding, and that at this first performance Queen Elizabeth assumed the very position of spectator-of-honour which Theseus mirrors within the play.

According to this interpretation, Elizabeth's assumed presence at the play's origin marks the text as a straightforward celebration of Tudor government, and reflects Shakespeare's assumed status as a spokesman of orthodoxy and hierarchy. But what happens if we situate *A Midsummer Night's Dream* instead in the commercial theatre? What if we consider rather the experience of an urban labourer, who would have paid a couple of pennies to watch and judge Shakespeare's play? Asking such questions may prompt us to perceive *A Midsummer Night's Dream* as a somewhat more dynamic text, which stages social tensions in a manner that is not so easily contained within the framework of a conservative ideology. If we attend to the experience of women in the play, for instance, we might note that their routine subordination to men does not go uncontested. It has, after all, taken military force to bring Hippolyta to the altar, while the Fairy Queen Titania is only reconciled with her husband's authority after a magically enforced humiliation. The silence of Helena and Hermia in the final act may also warrant further consideration; while they have married their chosen mates, they perhaps have time here to consider the costs of this process, including the unresolved rift in their own friendship.

And if we attend to the experience of the artisans, as Annabel Patterson has done, we might even identify within the play a strain of social radicalism which disrupts conservative interpretations. In several comic scenes in the middle of the play, Oberon's magic first gives Bottom an ass's head, then makes the fairy Titania dote on him. Bottom – whose name reminds us of his lowly status – subsequently makes sense of his miraculous experience by describing it as a dream. He says:

> I have had a dream past the wit of man to say what dream it was. Man is but an ass if he go about t'expound this dream. Methought I was – there is no man can tell what. Methought I was, and methought I had – but man is but a patched fool if he will offer to say what methought I had.

(IV.i.200–4)

As Patterson suggests, and as many members of a contemporary audience may have appreciated all too well, Bottom's visionary experience is one of social inversion, which radically revalues those members of society who are 'normally mocked as fools and burdened like asses'. And, as Bottom perhaps realizes, 'prudent readers, especially those who are themselves unprivileged, will resist the pressure to interpret the vision'.[8] Patterson's is a provocative argument, which leaves us with an unexpectedly problematic play. Yet it is an argument based on a simple premiss: that *A Midsummer Night's Dream* was written not for the court but for London's commercial theatres. At this point, then, it will be worth attending more closely to the nature of this theatre.

1.2 The London playhouses: traditions and innovations

The dominant anxiety underpinning Jonson's contract with the audience of *Bartholomew Fair* centres on the playhouses, which he perceived to be creating their own standards and conventions. But no literary movement exists in a vacuum, and when studying Renaissance drama it is important to understand its connections with pre-existent cultural and literary practices. While the commercial playhouse was an innovation, the concept of a 'play' was as old as civilization itself. Consequently, in this section we will consider the ways in which the London playhouses transformed existing cultural traditions, in order to meet the demands of a new institution and a new audience. Consideration of medieval dramatic practices, the expectations of Renaissance audiences, and the physical and political status of the theatres, may extend our appreciation of the plays themselves.

Before the Renaissance, English drama had been predominantly didactic, bound to the interests and teachings of the Church. Many towns in medieval England regularly staged cycles of biblical stories, which became known as 'mystery plays', because each constituent part was the responsibility of a particular trade guild (or, in contemporary terminology, 'mystery'). The cycles were typically performed on open carts in the streets of the towns, in a manner that underscored the intention to unite a community in an affirmation of its central beliefs. Since the actors were also amateurs, recognizable as members of the community, the relationship between performers and audience was typically loose and informal. In a sense the whole town was involved in the performance, just as the whole town shared a common knowledge of the biblical narratives. The mystery cycles were suppressed from the mid-sixteenth century, when Protestant reformers dismissed them as pernicious remnants of Catholicism. Nonetheless, they survived long enough to influence the early Renaissance playwrights, and lived on in popular memory. When Hamlet proclaims that a theatrical performance 'out-Herods Herod' (III.ii.12), 'he is alluding to the famously bombastic role of Herod of Jewry in the mystery plays'.[9]

In contrast to the mysteries, morality plays were embraced and adapted by the Protestant Church, and therefore survived into the era of Renaissance drama. Moralities stage a 'contest for the spiritual welfare of the mankind hero' (a 'psychomachia'), employing allegory to convey a moral lesson about religious or civil conduct.[10] Typically a central character, who is less an individual than a figure representative of humankind as a whole, is beset by various allegorized figures or representative social types, and must choose the correct path in life in order to be rewarded spiritually. For example, in the relatively late morality play *Enough is as Good as a Feast*, written by the Protestant reformer William Wager, the figure of Covetous leads the battle for the soul of Worldly Man. Before Worldly Man rejects Covetous, the danger he courts is underlined by the prophet Jeremiah, who emerges to warn of the 'weeping and gnashing of teeth' in hell (ll. 1185–8; 1195–1208). Like the mysteries, these plays were performed in local settings, such as market squares or halls; however, they were usually performed not by members of the local community but by travelling troupes of professional actors. Moreover, while the moralities maintain a traditional commitment to a didactic form of theatre, they became increasingly self-contained and distanced from the audience, as the playwrights in the latter half of the sixteenth century embraced more complex representations of social interaction.[11]

This line of theatrical development – from the mystery cycles, to the morality plays, to the Renaissance stage – might in some respects appear clear and smooth. But London's playhouses and playwrights were responsive also to a range of other influences, which helped in various ways to shape the texts we now read. Crucially, the theatre companies participated in a market for a whole range of entertainment, from music to bull-baiting. Indeed, the first commercial dramatic performances in Elizabethan London took place in inn-yards, while the early commercial theatres were commonly used for more than one type of spectacle. Most playhouses were built to versatile open amphitheatre designs; hall playhouses, such as the Blackfriars, were developed slightly later in the period, and remained smaller, more expensive, and more socially exclusive. Theatre companies and playwrights alike thus continued to focus their attentions on playhouses such as the Hope Theatre, which 'was designed from the start as a dual-purpose bull-and bear-baiting house with a removable stage', and in which an uneasy space-sharing relationship was maintained until around 1620.[12] This fact helps further to contextualize Jonson's contract with his audience at the Hope in 1614. As much as he wants to raise the status of his work, Jonson is painfully aware that *Bartholomew Fair* is to be staged in the same building as bull-baiting, and may perhaps be consumed by some of the same people, in the same boisterous spirit.

Other playwrights, particularly in the sixteenth century, were more appreciative of the resources of popular culture. George Peele's *The Old*

Wife's Tale is in fact staged as a story told on a winter's evening by a fallible and lively blacksmith's wife. The play's intertwined romance narratives rely heavily on magic and miracle, in accord with established ballad and prose traditions. Robert Greene's *Friar Bacon and Friar Bungay* is another example of popular romance brought to the stage, while Francis Beaumont's early seventeenth-century comedy *The Knight of the Burning Pestle* looks more sceptically on such writing. Written for the Blackfriars Theatre, Beaumont's play builds layer upon layer of dramatic artifice, as a London grocer appears to invade the stage and redirect the course of a perfectly respectable play, so that it accords with his plebeian tastes. Beaumont thus satirizes extravagant romances, and seeks to clarify boundaries between popular and elite tastes. Like Jonson's comparable effort in *Bartholomew Fair*, however, *The Knight of the Burning Pestle* is itself dependent on the support of the people, even as it sets out to mock them.

Other plays incorporate more particular elements of popular culture into the theatrical experience. For instance, the presence of stage clowns in a theatre company not only attracted spectators but also influenced playwrights. When Shakespeare created characters such as Sir John Falstaff or the incompetent constable Dogberry, he was probably creating roles for Will Kemp, a clown with a reputation for his dancing and knockabout extemporizing. By comparison, Kemp's departure from the company perhaps enabled Shakespeare to experiment in the latter half of his career with more sophisticated kinds of fool, such as Lear's sardonic companion. Further, it was commonplace throughout most of the period for a theatrical performance to be concluded with a 'bawdy knockabout song-and-dance farce' known as a 'jig'.[13] It seems that this form was also surprisingly malleable, and could be used for the purposes of topical comment and scurrilous satire.[14] Contemporary critics were concerned particularly by their immorality. As late as 1612 Middlesex magistrates complained about 'certain lewd jigs, songs and dances' at the Fortune, which were believed to attract 'diverse cut-purses and other lewd and ill-disposed persons'.[15]

Though focused specifically on jigs, the magistrates' statement is symptomatic of more widespread concerns about plays and playhouses. Indeed, the governors of the city of London saw the theatres as sites of disorder and immorality, agreeing roughly with many of the anti-theatrical arguments presented so forcefully in our extract from Stubbes. Consequently, the theatres were built only in areas known as 'liberties', over which the civic authorities had little or no control. Most were on the south bank of the Thames, an area long associated with popular entertainment and prostitution, while others survived in pockets of the city controlled by the court. Scholars such as Steven Mullaney have argued that this physical situation informed the nature of the plays written for the theatres. These marginal spaces, Mullaney suggests, provided a forum for the expression of unorthodox and 'divergent points of view'.[16] Yet this is not to say that the theatre was entirely uncontrolled. Censorship was a fact of life for all Renaissance writers, and all plays required a licence from the Master of Revels, the officer in charge of court entertainment. Jonson was one of many playwrights to feel the wrath of the authorities, when he was imprisoned in 1597 for his part in writing the purportedly seditious (though now lost) play *The Isle of Dogs*.[17] Shakespeare's company was more compliant when publishing early quarto versions of *Richard II*. These do not include the famous deposition scene, in which the king relinquishes his crown; such possibilities, it seems, were too sensitive in the final years of Elizabeth's life.

A play which articulates seditious arguments, or which represents acts of sedition, might be perceived as a threat to the state because it carries the potential to incite sedition. But the limits of allowable expression remain flexible, for the very reason that Jonson acknowledges in *Bartholomew Fair*: as much as the state might wish to impose its interpretations on plays, every spectator buys for himself or herself the right to determine meaning. With admission prices as low as one penny, the theatres provided a form of entertainment affordable for almost all members of London society, and it was these people who would keep a theatre company in business. Clearly these playgoers were more sophisticated than Stubbes would have us believe; witnessing the deposition scene in *Richard II* does not automatically convert a spectator into a revolutionary. Yet it is equally clear that the audiences of London's playhouses were willing to interpret – and, when circumstances changed, to reinterpret – a text. In 1601, when the Earl of Essex was preparing to stage an uprising against Queen Elizabeth, his conspirators paid Shakespeare's company to revive *Richard II*. How many people left the theatre freshly convinced of the legitimacy of rebelling against a weak monarch must remain a matter of conjecture. Since the Essex Rebellion failed so miserably, it is possible that the conspirators, like so many of their contemporaries, overestimated the power of the theatre and underestimated the intelligence of the common playgoer.

As has become apparent throughout this section, the changing conditions of English drama altered the nature of the plays we continue to read. Factors such as the location and structure of theatres, the expectations and demands of audiences, and the restrictions of licensing authorities, all helped to shape what we now know as Renaissance drama. These various pressures prompted playwrights to abandon the religious and ethical certainties of the morality plays in favour of a more rigorously secular attention to contemporary issues and identities. Hence in Jonson's *Volpone*, to take just one example, the morality form is stretched to breaking-point. Jonson initially invokes expectations of that form by proclaiming in a prefatory letter that literature should 'inform men in the best reason of living' ('Prefatory Epistle', l. 108), and then by introducing characters whose names apparently define their identities. Volpone's name means 'old fox'; his servant Mosca is 'any kind of fly'; Corbaccio is 'a filthy great raven'; whereas Bonario, whose name is derived from the Latin *bonus* ('good'), is signalled as the play's likely hero. For an audience, the codes are almost too simple.

In the Renaissance theatre, however, those codes cannot hold their shape. While Jonson gives us the moralistic ending the play proffers from the beginning, he does so only after providing glimpses, at the close of the fourth act, of an alternative, in which Volpone's skills of manipulation and dissimulation overcome the powers of the state and its legal system.[18] Significantly, it is not Bonario who effects the play's eventual conservative resolution; in fact Bonario's heroic rhetoric and black-and-white morality seem conspicuously misplaced – even outdated – in the civic world which Jonson creates. Instead, Volpone brings down the unreliable forces of justice upon himself, after he falls out with his equally unscrupulous servant. In Bonario's subsequent assessment of events, 'Heaven could not long let such gross crimes be hid' (V.xii.98). An audience, though, might well find this perception inadequate, and appreciate rather the play's intricate representation of a secular and brutally competitive world. In this world – as in Jonson's London – the comfortable narratives of the moralities were being rendered irrelevant, just as the playwright's status as teacher was giving way to a role as a producer of another commodity for another market.

1.3 Theatrical representation on the London stages

The example of Jonson's *Volpone* signals a newly sophisticated relationship between an audience and a play. While mystery plays tell familiar stories over and over, and moralities trace predictable moral lessons, the drama of Shakespeare and Jonson makes considerable demands of its audience. Shakespeare reminds his audience of these in the Prologue to *Henry V*, in which a player begs that the spectators might 'let us . . . / On your imaginary forces work' (ll. 17–18). As Shakespeare was well aware, the conditions of the London theatres created new possibilities for the business of theatrical illusion, and informed fresh approaches to the staging of characters and societies. In the final section of this chapter, we will consider more closely these changing practices of theatrical representation. An early Renaissance play, Marlowe's *The Jew of Malta*, will be particularly enlightening in this context, because of the way in which it reveals these forms in the very process of construction.

The 'imaginary forces' of Renaissance audiences were trained to accommodate the theatre's limited techniques of illusion. On the amphitheatre stages, performances were always in daylight, so the dramatic time of day was necessarily communicated verbally, while the state of the weather might further be signalled by conventional aural cues. Hence a play such as *Macbeth*, which opens with the witches meeting in a storm, and in which much of the significant action takes place in the dead of night, draws heavily on the imaginative powers of an audience. The theatrical representation of space, meanwhile, was as much emblematic as realistic. Traditionally, the brightly painted ceiling of the stage canopy represented the 'heavens', while the trapdoor on the stage represented an entrance to hell. Like many of his contemporaries, Shakespeare combines these conventions with a fresh realism; in *Measure for Measure*, for instance, the trapdoor is opened to reveal the prison cell of Barnardine, the irredeemable criminal who declares that he is too drunk to be executed.

Since there was almost no scenery used on the Renaissance stage, the representation of places also became flexibly suggestive. At most a couple of props (for instance, a bed or a tree) might be used to indicate place, while the invocation of foreign settings can seem at times almost random. (Famously, in Shakespeare's *The Winter's Tale* Antigonus lands his ship on the coast of Bohemia – where, as Jonson was quick to point out, 'there is no sea near by some 100 miles'.)[19] In a play such as *Volpone*, however, the associations of the purported setting help a playwright to focus attention on certain central concerns. In that play Jonson is unquestionably interested in practices and values within his own city; however, his decision to situate the action in Venice is no accident. A city associated in the English imagination with trade and luxury, Venice becomes a kind of social laboratory within which Jonson can explore the operations of rampant individualism and unfettered economic competition. Only a foolishly unobservant spectator would assume that such phenomena are exclusive to Venice.

In the absence of elaborate stage settings, the theatre's creation of spectacle was dependent rather upon action and costume. The entry of devils, in plays such as Marlowe's *Doctor Faustus* or Jonson's *The Devil is an Ass*, would generally be signalled by fireworks. The highly contrived scenes of multiple deaths at the end of numerous tragedies, meanwhile, typically combine the spectacular with elements of symbolism and allegory. The deaths at the end of plays such as Shakespeare's *Titus Andronicus* or

Thomas Kyd's *Spanish Tragedy* thus invite an intellectual act of interpretation even as they overwhelm the senses. And even the simple act of representing monarchs and courtiers on stage involved an impressive element of spectacle, at a time when a theatre company might well spend more on costumes than on scripts.[20] As I will discuss further in Chapter 2, many social commentators identified dress as a fixed sign of identity, and were deeply troubled by the sight of a common player in the robes of a king. Some of the better playwrights in fact incorporated such anxieties into their texts. In *King Lear*, for example, a play which insistently questions the relation between authority and individual identity, we can hardly overestimate the significance of Lear tearing away his clothes in the storm, and thereby choosing to search for meaning in 'unaccommodated man' rather than the 'lendings' of social status (III.iv.99–100).

A spectator, when watching such a scene, was also faced with linguistic demands. While the language of Shakespeare has undoubtedly become more difficult to grasp with the passing of centuries, his own contemporaries were required to comprehend his lines at much greater speed than we would expect today. Partly in response to the challenges presented by daylight staging and restless audiences, the players sought to seize attention through a rapid mode of performance. Playwrights, meanwhile, experimented with new approaches to dramatic language. It is not insignificant that Renaissance plays are longer and include more characters than we would find in moralities: this alone indicates their more rigorous attention to processes of social interaction. The innovative use of the soliloquy which becomes one of the definitive characteristics of Renaissance drama – serves further to construct characters as autonomous agents. As Catherine Belsey has argued, 'the moral conflicts externalized in the morality are internalized in the soliloquy and thus understood to be confined *within the mind* of the protagonist'.[21] Whereas the spectator of a morality is always aware of the correct path for the protagonist and is thus enlisted by the playwright in a public affirmation of good against evil, the audience in the Renaissance theatre might expect to engage more actively with a character. When Hamlet asks, 'To be, or not to be'? (III.i.58), Shakespeare invites the audience to sympathize with his dilemma rather than to stand back and condemn his contemplation of a sin.

This shift in the representation of characters and their worlds might be clarified by focusing on the Renaissance transformation of the conventional figure of the Vice. In the morality, the Vice plays the role of the tempter, in a fashion that is at once sinister and comic. He typically represents a single sin, and is clearly identified for the audience as an agent of moral corruption. Although he might disguise himself in an attempt to trick the everyman-protagonist – in Wager's *Enough Is as Good as a Feast*, for instance, the figure of Covetous disguises himself pointedly as 'Policy' – the audience is always aware of his essential identity. For Renaissance writers, though, the Vice figure offered a vehicle through which to examine in greater detail the workings of self-interest. The Vice is thus merged increasingly into the new theatrical phenomenon of a tragic hero who is fundamentally alone, and does not seem to fit into any of his society's neat structures of order. Shakespeare's Richard III invokes theatrical tradition when he compares himself to 'the formal Vice, Iniquity'; however, the play as a whole constructs him as a more complex individual, who relishes the idea of a 'world for me to bustle in' (III.i.82; I.i.152). Although Richard 'derives from the Vice', he 'grows beyond this role to become a heroic exemplar of humankind as beings able to exert will'.[22]

Barabas, Marlowe's protagonist in *The Jew of Malta*, provides an even clearer example of theatrical characterization in a state of transition. Barabas is identified as alien and threatening for the Christian audience simply by his Judaism, and it is almost certain that this difference was underlined on the Renaissance stage by grotesque dress. In accord with medieval traditions governing the representation of Jews, Barabas was probably dressed in a red wig and beard, an outrageously hooked nose, and a long gabardine coat. Moreover, he is first revealed to the audience 'in his counting house, with heaps of gold before him': a conventionally emblematic image, also used by Jonson in *Volpone*, which identifies the character as representative of the sin of covetousness (I.i.sd). Yet it soon becomes apparent that there is more to Marlowe's character than this restrictive stereotype allows. For Marlowe, like so many Renaissance dramatists, is concerned less with easy moral denunciation than with an interrogation of an entire society. Marlowe's subtle representation of Barabas highlights the extent to which he has been moulded by a society that shares his acquisitive desires but is simply better at masking them. Barabas might thus be situated, in Stephen Greenblatt's words, as 'the alienated essence of Christian society': a 'semimythical figure', whose activities actually stand at the heart of the society he inhabits, but which are figured by the (hypocritical) dominant culture as alien.[23]

Consequently, while the play offers a conventionally emblematic conclusion, as Barabas lands himself in a cauldron which prefigures the fires of hell, the audience might well perceive more than a Christian victory over evil. Barabas has not only provided the play's driving energy, but has also commanded a measure of the audience's sympathy. His early soliloquies indicate a subjectivity shaped in response to the unbending hatred of the dominant culture, while his confrontation with the Christian rulers pointedly demystifies their claims of superiority. 'Ay, policy, that's their profession,' he comments, 'And not simplicity, as they suggest' (I.ii.161–2). Indeed, the amoral codes of 'policy', introduced in the Prologue by the figure of Machiavel (a theatricalized image of the Florentine political theorist Niccolò Machiavelli), are increasingly revealed as the true motors of Maltese society. Ferneze, who is left in firm control at the end, and who closes the play thanking 'heaven' for his success, is perhaps merely a better practitioner of 'policy' than Barabas. *The Jew of Malta* therefore becomes something very different from the morality play that it might initially appear to be. It is in part a play about the dominant Christian culture's easy vilification of an alien culture; and as such, the figure of the alien, for all his excessive acts of violence, commands at least a measure of sympathy and admiration.

Notes

1 Don E. Wayne, 'Drama and Society in the Age of Jonson: An Alternative View', *Renaissance Drama*, new series, 13 (1982), 114.
2 See Richard Helgerson, *Self-Crowned Laureates: Spenser, Jonson, Milton, and the Literary System* (Berkeley and Los Angeles, 1983), ch. 3.
3 Andrew Gurr, *The Shakespearean Stage 1574–1642*, 3rd edn (Cambridge, 1992), p. 27.
4 Louis Montrose, *The Purpose of Playing: Shakespeare and the Cultural Politics of the Elizabethan Theatre* (Chicago, 1996), p. 54.
5 See *Renaissance Drama by Women: Texts and Documents*, ed. S. P. Cerasano and Marion Wynne-Davies (London, 1996).
6 *The Defence of Poesy*, in *Sir Philip Sidney*, ed. Katherine Duncan-Jones (Oxford and New York, 1989), p. 212.
7 Jean E. Howard, *The Stage and Social Struggle in Early Modern England* (London and New York, 1994), p. 5.
8 Annabel Patterson, *Shakespeare and the Popular Voice* (London, 1989), p. 69.
9 Stephen Greenblatt, 'General Introduction', *The Norton Shakespeare*, p. 30.
10 David M. Bevington, *From 'Mankind' to Marlowe: Growth of Structure in the Popular Drama of Tudor England* (Cambridge, Mass., 1962), p. 9.
11 Anne Righter, *Shakespeare and the Idea of the Play* (London, 1962), ch. 1; Bernard Spivack, *Shakespeare and the Allegory of Evil* (New York, 1958), chs 7–8; Bevington, *From 'Mankind' to Marlowe*, p. 141.
12 Gurr, *The Shakespearean Stage*, pp. 120–1.
13 Gurr, *The Shakespearean Stage*, p. 174; see further C. R. Baskervill, *The Elizabethan Jig and Related Song Drama*, rep. edn (New York, 1965).
14 See the texts in C. J. Sisson, *Lost Plays of Shakespeare's Age* (Cambridge, 1936), pp. 125–56.
15 Quoted in Gurr, *The Shakespearean Stage*, p. 175.
16 Steven Mullaney, *The Place of the Stage: License, Play, and Power in Renaissance England* (Ann Arbor, 1988), p. 38.
17 Gurr, *The Shakespearean Stage*, p. 43.

18 On issues of closure in this play, see Stephen Greenblatt, 'The False Ending in *Volpone*', *Journal of English and Germanic Philology*, 75 (1976), 90–104.
19 'Conversations with William Drummond', in *Ben Jonson: The Complete Poems*, ed. George Parfitt (Harmondsworth, 1975), p. 466.
20 Gurr, *The Shakespearean Stage*, p. 194.
21 Catherine Belsey, *The Subject of Tragedy: Identity and Difference in Renaissance Drama* (London and New York, 1985), p. 43.
22 John Jowett, 'Introduction' to his edition of *Richard III* (Oxford, 2000), pp. 10–11.
23 Stephen Greenblatt, *Learning to Curse: Essays in Early Modern Culture* (New York and London, 1990), pp. 48–9, 53.

2

'What a piece of work': issues of identity

In the Jacobean pamphlet *Haec Vir* (an extract from which is the document for this chapter; see pp. 147–8), a woman dressed in a masculine fashion confronts a man dressed in feminine fashion. The text is premised on a conservative argument that the world has been turned upside down in contemporary London, yet the mannish-woman (Hic Mulier) by no means emerges from the text as the figure of ridicule we might expect. On the contrary, as she rebuts the challenges of the womanish-man (Haec Vir), she presents some startling arguments about individual 'freedom'. Rules governing appearance, she claims, are nothing more than the imposition of 'custom', and they impose a 'miserable servitude' upon the free woman. Therefore, although it was written as part of a short lived controversy about dress and gender identities in London, this pamphlet also participates in more profound Renaissance debates about the very foundations of identity. People were asking: are the conventions which distinguish the appearance and behaviour of men and women, rich and poor, masters and servants, ordained by God or merely devised by society? In the terms employed by *Haec Vir*, is identity determined by nature or custom? For many contemporaries, the arguments raised by Hic Mulier were deeply disturbing. For London's playwrights, however, such questions of identity were already established as fundamental to their art.

In Chapter 1 we considered the ways in which the methods of theatrical representation on the Renaissance stage produced radically new kinds of dramatic characters. We also saw that some critics of the theatre found these developments threatening. In the light of Hic Mulier's arguments, it will now be helpful to examine more thoroughly the ways in which Renaissance plays participate in ongoing debates over the contours of selfhood. For there was apparent at this time, as various scholars have demonstrated, 'an increased self-consciousness about the fashioning of human identity as a manipulable, artful process'.[1] Within this context, playwrights involved themselves in the project of rethinking subjectivity: debating, that is, what it means to be human. Hamlet is driven to the point of madness by the paradox that man is a 'piece of work' at once 'noble in reason' yet materially reducible to a 'quintessence of dust' (II.ii.293–8). In *As You Like It*, Rosalind confronts a paradox akin to that raised in *Haec Vir*, as she explores the effect of a man's 'doublet and hose' on her woman's identity (II.iv.5).

This chapter pursues the implications of such questions and uncertainties. The first section surveys changing ideas and discourses of identity, focusing on the ways in which Renaissance tragedies stage the anxieties of an increasingly sceptical age. The second section examines issues of gender identity, and returns to questions raised by Hic Mulier as it considers comedies structured around cross-dressing. And the final section looks at Renaissance theories of the body: always the material foundation of human identity, but an object which is understood very differently within particular cultures. When the hero of John Ford's *'Tis Pity She's a Whore* seeks to demonstrate his grip on the heart of his sister by literally tearing the living organ from her body, we see a playwright interrogating centuries of intertwined physiological and erotic discourses.

2.1 Inventing the self: the coordinates of Renaissance subjectivity

'Man', claims the French philosopher and historian Michel Foucault, 'is an invention of recent date', the product of certain distinctive 'arrangements of knowledge'.[2] This arresting statement confronts our understandable preconceptions that identity transcends history: that, in simpler terms, because my body and mental capacity are roughly the same as those of an average inhabitant of sixteenth-century London, it might be safe to assume that my life has the same meaning as his. Foucault argues instead that subjectivity is contingent upon historical circumstances, and defined by contemporary structures of discourse. More specifically, he suggests that the discourses which have sustained modern notions of 'man' simply did not exist in the Middle Ages, and only gradually assumed a recognizable form in the course of the early modern period. Interestingly, in the years when Shakespeare and his contemporaries were writing for the stage, the quintessential genre of modern selfhood, autobiography, simply did not exist.[3]

Playwrights were therefore thinking their way beyond medieval knowledge of the self, and in the process helping to give shape to the modern equivalent. As several important critics have suggested, this helps to contextualize Hamlet's ever-mysterious claim, 'I have that within which passeth show' (I.ii.85). His assertion sets unreliable external appearance against a promise of hidden yet authentic interiority, in a manner that may seem unproblematic enough in a modern text yet leaves critics grasping at air when confronted by Shakespeare's curiously insubstantial hero. In one influential reading, Francis Barker identifies here the 'premature', and ultimately illusory, emergence of 'the figure that is to dominate and organize bourgeois culture'. Hamlet, in other words, gestures towards a modern notion of subjectivity; although, in fact, 'At the centre of Hamlet, in the interior of his mystery, there is, in short, nothing.'⁴ Others have helpfully modified such arguments by arguing the need to historicize ideas and discourses of interiority; to understand Hamlet, they have suggested, we must first understand what Shakespeare's contemporaries understood by both outwardly 'seeming' and inwardly concealing identity.⁵ We will return to *Hamlet* later in this section. First we must sketch out some of this context, by considering the significance of intertwined processes of intellectual, socio-economic and religious change upon the coordinates of early modern subjectivity.

According to orthodox doctrine set forth by Church and state alike in the sixteenth century, the individual subject was inscribed from birth within a rigidly hierarchical socio-political system. We will consider the implications of these theories for society as a whole in Chapter 4; here, by comparison, I want to focus on their implications for appreciations of individual subjectivity. Shakespeare's Ulysses famously appeals to such a model in *Troilus and Cressida*, when he attributes the failures of the Greek army to a collapse of universal structures of 'degree'. He proclaims:

> The heavens themselves, the planets, and this centre
> Observe degree, priority, and place,
> Infixture, course, proportion, season, form,
> Office and custom, in all line of order.
>   [. . .]
>   O when degree is shaked,
> Which is the ladder to all high designs,
> The enterprise is sick. How could communities,
> Degrees in schools, and brotherhoods in cities,
> Peaceful commerce from dividable shores,
> The primogenity and due of birth,
> Prerogative of age, crowns, sceptres, laurels,

But by degree stand in authentic place?
Take but degree away, untune that string,
And hark what discord follows.

(I.iii.85–110)

Though he is himself by no means an entirely reliable character, Ulysses here invokes a powerful ideological model that fixes every individual unproblematically within a strictly hierarchical society. Interconnected networks of authority and order, from the patriarchal family to the absolutist state, define identity as surely as the stars hold their assigned positions in the sky. Within an early modern context, moreover, the assumption that degree is a product of nature is underpinned further by Christian teaching. In particular, ideas of providence – which posit God directly involving Himself in human affairs – were commonly invoked to bolster theories of unshakeable degree.

The early modern state reinforced such notions of order with laws designed to ensure that identity should be not only fixed but also *legible*. 'Sumptuary laws' introduced in the reign of Elizabeth stipulated what clothes could be worn by people of different genders and social degrees. Types and colours of fabric, styles of dress and forms of adornment were scrupulously regulated in these laws.[6] For example, only knights and those with an annual income of over £200 were permitted to wear velvet in their gowns, while only the eldest sons of knights and those with an income of over £100 were allowed velvet in their hose and doublets. The premiss of these laws – which Hic Mulier is almost determined to explode – is that in any public place a practised observer should be able to register immediately differences of gender and gradations of degree. That observer might then select an appropriate mode of address, which will serve further to set an individual in his or her place. Although there is little evidence of the statutes being enforced, and they were eventually repealed in 1604, they remain one of the best examples of the early modern commitment to distinct signs of hierarchy.

Indeed, it is by no means insignificant that the sumptuary laws should have been introduced at a moment when many people felt that traditional lines of distinction were becoming troublingly unclear. As in any age, conservative rhetoric and legislation are typically evidence of aspiration rather than documents of actual circumstances. Ideologies are often expressed most clearly when they are under greatest threat; at other times what seems simply natural hardly requires definition. Even within the shadow of this ideology, then, individuals in early modern England were facing the possibility that identity might not be fixed so easily. Of course this was not a sudden change, nor was it clearly perceptible; yet playwrights, along with a host of other writers, from religious commentators to the authors of pamphlets such as *Haec Vir*, participated in the project of analysing and realizing its consequences. As we see in countless plays, this project centred attention on a perceived discrepancy between 'outer' and 'inner': between, that is, physical appearance and a sense of unique and mysterious interiority.[7]

The emergent preoccupation with interior sites of identity was informed by concurrent changes in religious doctrine. The Reformation of the mid-sixteenth century, informed by the teachings of Martin Luther, introduced the notion of justification by faith alone: that an individual would be judged, and raised to heaven or condemned to hell, solely on the basis of a unique spiritual commitment. No longer would a priest claim a mediating role between an individual and God, and no longer would good works on earth ensure salvation. What mattered, increasingly and urgently, was a personal relationship with God. As a result, Catholic practices of confession and absolution were translated into freshly rigorous strategies of self-examination, often imagined in strikingly physical terms. The Christian was repeatedly exhorted to look within; according to the Elizabethan theologian Richard Hooker, even people who have no access to the 'written law of God' nonetheless 'carry written in their hearts the universal law of mankind, the law of reason'.[8]

More specifically, the word 'heart' could also signify the conscience. As the Jacobean puritan Jeremiah Dyke explains, invoking Jeremiah 17.1: 'Conscience prints and writes so surely, so indelibly, yea it writes men's sins as Judah his sin was, with a pen of iron, with the point of a diamond, and they are graven upon the table of their hearts.'[9] His image conceives of the core of a person's identity as something scripted by the individual, which consequently stands witness to God as a record of the Christian life.[10] Crucially, this discourse holds the potential to subvert structures of social hierarchy: a point made in *The Changeling* (by Thomas Middleton and William Rowley) by De Flores. When Beatrice-Joanna, having employed De Flores as a murderer, attempts to pay him off and dismiss him from her service, the lowly servant justifies his sexual demands with radical claims of equality. For Beatrice-Joanna, difference is a matter of 'blood'; De Flores, however, advises her to 'Look but into your conscience . . . / 'Tis a true book. You'll find me there your equal' (III.iv.132–3). Moreover, as De Flores recognizes and Protestant theology consistently taught, it is the responsibility of the individual, rather than any external authority, to scrutinize and assess that record of selfhood. Hamlet, it is worth recalling, has studied at Luther's university, Wittenburg, and wishes at the outset of the play to return there.

The growing prominence of the theories of John Calvin intensified these shifts. Calvinist doctrine, which was embraced by the English Church for most of our period, insisted that individuals were marked indelibly from birth either for salvation or damnation. This theory of 'election' exacerbated anxieties about the self, and intensified exercises in self-scrutiny. How was a person to know whether he or she was one of the elect? Social degree could be signalled by clothing, but what were the signs of salvation? The Elizabethan puritan Phillip Stubbes speculated that such signs might be rendered visible, just as the criminal justice system inscribed physical marks on convicted felons. Stubbes proposed that adulterers and fornicators should be 'seared with a hot iron on the cheek, forehead, or some other part of their body that might be seen, to the end honest and chaste Christians might be discerned from the adulterous children of Satan'.[11] But this was no more than another version of the prevailing early modern fantasy of identities being rendered legible – and on the Renaissance stage, playwrights commonly exposed the limitations of such fantasies. In Jonson's *Bartholomew Fair*, for example, the hypocritical puritan Zeal-of-the-land Busy pompously declares that 'the fleshly woman which you call Ursula is above all to be avoided, having the marks upon her of the three enemies of man: the world, as being in the fair; the devil, as being in the fire; and the flesh, as being herself' (III.vi.32–5). Busy's own indulgence in the excesses of the fair, however, suggest that he is hardly a reliable judge.

Intellectual movements, unconnected to the Church, further contributed to anxieties about the illegibility and malleability of identity. Niccolò Machiavelli, whose work we will consider in Chapter 6, challenged the relation between religion and the power of the state. Echoes of his powerful demystification of secular authority may be heard in Richard III's claim that 'Conscience is but a word that cowards use, / Devised at first to keep the strong in awe' (V.vi.39–40). Conscience, according to this argument, is a mere myth foisted upon the people in order to keep potentially rebellious desires under check. The transgressive heroes of Marlowe's plays uniformly agree, in the process redefining heroism itself as a desire to reach beyond orthodox models of hierarchy and order. Francis Bacon's essays, written during a life of service at court, adapt and extend some of Machiavelli's arguments, particularly by dwelling (like Hic Mulier) on the concept of 'custom'. For Bacon, custom encompasses a wide range of orthodox religious and moral codes, and profoundly restricts the subject; men under the sway of custom function 'as if they were dead images and engines'.[12] To appreciate this, and to set aside the constrictions of custom, is to realize wondrous new possibilities for self-determination. In the words of Jean-Christophe Agnew: 'If custom could

... be conceived as a kind of costume – something to be put on and off at will – then man could literally make himself.'[13]

This process of making the self – or, in Stephen Greenblatt's influential coinage, 'self-fashioning' – was evident particularly in the court and city. At court, conduct manuals such as Baldassare Castiglione's *Book of the Courtier* proposed that 'the most becoming conduct relies on tactics of dissimulation'.[14] The courtier's self, therefore, becomes an unstable and infinitely protean construction: 'a being of astonishing flexibility because he lacks a fixed nature or a commitment to anything'.[15] In *King Lear*, Edmund, the bastard son of Gloucester, memorably asserts this potential, cloaking a complaint at 'the plague of custom' in the spurious form of a prayer to 'nature' (I.ii.1–22). In Ford's *Perkin Warbeck*, we are presented with an unsettling confrontation between a legitimate but unconvincing king, and a pretender who has the performance of royalty down to a fine art. Which man, we are prompted to ask, is the rightful ruler?[16] Within the city, the social fluidity created by increasingly aggressive mercantile practices threatened similarly to collapse assumptions of fixed and legible distinctions. What happens if a citizen grows wealthy through success in the market, and seeks to transform his identity accordingly, by purchasing land and newly opulent clothes? At what point does he become accepted as a gentleman, perhaps displacing in the process a traditional member of the gentry? City comedies relentlessly worry about such processes of transformation. Even in Thomas Dekker's early and relatively conservative *Shoemaker's Holiday*, the miraculous social rise of the artisan Simon Eyre is carefully underlined by his wife's purchase of new clothes. And there is a more than a hint of social radicalism in Eyre's repeated assertions, before and after his transformation, that 'Prince am I none, yet am I nobly born' (vii.48–9; cf. xxi.35–6). In the city, opportunity and desire offer to render all men – almost – equal.

On the stage, contemporary concern surrounding the protean self converges with its physical embodiment, the player. Critics of the theatre focused attention on the very practice of acting: of fashioning the self for theatrical performance, adopting the appearance and dress of another social rank, or (in the case of boy-players) another gender. As Jean Howard has argued, for such anti-theatrical writers the stage epitomizes 'fears about the "counterfeitability" of social identity in a world in which the visible marks of social status can be bought, sold, borrowed, or stolen'.[17] In turn, dramatists themselves dwell subtly on the manipulation of identity. Shakespeare's *Othello*, for instance, circles anxiously around the fashioning of selves and others. Cassio laments the loss of reputation, 'the immortal part of myself' (II.iii.247); Desdemona, in the course of the play, is 'bewhored' (IV.ii.118); and Othello himself (as we shall see further in Chapter 7) is somehow brought to conform to stigmatized images of savage Moors. Yet this play also, in accord with so much Renaissance drama, nags away at the question of an authentic yet hidden identity. Hence the frustration of characters and audience alike when Iago, the arch fashioner of selves, refuses to reveal his own motivations, taunting us with the opaque words, 'What you know, you know' (V.ii.309). Other plays use the soliloquy as vehicle of revelation; by comparison, perhaps the greatest challenge posed by *Othello* is to accept that identity may be no more than a series of masks. As Iago warns us at the outset: 'I am not what I am' (I.i.65).

Like Hamlet's 'I have that within which passeth show', Iago's lack of definition highlights again the unfixed and transitional status of identity on the Renaissance stage. Foucault's 'man' – or, in Catherine Belsey's more specific formulation, the 'liberal humanist subject', who stands as a 'free, unconstrained author of meaning and action' – was gradually and mysteriously taking shape on the Renaissance stage.[18] This helps to explain the boundless energies and desires of Marlowe's heroes, seizing opportunities to define themselves against the constraints of religion and society. Tamburlaine, after beginning life as a shepherd, marches relentlessly through two bombastic plays, defined by his seemingly endless series of conquests. Transgression and consumption shape this hero, and therefore he is effectively incapable of stopping: incapable of fixing himself within a political structure and reconciling himself to God. Instead, his cycles of violence and destruction are repeated over and over until an inevitable death.

A number of Marlowe's contemporaries were focusing rather on individuals confronted traumatically with failures of justice or disruptions of order. Revenge tragedies were heavily indebted to the Roman models of Seneca; however, they also had particular contemporary resonance, since they 'involved precisely the question of the obligations and responsibilities of the subject in the implementation of divine and human justice'.[19] For Francis Bacon, revenge is 'a kind of wild justice', which subverts the abstract legal and moral codes of civilized society.[20] But what if a man who has devoted his life to maintaining those codes is confronted with a devastating personal loss which demonstrates the limitations of justice? What if that man discovers that the murderers of his son are using their positions of authority to evade justice? This is the situation of Hieronimo, the hero of Thomas Kyd's *Spanish Tragedy*, one of the earliest and most influential of Renaissance revenge tragedies. Within a court dominated by a murderous prince, Hieronimo finds that his knowledge is almost literally unspeakable, and consequently descends into a form of madness which is characterized by a radical lack of faith in language and comprehension. He tears legal documents into shreds;

he stages a play in a cacophony of different languages; and, after killing the murderers, he bites out his tongue and spits it onto the floor at the feet of the king. Hieronimo resists to the end the king's efforts to inscribe him into an authoritative narrative; given a knife to sharpen his pen, he seizes the opportunity instead to become the author of his own death.

Hamlet, the greatest of all the revenge tragedies, places its hero in a comparable position. Even before the appearance of his father's ghost, Hamlet is disturbed and evasive, unsettled by his mother's hasty remarriage and his uncle's accession to the throne. Hamlet deploys sardonic wordplay in order to frustrate Claudius's efforts to reassert order:

> [*Claudius*:] But now, my cousin Hamlet, and my son –
> *Hamlet*: A little more than kin and less than kind.
> *Claudius*: How is it that the clouds still hang on you?
> *Hamlet*: Not so, my lord, I am too much i'th' sun.
>
> (I.ii.64–7)

The disrupted family, like the body politic, cannot be united by an easy declaration of kinship; there is, as Marcellus will declare, and Hamlet's obsessive imagery of rankness and corruption will reiterate, 'Something . . . rotten in the state of Denmark' (I.iv.67). Consequently, whereas earlier revenge tragedies had relied heavily on ghosts and other supernatural paraphernalia in order to underline the failings of human justice, the Ghost in *Hamlet* is not such a central presence. This play rather directs attention to a secular context, and looks sceptically at certain foundational discourses of identity.

Crucially, as much as the Ghost by its very existence might be taken to prove the existence of an afterlife, Hamlet confronts orthodox ideas of identity with a radical materialism:

> What piece of work is a man! How noble in reason, how infinite in faculty, in form and moving how express and admirable, in action how like an angel, in apprehension how like a god – the beauty of the world, the paragon of animals! And yet to me what is this quintessence of dust?
>
> (II.ii.293–8)

Hamlet unpicks myths of the grandeur of 'man' by focusing on the material basis of life, which is at once common to all humanity and disturbingly unreliable. His disgust, fuelled by his mother's apparent 'frailty' (I.ii.146), manifests itself ultimately in a misogynistic rejection of sexuality. Hence Ophelia is dismissed to a 'nunnery', while Gertrude is enjoined to avoid her new husband's bed (III.i.130; III.iv.166–7). Hamlet himself, meanwhile, confronts the force of Christian morality, which fills him with qualms about

committing a sin, and presses upon him residual anxieties about the afterlife. Thus, he concludes, 'conscience does make cowards of us all', as it dulls
a revenger's 'native hue of resolution' (III.i.85–6). Nowhere in revenge
tragedy is the pressure between classical codes of heroic action and
Christian doctrines of heroic forbearance more clearly articulated.
Shakespeare not only brings these discourses into conflict, but grants his
protagonist the self-awareness to question their relation, creating in the
process an effect that feels to an audience awfully like madness.

In a play which so powerfully centres attention on the uncertain relation
between life and death, it is appropriate that funerals should figure promi-
nently. Burial practices are designed to contain anxieties surrounding death.
The contemporary funeral service itself rehearses Christian doctrine concerning the immortality of the soul, while the site of the grave memorializes
the deceased person's place in society. Princes are elaborately entombed in
church buildings; paupers are hurried into overcrowded graveyards. At the
outset of the play, Hamlet is indignant that his father's death has not been
properly honoured; leftover 'funeral baked meats', he sneers, have served to
'coldly furnish forth the marriage tables' (I.ii.179–80). Yet Hamlet himself
later upsets the already precarious decorum at the funeral of Ophelia, who
has been allowed a truncated service and a grave in consecrated ground
despite overwhelming evidence that she has suicided. Hamlet's argument
that a man might trace 'the noble dust of Alexander till find it stopping a
bung-hole' (V.i.188–9) travesties the funeral service's solemn 'earth to earth,
ashes to ashes, dust to dust'.[21] Where the Church asserts meaning in the face
of physical disintegration, Hamlet reduces life to a grotesquely random circulation of matter. Nothing, he suggests, can fix the subject in place; nothing can reliably provide meaning to a life.

In the face of such scepticism, the play's conclusion with preparations for
Hamlet's own funeral is steeped in ambivalence, gesturing towards a re-
establishment of order yet naggingly recalling Hamlet's own image of a
heroic life transformed into a cork in a beer-barrel. Identity remains, to the
end, utterly mysterious. As Hamlet's dying words would have it, 'The rest is
silence' (V.ii.300).

2.2 The difference of gender; or the difference that gender makes

In the debate between Hic Mulier and Haec Vir, the participants tease away
at the foundations of gender difference in early modern England.

Distinctions of gender, we should remember, are not the same as those of sex: broadly speaking, while sexual difference is physiological, gender difference is socially constructed, marked by codes of dress, speech and behaviour. These codes are evident as powerful cultural assumptions within any society. In the early modern period they were further enforced by state regulations, and promoted by the teachings of the Church; one biblical text, favoured alike by proponents of sumptuary laws and opponents of the stage, stated that 'The woman shall not wear that which pertaineth unto a man, neither shall a man put on a woman's garment: for all that do so are abomination unto the Lord thy God' (Deuteronomy 22.5). The challenge that Hic Mulier makes to such codes is to suggest that they may be profoundly ideological, shaped in the interests of patriarchal power. Consequently, they may be neither 'natural' nor unchangeable – and this was a challenging and subversive suggestion, at a time when many contemporaries were acutely anxious about the boundaries between the masculine and the feminine.

Anxieties about gender difference were underpinned by prevailing theories of sexual difference. We will consider Renaissance discourse on the body further in the following section; at this stage, however, it is worth noting the perception in physiological tracts that male and female sexual organs were not essentially different but rather uncannily correspondent. 'In this view of sexual difference,' as Stephen Orgel explains, 'the female genitals were simply the male genitals inverted, and carried internally rather than externally.'[22] The fact that the male version protruded from the body was said to be caused by more heat being present at the time of conception – and, not surprisingly, this was claimed as a sign that the female body might be understood merely as a less perfect version of the male body. But since difference was not in any way essential, it was also seen to be unstable. Medical literature recorded cases of female genitalia literally popping out of the body, especially in adolescence and under the strain of extreme physical exertion.[23] This helps to explain concerns surrounding the period of youth: the phase of life in which sexual difference fully asserts itself, and that on which romantic comedy focuses its attention. It also contextualizes Renaissance drama's interest in the potential for gender to be counterfeited. If sexual difference is no more than the quirk of a fold of skin, then why should Hic Mulier not be capable of performing the role of a man? And why should Rosalind, when dressed as a man in Shakespeare's *As You Like It*, not be as much a man as the man she will marry, Orlando?

Orthodox gender codes were supposed to make such questions unthinkable. For Renaissance writers, subjectivity itself was implicitly gendered; when Hamlet considers 'what piece of work is a man', while he may be

thinking about humankind as a species, his fundamental assumptions about
the normative experience of that species are those of a man. Woman, by
comparison, is man's 'other' – a category which, in its very difference, helps
to define and stabilize the sex-gender system. So in early modern society
women were defined by their relations with men, as 'maids' (unmarried, vir-
ginal youths), wives or widows. Hence in Shakespeare's *Measure for
Measure*, when Mariana presents herself at court as neither a wife, maid,
nor widow, the Duke concludes in exasperation that she is 'nothing'
(V.i.170–6). Codes of behaviour were also shaped in the interests of male
authority. According to these codes, which were promoted in a wealth of
conduct books and moralizing literature, women were expected to be
chaste, silent and obedient. That is, they were enjoined to control their
bodies, their speech and their behaviour, shaping each in the interests of
patriarchy.[24]

Equally, male anxieties focused on stereotypes which represented inver-
sions of those ideals, such as the sexually incontinent 'whore', the verbally
unruly 'scold' and the ungovernable 'shrew'. Each is an image of excess;
according to patriarchal thinking, the nature of women required tight controls, especially once they had been introduced to sexuality. And since each
type was merely one manifestation of disobedience to male authority, they
were generally perceived as connected, or even collapsible into one other.
Hence, according to one saying of the time, 'the woman of fluent speech is
never chaste'.[25] And hence the somewhat confused misogyny of Vindice in
The Revenger's Tragedy (probably by Middleton), when he claims: 'Tell but
some woman a secret overnight, / Your doctor may find it in the urinal i'th'
morning' (I.iii.82–3). In Jonson's *Epicene*, meanwhile, male fears of transgression are embodied in the 'collegiate ladies', who reject the authority of
men by assuming rights at once to free speech and free movement about
town. Their central challenge to men is their assertion of authority over
their own bodies, epitomized most clearly in their claim to have discovered
a reliable contraceptive, which will allow them to wrest from men control
over their own sex lives.

As this example demonstrates, Renaissance comedies commonly revolve
around anxieties about the containment of women. Numerous romantic
comedies end with images of hitherto vibrant and independent young
women ceding control of their lives to men. In *As You Like It*, for example,
Rosalind turns first to her father and then to her betrothed, repeating the
words, 'To you I give myself, for I am yours' (V.iv.105–6). Female autonomy
is reduced here to the power to give oneself away. Other plays, such as *A
Midsummer Night's Dream*, figure the patriarchal enclosure of female will
by the collapse of women into almost total silence after the point of

betrothal. Yet playwrights are equally drawn to images of excess and transgression, which test the limits of male control. *Measure for Measure*, a play redolent with concerns about female sexuality, presents the bawd Mistress Overdone, whose own voracious sexuality is signalled by the fact that she has consumed nine husbands; she is, as Pompey puns, 'Overdone by the last' (II.i.181). Not only do the forces of authority in this play fail to contain Mistress Overdone and the disorder she represents, their efforts to appropriate the chaste heroine, Isabella, are also left notably unresolved. Here silence does not necessarily mean female acquiescence. From the point at which the Duke reveals the brother Isabella had believed to be dead, and turns to her with the request (that sounds awfully like a command), 'and for your lovely sake / Give me your hand, and say you will be mine' (V.i.485–6), Isabella says nothing at all.

The control of women is equally a matter of masculine self-assertion. In *Measure for Measure*, the Duke's proposal to Isabella thus represents an effort to reassert himself not only as the legitimate ruler but also as the potent and regenerative patriarch. Similarly, when Katherine in *The Taming of the Shrew* presents her notoriously categorical speech of submission to the values of male authority, her performance wins her husband a wager with other men, and thus marks him as the play's apparently successful figure of masculine strength (V.ii.140–83). Having 'tamed a curst shrew', Petruccio leads her, not surprisingly, 'to bed' (V.ii.192, 188). Yet even this play is not necessarily without a certain play of irony, which might be exploited in performance so as to expose as unstable dominant myths of male authority, and other plays admit more open scepticism. In Shakespeare's *Troilus and Cressida*, the purportedly heroic war waged over a stolen woman degenerates into strikingly shaky performances of masculine strength. Focusing on contemporary settings, city comedies produce characters such as Otter in *Epicoene*, who abuses his wife behind her back yet pliantly submits to her authority at home. In the same play, the comic posturing of the fops John Daw and Amorous La Foole invites the still more radical perception that masculinity may be no more than an unreliable performance.

The contours of such performances were never more apparent than on the stage. Given that there were no female actors in the English Renaissance theatre, male actors were daily involved in the personation of femininity – boys or young men playing most female roles. For critics of the theatre (such as Phillip Stubbes, whom we encountered in Chapter 1), the very act of using on the stage 'garments [which] are set down for signs distinctive between sex and sex ... is to falsify, forge, and adulterate, contrary to the express rule of the word of God'.[26] For modern readers of Renaissance drama, while we might assume that this must generally have been accepted by audiences as a basic condition of theatrical personation, it would be a mistake to assume that such performances were universally unproblematic. Hence it is fair to assume that the boy playing the role of Juliet was always discernible as a boy, and that this gap between performer and performance was always at least a potential source of interest or friction. Moreover, numerous plays explicitly focus attention on the performance of gender, by incorporating narratives of cross-dressing into their plots. A boy playing a woman might be accepted as a mere theatrical convention; a boy playing a woman who dresses herself as a man, by comparison, centres an audience's attention on the problematics of gender-impersonation.

Acts of cross-dressing are indeed pivotal within several of Shakespeare's romantic comedies. In *Twelfth Night*, for instance, the twins Viola and Sebastian are effectively indistinguishable when Viola dresses herself as a young man. Order is apparently restored when Sebastian appears at the end, oozing the machismo that Viola's performance as Cesario has notably lacked, and taking the place of Cesario at the wedding planned for 'him' by the besotted Olivia. In Sebastian's untroubled view, the resolution is entirely natural: if Olivia has married the wrong 'man', it is because 'nature to her bias drew in that' (V.i.253). Yet in the course of the play desire itself has been represented as remarkably unstable, and a subtle performance will reveal the complex reactions of both Olivia and Orsino at the end of the play, when they each realize that the object of their desires has not been what s/he seems. Olivia, who never responds to Sebastian's assertion about her unconscious observance of a natural bias, has not got the coy and submissive boy-girl she had courted, while even Orsino wants to see his beloved in her rightful 'woman's weeds' before he will accept what has been revealed (V.i.266).

As You Like It takes the interrogation of gender roles a step further, as Rosalind first dresses as a boy and then performs for her bewildered lover, Orlando, the role of Rosalind. Though a central source of the play's humour, these multiple performances also have some important effects, especially as Rosalind uses them to confront and remould Orlando's preconceptions about women. She is, in Jean Howard's words, 'theatricalizing for her own purposes what is assumed to be innate, teaching her future mate how to get beyond certain ideologies of gender to more enabling ones'.[27] Hence, when she ultimately 'gives' herself to her father and future husband, she is not necessarily abandoning the degree of agency and vitality she has assumed in the course of the play, in order to conform meekly to a stereotype of female submission. Rather, one might well argue that she and

Orlando ultimately represent an approach to gender roles in marriage that differs, subtly yet significantly, from early modern orthodoxy.

City comedies of the early seventeenth century translate romantic cross-dressing narratives into an urban, mercantile context. In Jonson's *Epicene*, for example, a boy is employed to play the role of a woman, in order to dupe the miserly Morose into giving money to his canny and acquisitive nephew, Dauphine. There is no love in this world. Instead, Morose is initially attracted to Epicene because s/he performs impeccably the stereotypical woman of male fantasy: chaste, obedient and almost perfectly silent. He subsequently rejects her, and submits to the authority of his nephew, when Epicene switches into the role of the shrewish wife, which s/he plays equally well. There is a disturbingly subversive logic at work here. For, if a boy can perform the positive and negative female stereotypes better than any woman, then perhaps those stereotypes may be no more than the products of male fantasy. And fantasies, in a mercantile environment, may be traded like any other commodity. This point is underscored elsewhere in the play, most notably in Otter's misogynistic rant about the cost of sustaining his wife's appearance: 'All her teeth were made i'the Blackfriars, both her eyebrows i'the Strand, and her hair in Silver Street. Every part o'the town owns a piece of her' (IV.ii.93–6). In this satiric vision, not only the beauty of women but their physical being is depicted as the product of a grotesque marketplace. For the purposes of the satire, the grammatical structure of the sentence is significantly pointed: Mrs Otter does not herself own her beauty; instead she is owned piecemeal by the 'town'.[28]

Perhaps the most rigorous reassessment of romantic cross-dressing plots is offered by the relatively late city comedy, *The Roaring Girl*, co-written by Middleton and Dekker. Here the cross-dressing woman is not the apparent romance heroine, Mary Fitz-Allard, whose desired marriage is being blocked unreasonably by the father of her lover. Instead, 'the roaring girl' is Moll, a woman with a dubious background in the London underworld, who emerges as the play's undeniable centre of comic energy as she helps to bring the lovers together. Yet Moll is not a typical comic cross-dresser: firstly because most people in the play know that she is a woman, even when she is performing the part of a man; and secondly because she chooses to dress as a man not as a means to a romantic end, but rather as an ongoing effort to evade the constrictions of gender codes. From this ambiguous subject-position she presents an incisive critique of male expectations of women, especially in her humiliation of the braggart Laxton. He makes the mistake of interpreting her transgressive dress and unfettered speech as signs of sexual looseness. In response, as she physically beats him she also makes a subtle point about language. Masculine romantic discourse, she argues, is self-interested and exploitative, and repays the 'good thoughts' of women only with a 'blasted name' (III.i.83). Given such assumptions, she suggests, there is simply no legitimate place in contemporary culture for either female speech or female desire.

The Roaring Girl has a conservative comic momentum, as the thwarted lovers are brought together and Moll helps to discipline those who threaten the precarious domestic stability of the city. In some respects she even endorses existing gender codes, teaching the men to be men and the women to be women. Yet the play is striking in its appreciation that there is no place in this society for someone who herself challenges these codes. Moll, therefore, remains an outsider. She says, cryptically, 'I have no humor to marry. I love to lie o'both sides o'th'bed myself' (II.ii.37–8) – a comment that reflects grimly on the powerlessness of women within marriage, while possibly also hinting at an unstable sexuality that would be stifled within the bounds of enforced heterosexuality. Her challenge is thus decisively limited, and these limits are particularly pressing on her sexual identity. 'Except in her dreams,' Howard argues, 'Moll cannot be a free sexual subject and escape being called a whore.'[29]

2.3 The Renaissance body

It is often said that the past is a foreign country, with its own beliefs and codes which are in some respects familiar, yet in others entirely alien. Although by modern standards it is easy to think that the people there knew *less*, it is more profitable to approach the past as an anthropologist approaches another culture, on the understanding that the people simply knew different things and thought in different ways. This is never more evident than when we encounter Renaissance ideas about the body, and attempt to appreciate the effects that these had on constructions of identity. It is worth remembering, for instance, that Shakespeare wrote all his plays before the circulation of blood had been demonstrated, and at a time when most physiological theory accepted Aristotle's location of sensory knowledge and imagination in the heart rather than the brain. So while bodies have not changed much physiologically since the sixteenth century, the ways in which bodies are understood have been entirely transformed.

Renaissance physiological knowledge rested on the theory that the body was governed by four 'humours': blood, phlegm, yellow bile and black bile. Each humour was related at once to physical and psychological conditions. For example, a melancholy state is one dominated by black bile, which is excessively dry and cold, whereas a phlegmatic state is excessively watery, cold and dull. (We can see here the origin of our term for the common 'cold'.) Humoral theory also explains differences of gender and age. Female bodies were thought to be more wet and cold than male bodies, just as youthful bodies were more wet than those of the aged. For writers, humoral theory afforded a rudimentary way of representing individual characteristics and eccentricities; indeed, it provided the basis for Jonson's plays, *Every Man in his Humour* and *Every Man out of his Humour*. But while Jonson, as a satirist, revelled in the depiction of extreme types of human behaviour, the average person was urged by medical theory to monitor his or her humours, with the goal of maintaining a rough state of balance. This explains, of course, the common practice of blood-letting. It also underpinned a culture of self-scrutiny, which encouraged each person to engage in a constant examination of his or her body, looking vigilantly for signs of disorder.[30] In this respect physiological theory coalesced with the religious doctrine examined earlier in this chapter, which encouraged the individual to search for signs of God's favour. For one puritan diarist, disease should prompt the sufferer to 'labour to find the cause why and to what purpose God doth follow you in such a kind'.[31]

These theories also affected the ways in which the identities of other people were interpreted. Stubbes, as we have already seen, fantasized that signs of moral turpitude might be made visible on the face of a sinner. In cases of witchcraft, a comparable logic impelled invasive searches of the female body, in efforts 'to find a "witch's mark," a hidden nipple in her "secret parts" at which she is supposed to suckle her [devilish] familiar'.[32] Attacks on Richard III were informed by a similar belief that qualities of an individual's character might be legible on the surface of his or her body: a belief, that is, in physiognomy. Interestingly, while Shakespeare invokes such beliefs, his play resists a clear endorsement of them, therefore leaving identity itself as a construct infinitely more complex than the science of physiognomy would allow. For Queen Margaret, the hunch-backed Richard is a man upon whom 'Sin, death, and hell have set their marks' (I.iii.291). But Richard himself reverses Margaret's apparently straightforward logic of cause and effect, suggesting that since he has been 'Cheated of feature by dissembling nature', and is therefore unfit for the regular pastimes of a courtier, he shapes himself for evil: 'determined', he says, 'to prove a villain' (I.i.19, 30). As we might expect from Shakespeare, identity becomes more problematic in this play, and presents challenges for characters and audience alike. Margaret's moral absolutism seems woefully inadequate in such a world.

As Shakespeare's physiognomic scepticism suggests, many contemporaries were all too well aware of the limitations of their knowledge of the body. Humoral theory at times seemed to beg as many questions as it answered. John Donne, ever concerned about the science of the self, asked:

> Know'st thou but how the stone doth enter in
> The bladder's cave, and never break the skin?
> Know'st thou how blood, which to the heart doth flow,
> Doth from one ventricle to th' other go?
> And for the putrid stuff, which thou dost spit,
> Know'st thou how thy lungs have attracted it?
>   [. . .]
> What hope have we to know our selves, when we
> Know not the least things, which for our use be?[33]

In the face of such doubts, the emergent art of anatomy promised a new kind of bodily knowledge, based on investigations beneath the surface of the skin.[34] Anatomy was still a controversial and relatively uncommon practice in England in the early seventeenth century, and as a result attracted intense interest. Anatomy 'theatres' were sites of public performance, in which 'thing[s] within that passeth show' were incontrovertibly exposed to the gaze of an audience. For some observers, anatomy threatened to expose secrets which should be the exclusive province of God; for others, though, this arena fuelled freshly potent fantasies of revelation and control.

A late Renaissance play, Ford's *'Tis Pity She's a Whore*, spectacularly interrogates the desire to find hidden truths of identity within the body. At a time when the English were becoming increasingly accustomed to the achievements of anatomy, this play asserts afresh the limitations of investigation. Most notably, the word 'heart' resonates through the play, used more than 35 times in total. There was no more mysterious bodily organ than the heart, and none more loaded with metaphorical and metaphysical significance. As noted above, in Aristotelian thought the heart performed many of the functions we now attribute to the brain, while in Christian doctrine it was accepted as a vital centre of spiritual identity. The heart had thus come to signify the source of one's innermost thoughts and secret feelings, the seat of emotions, and the source of desire and truth.[35] And within this context, anatomy promised to expose to view the faultline between metaphor and reality. At the Elizabethan court in 1600, for instance, a woman who died in grief, soon after her brother's death, was given a crude autopsy at the command of the queen. All was found to be 'well and sound' except for 'certain strings striped all over her heart'.[36] It was, it seemed, broken.

Giovanni, the unhinged protagonist of *'Tis Pity She's a Whore*, fixates on the heart as an essential site of identity. Early in the play, declaring his incestuous love for his sister, Annabella, he offers her a dagger, daring her: 'Rip up my bosom; there thou shalt behold / A heart in which is writ the truth I speak' (I.ii.210–11). This performance seems at the time a mere act of emotional hyperbole; however, it gathers a menacing significance as a range of characters variously speculate on secrets hidden in hearts, and Annabella's husband threatens to 'rip up [her] heart' in search of truth (IV.iii.53). In the play's extraordinary climax, Giovanni himself turns into a debased anatomist, tearing Annabella's heart from her chest and marching into a banquet with the dripping organ impaled on his dagger. The subsequent dialogue is even more remarkable. What Giovanni had imagined as a moment of tragic triumph threatens to collapse into farce as the other characters fail to grasp the significance of his bloody trophy. Moreover, as much as he declares that ''Tis a heart, / A heart . . . in which is mine entombed' (V.vi.26–7), the play itself suggests an unsettling alternative interpretation. In a text which has depicted characters variously tormented by neurotic desires to know – or, quite literally, to see – the truth of another person's identity, the shock is palpable. Annabella's heart simply bears 'none of the secret signs of inner truth'. Instead, in 'its appalling blankness, its resistance to allegoric inscription, it becomes a sign of indistinction and undifferentiation'.[37]

This stunning dramatic spectacle presents a grotesque counterpoint to Hamlet's boast that he has 'that within which passeth show' (I.ii.85). Throughout this chapter we have been concerned with the various ways in which playwrights explore the mysteries of identity. There has been no consensus, but rather evidence of a lively contemporary debate, with arguments ranging from Hamlet's claim to an indefinably unique subjectivity through to Ford's image of materialist indistinction. As I am arguing throughout this book, it is precisely these uncertainties – these traces of intellectually sophisticated writers tackling the greatest questions of their time – that give Renaissance drama much of its power and mystery. For us, living at a time when heart transplants are almost routine, if we are to grasp the significance of Ford's dramatic image, it is critical that we should historicize the heart. Though it is, of course, equally important that we should feel the sheer horror of this remarkable scene.

Notes

1 Stephen Greenblatt, *Renaissance Self-Fashioning: From More to Shakespeare* (Chicago and London, 1980), p. 2.

2 Michel Foucault, *The Order of Things* (London, 1970), p. 387; quoted in Catherine Belsey, *The Subject of Tragedy: Identity and Difference in Renaissance Drama* (London and New York, 1985), p. 13.

3 Paul Delany, *British Autobiography in the Seventeenth Century* (London, 1969), p. 1.

4 Francis Barker, *The Tremulous Private Body: Essays on Subjection* (Ann Arbor, 1995), pp. 32–3.

5 Katharine Eisaman Maus, *Inwardness and Theater in the English Renaissance* (Chicago and London, 1995), esp. pp. 1–6.

6 See Lisa Jardine, *Still Harping on Daughters: Women and Drama in the Age of Shakespeare* (New York, 1983), ch. 5; <http://ren.dm.net/sumptuary/index.html>.

7 See Maus, *Inwardness and Theater*, p. 13.

8 *Of the Laws of Ecclesiaticall Polity*, ed. Arthur Stephen McGrade (Cambridge, 1989), p. 124.

9 *Good Conscience: Or a Treatise Shewing the Nature, Meanes, Marks, Benefit, and Necessity thereof* (1624), pp. 12, 14.

10 Robert A. Erickson, *The Language of the Heart, 1600–1750* (Philadelphia, 1997), p. 38.

11 *Anatomie of Abuses* (1583), 1.99; quoted in Peter Stallybrass, 'Reading the Body: *The Revenger's Tragedy* and the Jacobean Theater of Consumption', *Renaissance Drama*, 18 (1987), 122.

12 *Essays*, ed. John Pitcher (London, 1985), p. 179; see Jonathan Dollimore, *Radical Tragedy: Religion, Ideology and Power in the Drama of Shakespeare and his Contemporaries*, 2nd edn (New York, 1989), esp. pp. 9–17.

13 Jean-Christophe Agnew, *Worlds Apart: The Market and the Theater in Anglo-American Thought, 1550–1750* (Cambridge, 1986), p. 84.

14 Daniel Javitch, *Poetry and Courtliness in Renaissance England* (Princeton, 1978), p. 55.

15 Stephen Greenblatt, *Sir Walter Raleigh: The Renaissance Man and his Roles* (New Haven and London, 1973), p. 40.

16 We might usefully compare this text to the considerably earlier, and more conservative, *Friar Bacon and Friar Bungay*, in which a jester consistently fails to convince in his impersonation of the king.

17 Jean E. Howard, *The Stage and Social Struggle in Early Modern England* (London and New York, 1994), p. 32.

18 *Subject of Tragedy*, p. 13.

19 Belsey, *Subject of Tragedy*, p. 111.

20 *Essays*, p. 72.

21 'The Order for the Burial of the Dead', from *The Book of Common Prayer* (1559); <http://justus.anglican.org/resources/bcp/Burial_1559.htm>

22 Stephen Orgel, *Impersonations: The Performance of Gender in Shakespeare's England* (Cambridge, 1996), p. 20.

23 See Stephen Greenblatt, *Shakespearean Negotiations* (Oxford, 1988), pp. 73–86.

24 See Sara Mendelson and Patricia Crawford, *Women in Early Modern England* (Oxford, 1998), pp. 65–71.

25 Quoted in Jardine, *Still Harping on Daughters*, p. 57; see further Peter Stallybrass, 'Patriarchal Territories: The Body Enclosed', in *Rewriting the Renaissance: The Discourses of Sexual Difference in Early Modern Europe*, ed. Margaret W. Ferguson *et al.* (1986), pp. 123–42.

26 Stephen Gosson, *Playes Confuted in Five Actions* (1582), sig. E3v; quoted in Howard, *Stage and Social Struggle*, p. 40.

27 Howard, *Stage and Social Struggle*, p. 119.

28 See further Karen Newman, *Fashioning Femininity and English Renaissance Drama* (Chicago and London, 1991), pp. 129–43.

29 Howard, *Stage and Social Struggle*, p. 125.

30 See further Michael E. Schoenfeldt, *Bodies and Selves in Early Modern England:*

Physiology and Inwardness in Spenser, Shakespeare, Herbert, and Milton (Cambridge, 1999), pp. 1–39.

31 Nehemiah Wallington, quoted in Andrew Wear, 'Puritan Perceptions of Illness in Seventeenth Century England', in *Patients and Practitioners: Lay Perceptions of Medicine in Pre-Industrial Society*, ed. Roy Porter (Cambridge, 1985), p. 71.

32 Maus, *Inwardness and Theater*, p. 115.

33 'Of the Progress of the Soul: The Second Anniversary', ll. 269–80; in *John Donne: The Complete English Poems*, ed. A. J. Smith (London, 1986), p. 295.

34 See Jonathan Sawday, *The Body Emblazoned: Dissection and the Human Body in Renaissance Culture* (London and New York, 1995).

35 Erickson, *The Language of the Heart*, p. 11.

36 Quoted in Michael Neill, ' "What strange riddle's this?": Deciphering *'Tis Pity She's a Whore*', in *John Ford: Critical Revisions*, ed. Neill (Cambridge, 1988), p. 156.

37 Neill, ' "What strange riddle's this?" ', p. 168.

|3|

Of love: desire and domesticity

This chapter's document, taken from William Gouge's *Of Domesticall Duties* (see pp. 149–51), considers the relation between individual desires and social responsibilities. Like a wealth of other material from this era, much of it written by clergymen such as Gouge, this book as a whole is concerned broadly with the place of *affect* (emotional feeling or desire) in society. Hence he suggests that 'mutual love and good liking' provide an important basis for a marriage, but not if these concerns override 'what is honest and meet': in other words, if the couple are of differing social degrees, or if their families and friends otherwise disapprove of the match. In such cases, Gouge translates 'mutual love' into the 'violence of lust'. According to his theory – shaky as it may seem – it is simply inconceivable that true love could ever threaten prevailing notions of hierarchy and social order. Love must, by definition, serve the interests of 'the order which God hath established'. Although his book consistently acknowledges interests of affect, it is ultimately a manual of instruction for a godly life; it defines, at considerable length, domestic *duties*.

Gouge is often described as a puritan; however, he wrote at a time when there was no great difference between puritanism and Protestant orthodoxy, and his work was undeniably popular and influential throughout his society. It would be a mistake, however, to accept his arguments as entirely uncontroversial. For example, his commitment to the role of 'mutual liking' between a couple before their marriage implicitly sides with those who dared to criticize the courtly practice of arranged marriages. Just a few years before Gouge's book was published, Sir Edward Coke, one of the finest legal thinkers of the century, battered down a door in order to seize his 15-year-old daughter, intending to marry her against her will to the foolish brother of the king's court favourite.[1] Further, Gouge's arguments about the importance of parental approval would hardly have appealed to the recently installed Dean of St Paul's, the poet John Donne, who had secretly married the daughter of his employer in 1601. More importantly in the present context, we might imagine that Gouge's views would have made him a dull critic of contemporary literature – of, for instance, Donne's rapturous love poetry, or Shakespeare's representation of passionate love between young members of rival households in *Romeo and Juliet*. Literature, thankfully, is rather more complex than Gouge's sermonizing.

Turning to the drama of Gouge's era, we find playwrights consistently addressing the issues he raises. Countless plays, that is, explore the demands of affect in human life, and its relation to structures of 'order'. But while Gouge presents arguments, plays stage debates; and while Gouge defines uneasy compromises, plays juxtapose polarized views. Hence Juliet's classic statements of love and desire clash with her father's perception of a daughter's duty to comply with patriarchal will. In this chapter, then, we will consider three aspects of affect. Firstly, we will explore ideas of love, a fundamental concept which itself demands to be recognized as in part a cultural construction. Secondly, we will attend to marriage and its place in society. And thirdly, we will discuss relations between parents and children. In all areas we will discern playwrights struggling – sometimes anxiously, sometimes insistently – to define a legitimate place for affect in human relations.

3.1 'This weak passion': historicizing love

The idea of historicizing love is one that many people will want to resist. Love certainly *seems* transcendent and ahistorical; the love of Romeo and Juliet, for instance, seems so easily translatable into a modern context. But the more we study Renaissance discourses of love, the more alien and uncertain the concept becomes. Francis Bacon, for example, considers love a 'weak passion', which will of necessity be avoided by 'great spirits', in the interests of their 'great business'. Indeed, he begins his essay 'Of Love' by drawing a clear distinction between theatre and life: 'For as to the stage, love is ever matter of comedies and now and then of tragedies; but in life it doth much mischief, sometimes like a siren, sometimes like a fury.'[2] Reading Bacon, it becomes evident that, while sexual desire may be ahistorical, the ways in which a culture ascribes meaning to it, or turns it into discourse, are not. Love is a cultural construction, and its meaning in some respects has never been less clear than it was in the Renaissance. In this section, while centring the discussion on love, we will consider also desire and sexuality; though they are connected in various ways, it will be important to maintain a sense of the differences between these three concepts.

It is possible to identify a range of different discourses of love in the Renaissance, each of which encodes variant meanings. At the conclusion of his essay, Bacon distinguishes three types, arguing that 'Nuptial love maketh mankind; friendly love perfecteth it; but wanton love corrupteth and embaseth it.'[3] Forming a rough hierarchy of value, he thus suggests that sexual desires outside of marriage threaten both the individual and the state, love within marriage is necessary for the health and continuation of the state, while love between friends underpins an ideal state. His position is not without religious support. Gouge, as we have seen, argues that marriages should bolster existing social structures: couples should be of similar status, and their decisions should be endorsed by parents or friends. Further, the famous passage in 1 Corinthians 13, which is translated in modern versions of the Bible as a celebration of love (and consequently read at countless weddings), is routinely translated in the Renaissance as an endorsement instead of 'charity': a godly and generous love of one's neighbours, as opposed to an amorous love of one particular person.

At the Renaissance court, ideas of love were given further, subtly different inflections. Codes of courtly love, largely derived from the continent, posited a distant and unattainable woman as an object of intense desire. As a result, these codes produced a wealth of poetry in which male writers describe their lovers in a conventional language of adoration, and beg abjectly for signs of favour. Much of the great English love poetry of the sixteenth century was written within this context, while some of the very best is concerned also to interrogate its underlying premisses. Therefore in Shakespeare's 'Sonnet 130', his 'mistress' eyes are nothing like the sun'; and yet, the speaker concludes, 'I think my love as rare / As any she belied with false compare'. For those involved in the quest for career advancement at court, meanwhile, 'love' also had other meanings. In particular, this malleable word had always signified political favour – one rises, that is, through the 'love' of one's patron – and this discourse was intensified in the reign of Elizabeth, when male courtiers vied for the attention of a notoriously vain female monarch. Consequently, distinctly different discourses of love were available at any one time, and may even mix within a single text.[4]

For the general population beyond the court – the very people who constituted the bulk of an audience at a playhouse – it is possible that this range of meanings was somewhat more restricted. There is in fact historical debate on this point. On the one hand, Lawrence Stone characterizes England in the period 1450 to 1630 as a 'low affect' society, in which relationships between sexual partners, spouses and close family members were less emotionally intense compared with such relationships in later centuries. He attributes this to a range of factors, including the relatively short and uncertain life-spans of the time, the widespread perception that marriage was in part a business arrangement, and the fact that children and youths commonly spent years living apart from their parents. As a consequence, he argues, an Elizabethan audience of *Romeo and Juliet* would have identified the source of the tragedy 'in the way [the lovers] brought destruction on themselves by violating the norms of the society in which they lived'.[5] On the other hand, Keith Wrightson argues that Stone is overly swayed by evidence of the social elite, and amasses a considerable range of counter-evidence that indicates great depth of feeling in affective relationships.[6] Others still, in accord with Gouge's vision, suggest that affective relationships were more tightly located within the context of local peer groups, and hence lacked the intimacy and exclusiveness that we might assume of such bonds.[7]

Since valid evidence is raised in support of each argument, perhaps the crucial lesson for us is that there were at this time a range of different attitudes towards affective relations, and a range of available discourses. In some plays, especially those aimed at a cultural elite, the exploration of these different options assumes formulaic dimensions. For example, John Lyly's *Endymion*, first performed before Queen Elizabeth, establishes a clear hierarchy between types of love. Eumenides is forced to prioritize his love for a woman and his love for his male friend, Endymion, and concludes that, 'The love of men to women is a thing common, and of course; the friendship of man to man infinite, and immortal' (III.iv.119–21). Endymion himself privileges an even purer form of love, which he feels for the unattainable queen, Cynthia. We can virtually feel the playwright gesturing ever so respectfully to his own queen, as Endymion declares that:

> Such a difference hath the gods set between our states that all must be duty, loyalty, and reverence; nothing, without it vouchsafe Your Highness, be termed love.
>
> (V.iv.156–9)

At the court of Charles I, who assumed the throne in 1625, discourse on love again assumed the dimensions of a cult, and was explored particularly in pastoral comedies and tragicomedies. In the early 1630s, John Fletcher's *The Faithful Shepherdess*, which had failed in the public theatre in 1610, achieved a successful revival, alongside plays such as William Montagu's *The Shepherd's Paradise* and Joseph Rutter's *The Shepherd's Holiday*.

Lower in the social order, while emotions were not necessarily codified and intellectualized with such clarity, people were equally moved by their emotions. One seventeenth-century apprentice, for instance, seemed deeply unnerved by the strength of his feelings for a particular woman, stating in his diary that 'my affections ran out violently after her, so as that I was never contented one day to the end unless I had seen her, and chiefly my affections were set upon her virtues and womanly qualities'.[8] For such a man, the experience of seeing a play such as *Romeo and Juliet* (as he may well have done) might have been a more complex experience than Stone would admit, since the drama of this period was staging the very debates about love and desire that he appears to have been posing within his own mind. He might have puzzled in particular over Friar Laurence's neatly conventional moralizing on the lovers:

> These violent delights have violent ends,
> And in their triumph die like fire and powder,
> Which as they kiss consume.

> (II.v.9–11)

While this judgement accords with the views of Bacon, and even with those of Lyly, it seems in many respects inadequate as an assessment of Shakespeare's lovers. For the apprentice, like many others in Shakespeare's audience, it represented merely one position among a spectrum of contemporary attitudes.

Interestingly, the apprentice did not articulate his emotions in a discourse of 'love'; instead, he was concerned by the simple yet urgent promptings of desire. Essentially unpredictable and uncontainable, desire presents a problem for any society wishing to base itself on Gouge's principles of order. Conventional poetic imagery of the time underlines this point. Edmund Spenser depicts his waylaid hero in *The Faerie Queene* lying by a fountain, making 'goodly court' to his lady, 'Pourd out in loosnesse on the grassy grownd, / Both carelesse of his health, and of his fame'. Similarly, John Milton describes Adam and Eve in Eden immediately after the Fall, as 'They swim in mirth', with 'Carnal desire inflaming' their minds.[9] In each case desire is figured as fluid and unstable, and is implicitly set against substantial values of reason and heroism. As such, desire is often represented as a threat to masculine identity: as, in fact, a potentially effeminizing influence. When Mark Antony laments in Mary Sidney's *Tragedy of Antonie*, that 'In wanton love a woman thee misleads, / Sunk in foul sink' (I.120–1), his sexually loaded misogyny precisely echoes that of Sidney's own time. By contrast, he subsequently lauds 'the love, the never-changing love', through which his 'heart' is 'bound' to that of a male comrade (III.99–100).

Antony was in fact one of Bacon's examples of a man who failed to recognize the superiority of 'friendly love' over 'wanton love'; he was 'indeed a voluptuous man and inordinate'.[10] Plays, however, stage Bacon's discourse in dialogic and contestatory ways, as we might observe more closely in Shakespeare's version of the same narrative. The imagery of *Antony and Cleopatra* is tightly constructed into interlocking binaries: male and female, reason and passion, land and water, Rome and Egypt. Hence Antony's desire for Cleopatra is intimately connected to his loss of military and political power; he becomes, in the words of one of his followers, 'so leaky / That we must leave thee to thy sinking' (III.xiii.63–4). More pointedly, the verb 'melt' recurs at crucial moments. Antony opens the play defiantly committed to Cleopatra, declaring, 'Let Rome in Tiber melt, and the wide arch / Of the ranged empire fall. Here is my space' (I.i.35–6); later, he laments that 'Authority melts from me of late' (III.xiii.90).[11] But this is not to say that the play necessarily endorses the cultural association of desire with effeminacy. At the point of death Cleopatra proclaims herself 'marble-constant' (V.ii.236), an image of remarkable strength and solidity that belies the misogynist attacks on her. Moreover, despite their excesses, the lovers make the values of Roman masculinity appear by comparison hard and sterile. The play thus allows its audience, as Catherine Belsey argues, 'no single, unified position' from which to judge either its central characters or the value of desire itself.[12] We are forced instead to weigh the different discourses against one another, appreciating in the process the absorbing tensions between them.

If desire was a potential threat to order, the channelling of it into legitimate paths became a fundamental social goal. Hence the institution of marriage and the acceptance of 'courtship' as a phase leading towards an acceptable end; and hence Gouge's forthright rejection, elsewhere in his book, of bigamy, incest, the 'sin of buggery with beasts', and 'unnatural commixtions of parties of the same sex'.[13] The prevailing discourses of heterosexual desire were also distinctly gendered, positing the man as the desiring subject and the woman as the desired object. This model is typified in the opening scene of *Much Ado About Nothing*, in which Claudio professes his love for Hero to his male friends, before he has spent so much as a minute alone with her or exchanged so much as a single word with her. His rhetorical question, 'Can the world buy such a jewel?' (I.i.146), betrays his entirely conventional objectification of the female. She is a jewel or a prize, the possession of which promises to lift Claudio's status in the eyes of his peers; in the words of a Proverb cited by Gouge, 'a virtuous woman is a crown to her husband' (Proverbs 12.4).[14] Inevitably, given the preconceptions underlying this discourse, when Claudio is convinced that Hero has been unchaste, the 'rich and precious gift' is immediately transformed in his eyes to a 'rotten orange' (IV.i.26, 30).

This makes the articulation of *female* desire a distinct cultural problem. Female poets in this period courted accusations of sexual looseness if they tried to write within the conventional structures of love poetry that had been established by male writers. This concern also appears to lie behind the lament of Moll, in *The Roaring Girl*, that if a woman should happen to 'cast a liberal eye' upon a man, he will think her a 'fond flexible whore' (III.i.74–5).[15] A number of contemporary tragedies similarly challenge audiences to reassess their assumptions about female desire, as they combine narratives of moral downfall with glimpses into more complex subjectivities. In Thomas Middleton's *Women Beware Women*, for example, the experienced courtier Livia makes the apparently innocuous argument that before their marriage, 'Maids should both see and like' (I.ii.34). She continues more provocatively, arguing that a man

> tastes of many sundry dishes
> That we poor wretches never lay our lips to –
> As obedience, forsooth, subjection, duty, and such kickshaws,
> All of our making, but served in to them.
> And if we lick a finger then sometimes,
> We are not to blame; your best cooks use it.
>
> (I.ii.42–7)

After a powerful assault on the sexual double-standard, Livia's sting lies in the sexual innuendo of the final lines, which foreshadows her own sexual assertiveness in the play. While Livia gets her tragic comeuppance – poisoned in a spectacularly murderous masque at the end of the play – it would be misguided to dismiss her arguments as those of an immoral woman. Instead, the teasingly compelling logic of her speech resonates throughout the text.

Like all the plays presented in the Renaissance theatres, Livia is a character written by a man, to be performed by a man. Although surviving play-texts written by women are rare, Elizabeth Cary's *Tragedy of Mariam* provides a more complex, and in many respects more radical, critique of the sex–gender system. Cary juxtaposes two women who are unhappy in their marriages: Salome, who wants to divorce Constabarus, and who presents some trenchant arguments about sexual double-standards in support of her position; and Mariam, who responds to her moral disgust for Herod by withdrawing herself entirely from sexual relations. Although each woman operates by very different moral codes, they share a common 'desire for power over their own bodies'.[16] In Salome's words, such unconventional attitudes offer 'To show my sex the way to freedom's door' (I.iv.50). Interestingly, while Herod is sympathetic to Salome, he simply has no way of accommodating Mariam's intention, and so interprets her arguments as a mere cover for adulterous desires. For him she is a 'white enchantress', while even the supportive Sohemus concludes that 'Unbridled speech is Mariam's worst disgrace' (IV.iv.18; III.iii.65). The very act of female self-assertion, as we have seen in Chapter 2, is all too easily aligned with sexual immorality. As Herod declares: 'She's unchaste; / Her mouth will ope to ev'ry stranger's ear' (IV.vii.77–8).

The normative heterosexuality which underpins Renaissance discourses of sexual love also presents challenges for the representation of homo-eroticism and homosexual relationships. In this period, nobody identified themselves as 'homosexual'; that identity, or way of understanding and shaping subjectivity, only became available in Western culture towards the end of the nineteenth century. Legally, homosexual acts between men, known as sodomy, were at this time capital offences; although, curiously, very few cases ever made their way to court.[17] Homosexual acts between women, meanwhile, were sufficiently unthinkable that they were not even covered by the law. And yet, in a society in which people of the same sex often lived in very close proximity, commonly sharing living quarters and beds, there is good reason to believe that homosexual acts were not at all uncommon. Hence the naive Martha in Richard Brome's *The Antipodes*, recalls how

> A wanton maid once lay with me, and kissed
> And clipped and clapped me strangely, and then wished
> That I had been a man to have got her with child.
>
> (I.i.254–6)

While Martha is represented as comically ignorant about sex, her innocent inquisitiveness is telling. She reminds us that lesbianism existed, though it was neither understood nor expressed in the way it is today.[18]

Authors were therefore involved in a process of exploring these shadowy areas of sexuality, and looking for ways of articulating desires that were officially outlawed yet widely evident. As a consequence, homoeroticism is often encoded in ways we might not immediately recognize. For instance, critics have argued for centuries about the nature of the love between men that is figured in the first 126 of Shakespeare's *Sonnets*. Is this a conventional language of patronage, or a forthright exploration of homosexual love? Faced with such questions, Bruce R. Smith, one of several recent critics to explore this field, identifies certain 'myths' which, he argues, encode homoeroticism in the Renaissance – such as the myth of 'the passionate shepherd', or that of 'combatants and comrades'.[19] Such myths – and Smith's list should not be seen as in any way exhaustive – provide codes through which homosexual desire may be represented. They provide the resources necessary to bring hidden and unsanctioned desires into language.

We might, then, think in this context about the obviously sexualized bond between the 'combatants and comrades' Achilles and Patroclus in Shakespeare's *Troilus and Cressida*, or even the compulsive attraction Aufidius admits for Coriolanus when the former foes unite:

> Know thou first,
> I loved the maid I married; never man
> Sighed truer breath. But that I see thee here,
> Thou noble thing, more dances my rapt heart
> Than when I first my wedded mistress saw
> Bestride my threshold.
>
> (Shakespeare, *Coriolanus*, IV.v.112–17)

While Aufidius does not have any form of sexual relationship with Coriolanus, his words betray an attraction that seems overwhelming and uncontrollable – and that, perhaps, feeds the fury of his final murderous assault on the man.

Other critics have drawn attention to the unstable and ambiguous discourses of desire in certain plays, especially comedies involving cross-dressing. Stephen Greenblatt thus focuses attention on the 'mobility of desire' in *Twelfth Night*, in which Orsino and Olivia each fall in love with a woman dressed as a boy.[20] Admittedly this play, like many others, provides an ostensibly conservative heterosexual closure; however, while closure may depend on 'closing off the glimpsed transgression', the experience of the play has been altogether more ambiguous, or 'plural', than the ending might admit.[21] And what, finally, are we to make of the loose ends? The sea captain, Antonio, has risked his life in order to spend three months, 'day and night', with Sebastian, a man whom he professes to 'love without retention or restraint' (V.I.91, 75). At the end of the play he remains distinctly uncoupled: a silent reminder, perhaps, of other forms of love and other biases of nature.[22]

Christopher Marlowe's history play, *Edward II*, demonstrates vividly the range and complexity of discourses of love on the Renaissance stage. Marlowe himself was a transgressive figure, alleged to have asserted that 'all they that love not tobacco and boys were fools', and that 'St. John the Evangelist was bedfellow to Christ and ... used him as the sinners of Sodom'.[23] *Edward II*, which focuses on power struggles surrounding the controversial relationship between the king and his favourite, Piers Gaveston, provides some of the most compelling language of homoeroticism in the entire body of Renaissance drama. In the opening scene, Gaveston declares:

> I must have wanton poets, pleasant wits,
> Musicians that with touching of a string
> May draw the pliant king which way I please.
> Music and poetry is his delight;
> Therefore I'll have Italian masques by night,
> Sweet speeches, comedies, and pleasing shows;
> And in the day, when he shall walk abroad,
> Like sylvan nymphs my pages shall be clad;
> My men, like Satyrs grazing on the lawns,
> Shall with their goat feet dance an antic hay.
> Sometime a lovely boy in Dian's shape,
> With hair that gilds the water as it glides,
> Crownets of pearl about his naked arms,
> And in his sportful hands an olive tree
> To hide those parts which men delight to see,
> Shall bathe him in a spring
> [. . .]
> Such things as these best please His Majesty.
>
> (I.i.50–70)

It was an accepted fact of court life that monarchs should have their favourites. What Gaveston does, though, is draw to the surface the implicit homoeroticism of such relationships, as he lovingly imagines the 'things' that will 'best please his majesty'. In this way, the relation between 'master and minion', which always carried homoerotic potential, becomes overtly – and, for the other courtiers, confrontingly – sexual.

It is therefore easy to assume when viewing the play – or, especially, when watching Derek Jarman's 1991 cinematic translation of Marlowe's text into a modern context of gay-rights agitation – that Edward and Gaveston are victimized on account of their sexual transgression. The play might thus be interpreted as a fable of homophobia, inviting sympathy for a couple who are vilified on account of their illicit love. But Marlowe's play is more complex than this, largely because of the way in which it explores the interconnections between desire and power. Gaveston's imagined pleasures, we should note, have a political end; he wants to 'draw the pliant King which way I please'. Moreover, it is striking how little the other courtiers, when expressing their grievances about Gaveston, mention the erotic nature of his relationship with Edward. Rather, they are furious that a man of lowly birth is rising to such a position of power at court; the word 'minion', as Smith notes, 'seldom passes their lips without a qualifying [adjective] "base" '.[24] This anxiety about social hierarchy, coupled with the ambition of the

younger Mortimer, creates the conditions in which the evidently sexual relationship between the king and his favourite might be *made* to matter.
Edward and Gaveston, that is, are for political reasons stigmatized as
sodomites – an identity violently inscribed onto the monarch's body in his
assassination, which is effected by anal penetration with a red-hot poker.

One striking aspect of courtly discourse in this play is the extent to which
a range of characters use the word 'love'. While the love of Edward and
Gaveston provides the central focus, the queen equally professes her 'love'
for Edward, and several courtiers invoke the 'love' that should bind the king
with his people. The audience is invited to compare the various significa-
tions of this vital word, just as Bacon does in his essay 'Of Love'. For
Mortimer Senior, the situation is simple; 'If you love us', he declares to
Edward, 'hate Gaveston' (I.i.79). In his view, which accords with Bacon's
arguments, Edward's eroticized love for Gaveston has distracted him from
his duties, and has caused him to neglect the forms of love that should unify
the court and the nation. Yet this play, like so many of the period, insistently
foregrounds the intensity of the central affective bond, by comparison with
which the courtiers' professions of love seem self-serving, or even hypocritical. The ending of the play, in which first Edward is swept aside by the
usurping Mortimer Junior and then Mortimer Junior is purged by the young
Edward III, might possibly be read as a triumph for a form of love that is
rational and socially unifying. Such a reading, however, cannot account for
the palpable sense of loss: registered linguistically, in the absence of the lavish speech patterns of Edward and his favourites; and also dramatically, in
the brutal assassination of a man who ultimately assumes the status of a
tragic hero. And there is a final, understated irony in the fact that the resolution is achieved by a pre-pubescent boy, who is yet to encounter the unpredictable urgings of desire.

3.2 'Every Jack shall have Jill': marriage

When Gouge turns in *Of Domesticall Duties* to consider the purposes of
marriage, he rehearses three points familiar to his readers, from the standard wedding service of the time. In Gouge's words, these are:

1. That the world might be increased: and not simply increased, but
   with a legitimate brood, and distinct families ...
2. That men might avoid fornication (1 Cor. 7.2) and possess their
   vessels in holiness and honour ...
3. That man and wife might be a mutual help one to another (Gen. 2.18).[25]

Interestingly, there is no mention of 'love' here; the early modern English Church manages to turn marriage into an arrangement that is predominantly functional rather than affective. As the fairy Puck says with a shrug of his shoulders, as he uses his powers to manipulate the confused youths of *A Midsummer Night's Dream* into an acceptable set of couples, 'Jack shall have Jill, / Nought shall go ill' (III.iii.45–6). Yet there is also something inadequate about such statements, especially when we are faced with the affective intensity of relationships on the Renaissance stage. Hence, while Benedict might well be correct in terms of religious doctrine when he accepts marriage in *Much Ado About Nothing* on the grounds that 'The world must be peopled' (II.iii.213–14), no audience can miss his comic effort to delude himself about his emotional attachment to Beatrice. There is, of course, much more to this relationship than the cool words of the Church can encompass.

When considering the history of marriage in early modern England, it would be misleading to concentrate on the practices of the elite. Among the nobility and gentry arranged marriages were not uncommon, and many were arranged when the parties involved were children. This pattern is presented in countless Renaissance plays, so many of which are set at court. But playwrights and audiences alike would not necessarily have approved of such practices, which were controversial to the extent that they ignored the goal of 'mutual liking'. Many no doubt agreed with the provocative Sebastian in Cyril Tourneur's *The Atheist's Tragedy*, who greets his brother's wedding with a cry of 'rape', arguing that the arranged marriage 'forces [his bride] to lie / With him she would not' (I.iv.128–31). For Winifred, in John Webster's *The Devil's Law-Case*, such matches pervert and corrupt the course of an emotion she feels every right to crave; 'they make us loathe', she declares, 'The most natural desire our grandam Eve ever left us!' (I.ii.190–1).

By contrast, commoners exercised a considerable degree of choice in their search for partners. While the approval of parents and peers was by no means unimportant, and while marriage arrangements could include intricate exchanges of property between families, interests of affect were almost always considered relevant.[26] The common people also married surprisingly late. Marriage was perceived as an entry into adulthood and adult responsibilities, so most men would not consider seeking a wife until they were in a position to establish an independent household. As a result, ages at marriage could vary between people of different social degrees, and could also vary from one place or time to another; however, the average ages appear to have been the late twenties for men and the mid-to-late twenties for women. A significant minority could never afford to marry at all.[27]

Despite Gouge's formulaic assessment of the purposes of marriage, there is also evidence that people in early modern England were prepared to question the significance of marital bonds. Many unions undoubtedly bore testament to a spirit of raw pragmatism, which some historians perceive as the dominant force behind marriages in the period.[28] Moreover, moralists such as Gouge almost universally adhered to the principle that a wife should accept a subordinate role to her husband, even if he proves himself to be foolish or violent.[29] The law certainly supported such views: except for some technical exceptions, a woman's property became the property of her husband at marriage, while marital rape was legally inconceivable because a wife's body was considered the property of her husband. But shifts are nonetheless apparent – partly as a result of developments in Protestant theology, which attributed a greater spiritual integrity to women. For the influential godly writer William Perkins:

> The mutual duties of marriage extended . . . beyond mere cohabitation to what he called 'communion', a condition which ranged from the 'right and lawful use of their bodies or of the marriage bed', through 'cherishing one another' with goods, labour and counsel, to 'an holy kind of rejoicing and solacing themselves each with other in a mutual declaration of the signs and tokens of love and kindness'.[30]

In the mid-seventeenth century, Milton would contribute to the development of this new discourse on marriage, most notably in pamphlets arguing for a change in divorce laws. When the spiritual harmony of souls is lost, Milton argued, a marriage is effectively over, and the law should recognize this fact. Marriage, therefore, was being refashioned as 'a union of minds in the exclusive bond of true love'.[31]

Literature also contributed to this process of reassessment. The love poetry of John Donne, much of which was known to have been written for his wife, helped to effect what one critic has described as a 'reinvention' of love.[32] On the stage, while the representation of struggles over marriage among members of elite groups must often have appeared strange and alienating for an audience of commoners, the fundamental issues at stake in most such plays were entirely relevant to the English population at large. For example, although arranged marriages were principally an elite phenomenon, dramatic conflicts over marriages serve to highlight and clarify debates concerning the purpose and significance of marriage. It is indeed impossible to miss the cold political pragmatism that prompts Shakespeare's Antony to marry Octavia, thereby producing one of the bleakest images of marriage afforded by Renaissance drama. When Shakespeare turns to English history, it is by no means insignificant that he labours hard to represent the marriage of Henry V and the French princess Catherine as something very different. Here, military conquest is dressed up as true love. Catherine effectively has no choice – she is a dynastic jewel, the ultimate prize of the Battle of Agincourt – yet Shakespeare's King Harry woos her in a comically flirtatious bilingual scene, declaring finally, 'By mine honour, in true English, I love thee, Kate' (V.ii.206–7). Even under extreme circumstances, affective union remains in the theatre as a basic goal, which must be pursued by the heroic English king.

Romantic comedies focus more consistently on affective marriage, often by setting the emotional motives of young lovers against the calculating minds of their parents. Such plays depict young men and women in the period of youth, which was accepted in English culture as a distinct phase of life, lasting roughly from a person's early teens until their mid-to-late twenties.[33] Youth was appreciated as a preparative period, in which individuals developed themselves to be capable of full participation in the adult world of work, commerce, marriage and parental responsibility.[34] It was also a time of experimentation and improvisation, as young people tried out different social roles. On the stage, these years are of necessity concentrated into a much more condensed period of time, while the mood of turbulence and transformation is often underscored by use of setting (as we find in the forest environments of *A Midsummer Night's Dream* and *As You Like It*). In the latter, Rosalind looks forward to an enforced exile with a sense of excitement and opportunity. She proposes to 'devise sports' for herself and her cousin: 'Let me see, what think you of falling in love?' (I.ii.20–1). Crucially, however, while the wilfulness of youths in these plays commonly sets them against their parents, the conflicts over choices of marriage partners are almost always eminently resolvable, because the youths typically make choices that are not only emotionally satisfying but socially acceptable. In this respect romantic comedies are socially conservative, and rarely challenge Gouge's arguments that people should choose partners of similar social degree.

City comedies offer disturbing variations on this model. The quintessential landscape of city comedy is the marketplace, and numerous plays depict young and powerless women as objects of acquisitive desire, attractive mainly on account of their wealth. Shakespeare's *Merry Wives of Windsor*, which is one of the most benign of city comedies, resolves this pattern by having the spendthrift young courtier Fenton reform himself and form a genuine emotional attachment to the woman he initially saw as an answer to his financial problems. He tells her that, 'wooing thee, I found thee of more value / Than stamps in gold or sums in sealed bags' (III.iv.15–16). In Ben Jonson's *Bartholomew Fair*, by comparison, the position of the heiress

Grace Wellborn is much more constricted. Orphaned, Grace has been made a ward of Adam Overdo, who intends to profit from this notorious system of quasi-parental control by marrying her to the doltish Humphrey Cokes. While she evades this fate, her success is a triumph of pragmatism rather than romance. When the opportunistic young gentlemen Quarlous and Winwife arrange for the theft of the marriage licence with her name on it, and both men want to marry her in place of Cokes, she arranges a simple game of chance to determine a 'winner'. Her cool, unemotional language underscores the fact that she has not escaped the forces of the market, but has simply adapted herself to them; she intends, she says, to 'safely tender myself' (IV.iii.61). The wish-fulfilment of Shakespearean romance is thus translated into the harsh contemporary satire of city comedy.

Further, whereas romantic comedies tend to treat marriage as a marker of dramatic closure, city comedies regularly explore power dynamics within existing marriages. For Gouge, as for virtually all other contemporary commentators on marriage, domestic order depended on the wife's subordination to her husband's will. In Thomas Dekker's *The Shoemaker's Holiday*, the central marital relationship is rendered with a form of pantomime humour, which nonetheless carries an edge of brute force. The shoemaker Simon Eyre puts his wife in her place by calling her 'kitchen-stuff' and 'brown-bread tannikin', reminding her that he brought her into his household from the more humble occupation of 'selling tripes in Eastcheap' (vii.65–7). Although she is not sympathetically portrayed, we might detect an effort of almost unconscious repression in her curious verbal tic: 'but let that pass'. She has, simply, no other option. Other city comedies involve plots of infidelity, which explore male fears of being rendered a cuckold. In Jonson's *Volpone*, an old husband's anxiety about his control over his young wife prompts him to keep her like a prisoner – at least until he decides that he can use her body as an investment, which might bring him greater financial rewards if proffered up to the con-man Volpone. There is no clearer example in Renaissance drama of the process through which market forces tend to turn women into commodities.

The honour of the virtuous wife in *Volpone* is salvaged at the end of the play, as the court orders that her husband return her to the care of her father, 'with her dowry trebled' (V.xii.144). But such miracles belong to the world of comedy. By comparison, domestic dramas, some of which were based on contemporary crimes, represent more brutal solutions to marital disharmony, at a time when divorce was available only to rare members of the social elite. *Arden of Faversham*, for instance, depicts the 1551 murder of Thomas Arden by his wife and her accomplices. Predictably, the wife is figured as a woman driven by lust, whose commitment to a lover is irrational and subversive. More interestingly, Thomas Heywood's *A Woman Killed with Kindness* traces a relationship in which a man responds to his wife's infidelity by affording her all necessary material comforts, but cutting her off entirely from her family. Distraught, she starves herself to death. Although the play ends with a touching scene of reconciliation and forgiveness, the death fits neatly into a moral universe which perceives her adultery as a form of 'treason' (vi.86). In the play's closing speech, her husband proclaims his plans for her 'marble tomb', which will describe enigmatically a woman killed by 'her husband's kindness' (xvii.140). At times such as these in Renaissance drama, male anxieties about female sexuality are so overpowering that men seem altogether more comfortable with the idea of a dead woman than a live one.[35]

Romeo and Juliet, a play that is in so many ways central to the concerns of this chapter, is structured around power dynamics familiar from contemporary comedies. This play might so easily have become a comedy (a point the Friar appreciates, as he attempts to manipulate events towards a comic resolution), based as it is on a narrative of generational conflict over a choice of spouse. But the fact that it does not become a comedy is not a mere matter of chance; rather, Shakespeare's play reflects consistently on the potential dangers inherent in his society's structures for the management of desire. The profoundly social causes of this tragedy are signalled in the details Shakespeare provides about the ages of various characters. The Nurse's rambling family history establishes that Juliet's age is 13 years, 49 weeks, and several days (I.iii.12–38). Lady Capulet, who tells her daughter, 'I was your mother much upon these years / That you are now a maid', is therefore either 27 or 28 (I.iii.74–5). Juliet's father, by comparison, is old; he concedes that it is between 25 and 30 years since he has danced in a masque, and that he is now incapable of doing so (I.v.14–37). These facts demonstrate that Romeo and Juliet are trapped in a society shaped not only by a vicious family feud, but equally by a habit of arranging the marriages of young girls, just entering the phase of youth, to significantly older men.[36]

Indeed, *Romeo and Juliet* might be read as a tragedy produced by the excesses of patriarchy. The opening scene, in which servants of the rival households begin a street brawl, deftly outlines this context; as the Capulet servant Samson declares, he intends to 'push Montague's men from the wall, and thrust his maids to the wall' (I.i.15–16). Rape, he assumes, is a legitimate expression of masculine strength. Within the nuclear family, comparable preconceptions underpin the attitude of Capulet towards both his young wife and his even younger daughter. Their wills simply do not matter; 'An you be mine,' he warns Juliet, 'I'll give you to my friend. / An you be not, hang, beg, starve, die in the streets' (III.v.191–2). Meanwhile, the loom-ing tragedy is heightened by the way in which Romeo and Juliet are capable of thinking beyond the strictures typified by men such as Samson and Capulet, and of framing instead a radically new discourse of desire. This is evident in their first meeting, when Romeo first views Juliet from afar, describing her in conventional terms as 'a rich jewel' whose 'Beauty [is] too rich for use' (I.v.43–4). Their first lines of speech then form a perfect sonnet – applying the genre and discourse of courtly love to their situation, though turning it into a dialogic experience rather than a masculine expression of desire (I.v.90–103). And then, crucially, Juliet admonishes: 'You kiss by th' book' (I.v.107). Stale metaphors – and, more importantly, conventionally gendered discourses for the expression of love – are from this point not good enough, and as the relationship develops Juliet regularly takes the lead, fash-ioning in the process some stunning statements of female desire. This is the lovers' greatest achievement; and this is also why their society can never accommodate them.

Veronese society's eventual response to the deaths of Romeo and Juliet, though generally interpreted as a commitment to learn from the young lovers, might be seen in this light as altogether less positive. Certainly, Capulet and Montague agree to bury their feud:

> *Capulet.* O brother Montague, give me thy hand.
> This is my daughter's jointure, for no more
> Can I demand.
> *Montague.* But I can give thee more,
> For I will raise her statue in pure gold,
> That whiles Verona by that name is known
> There shall no figure at such rate be set
> As that of true and faithful Juliet.
> *Capulet.* As rich as Romeo's by his lady's lie,
> Poor sacrifices of our enmity.
>
> (V.iii.295–303)

The promise of solid gold statues is a bold gesture; however, it entirely misses the point of what Romeo and Juliet achieved, and what they hoped would give shape to their marriage. In a play so closely concerned with the eroticism and physicality of love, there is in fact something closed and ster-ile about the image, recalling as it does the objectifying language that Romeo learned *not* to use. Moreover, the efforts of Montague and Capulet to match each other in their lavish monumental displays indicate that the competitive patriarchal structures of this society remain entirely untouched by the tragedy. While the feud may be buried, there is no reason to expect that the excessively patriarchal order will not continue to warp young lives, forcing males and females into equally restrictive and ossifying roles. In its social vision, this is a devastatingly perceptive tragedy.

3.3 Parents and children

Ben Jonson survived all three of his children: one died as an infant, one as a child and one as a young adult. Though unfortunate, his experience as a parent was by no means atypical, at a time when family life was a much less predictable business than it is today. Since medical knowledge of the process of conception was poor, and practices of obstetrics far from reliable, reproduction itself was chancy and precarious. The early years of life were equally uncertain – especially in the cities and among the poor – and roughly a quarter of all children died by the age of 10.[37] Many of those who did survive spent a surprisingly brief amount of time with their parents. Infants of the elite were commonly sent out to wet-nurses for the first 12 to 18 months of their lives, while the period of youth, especially for those of middling degree, was most commonly spent in another household, generally in service or apprenticeships.[38] While historians continue to debate the effects that such conditions had on relations between parents and children, students of literature would at least do well to set aside modern preconceptions about the family. We might, for instance look afresh at efforts to interpret relationships on the Renaissance stage in the light of the theories of Sigmund Freud. Instead, when we examine the plays within their historical contexts, what we find are remarkably complex representations of family life, which repeatedly explore the faultline between affect and pragmatism.

Certainly, parents who view their children as servants or commodities are not hard to find in the period's drama. In Marlowe's *The Jew of Malta*, for instance, Barabas employs his daughter, Abigail, as a tool in his plots to wreak vengeance on his Christian enemies. When she finally resists his authority he turns viciously against her, declaring that she is 'False, credulous, inconstant', and plotting her death without so much as a whimper of remorse (III.iv.27). Shakespeare's *The Merchant of Venice* follows a similar plot, as Jessica, the daughter of Shylock, deserts him to marry a Christian. In the reaction which is gleefully reported by a gentleman of Venice, Shylock could hardly tell the difference in value between his daughter and the money she took with her: 'My daughter! O, my ducats! O, my daughter! / Fled with a Christian! O, my Christian ducats!' (II.viii.15–16). But these characters are in most respects intended as objects of ridicule, and Shylock's equation of human life with money makes an obvious satiric point. Moreover, the playwrights interestingly complicate their representations, suggesting at critical moments a wealth of emotion which the fathers seem barely able to express. Shylock, for example, laments that his daughter is 'my flesh and blood', and he underscores his solitude when he reflects on the news that Jessica has exchanged a ring for a monkey. Remembering his dead wife, he says: 'It was my turquoise. I had it of Leah when I was a bachelor. I would not have given it for a wilderness of monkeys' (III.i.32, 100–2). For all his obsession with money and revenge, this comment gestures subtly yet profoundly towards a lost domestic space, which was founded on very different values than those he professes in the marketplace.

Many comedies concerned with the citizens of London explore a similar dynamic. One of the most disorienting of such texts, Middleton's *A Chaste Maid in Cheapside*, represents family relations in a register of satiric excess. Here, the citizen Allwit happily prostitutes his wife to the egregious Sir Walter Whorehound, and raises a brood of children who seem genuinely confused about their parentage. Meanwhile, Sir Oliver Kix, who is unable to impregnate his wife, purchases a mysterious fertility potion, which only he seems unable to appreciate as a sham. Instead, the man selling it is himself famously fertile, and performs the task of impregnation while Sir Oliver is distracted with the potion. And at the centre of the play, in an odd comic sketch that might easily be overlooked, two men are tricked into taking a baby in a meat-basket. Rather than rejecting it, as one might expect, they leave the stage calculating the cost of rearing it. While Middleton's satire is directed at the tendency of a market-oriented culture to reduce human relationships to financial terms, there is more to the text than this. The play's peculiar relationships and sexual arrangements are underpinned throughout by a prevailing spirit of festivity, which is by no means devoid of affect. Notably, when Sir Walter Whorehound eventually repents of his sins, and denounces his companions in outraged tones of Christian moralism, they blithely ignore him and continue with the messy business of living. The goldsmith Yellowhammer grasps the mood more accurately in the play's final speech, in which he accepts the marriages of his two children, one against his wishes and the other to a woman who has been revealed as a whore:

> So Fortune seldom deals two marriages
> With one hand, and both lucky. The best is,
> One feast will serve them both. Marry, for room,
> I'll have the dinner kept in Goldsmiths' Hall,
> To which, kind gallants, I invite you all.

(V.iv.125–9)

While his mercantile mind calculates the cost of a combined wedding feast, Yellowhammer embraces at the end his role as a father, and acknowledges the significance of the family within his society. For all of its satire, the play's conclusion, with its general invitation to a feast, is apt.

The brute realities of death provide more pressing occasions for reassessments of emotional relationships. Jonson, though not generally given to the display of close personal feeling in his poetry, wrote poems on the deaths of each of his two children who died at a young age. The opening lines of 'On My First Son' struggle vainly with contemporary religious teachings that a parent should not become too devoted to a child: 'Farewell, thou child of my right hand, and joy; / My sin was too much hope of thee, loved boy'. Wishing tenderly that the boy may 'Rest in soft peace', Jonson toys himself with the momentarily attractive idea of escape from the very condition of parenthood: 'O, could I lose all father, now'.[39] On the stage, King Lear's lament for the dead Cordelia eventually abandons language altogether:

> And my poor fool is hanged. No, no life.
> Why should a dog, a horse, a rat have life,
> And thou no breath at all? O, wilt thou come no more.
> Never, never, never. – Pray you, undo
> This button. Thank you, sir. O, O, O, O![40]

And this speech, of course, provides a fittingly moving conclusion to a play which is so much concerned with relations between parents and children. Lear dismisses Cordelia in the first act because she resists his demand to turn filial love into a public performance. It takes Lear much of the remainder of the play to appreciate that the conventional language of devotion and duty is simply inadequate to encompass the meaning of his bond with Cordelia. In the end, an inarticulate cry is the most meaningful expression of all.

Shakespeare's romances focus with enlightening consistency on relations between generations. As a genre, romance is concerned with the restoration of order and the reuniting of families, often after disruptions stretching broadly across time and space. In some cases this is achieved through miracles which are observed in a detached, almost comic register. The lost sons of Cymbeline thus reappear heroically in a battle, thereby fulfilling a prophecy that branches lopped from a 'stately cedar' will 'revive, be jointed to the old stock, and freshly grow' (V.vi.438–40). Having been raised in a cave in Wales, they are wondrously princely, yet this is figured purely as a product of their irrepressible royal blood. Shakespeare is concerned with assertions about nature rather than an examination of nurture. By comparison, the enforced proximity of Prospero and Miranda in *The Tempest*

affords a more subtle study in the psychology of parental attachment, especially when Miranda meets her future husband, Ferdinand. This is a carefully contrived and politically advantageous match, so Prospero fittingly
proffers Miranda as a 'rich gift' (IV.i.8). But the accompanying note of
paternal irascibility betrays a fathomless anxiety of separation. If Ferdinand
and Miranda should dare to have sex before the day of their marriage,
Prospero savagely predicts: 'barren hate, / Sour-eyed disdain, and discord.
shall bestrew / The union of your bed' (IV.i.19–21). This is an unreliable
guide to the attitudes of early modern people to sex in the period between
betrothal and marriage, which were in fact remarkably liberal. It is, though,
much more telling as an insight into one unique dramatic relationship, as a
father prepares to give up his control over his daughter.

The Winter's Tale encompasses a still wider affective range, especially in
its juxtaposition of parallel relationships between father and son, and
mother and daughter.[41] Leontes frets from very early in the play about his
relationship with his young son, Mamilius. Unsettled by unjustified anxieties about the fidelity of his wife, Hermione, Leontes repeatedly studies the
boy's face for signs of resemblance between father and son. '[T]hey say we
are / Almost as alike as eggs', he comments, before recoiling into a doubt
founded on misogyny: 'Women say so, / That will say anything' (I.ii.131–3).
What he wants to see is a child who is straightforwardly 'a copy out of mine'
(I.ii.124). His image, like that in some of Shakespeare's *Sonnets*, expresses a
male fantasy of parthenogenesis: reproduction in which the mother contributes nothing to the genetic composition of the child. And what unsettles
him – perhaps even more than the rather innocuous interaction between his
wife and his best friend – is the sight of Hermione heavily pregnant. She will
experience the mystery of birth apart from Leontes; like all early modern
mothers, she will be confined instead with an entirely female coterie. When
Leontes' neurotic suspicions overcome him and he turns violently upon
Hermione, Mamilius dies, overcome with 'fear' of his mother's fate
(III.ii.142). Like Capulet's outbursts of rage towards his daughter, this is
another instance of patriarchal excess, and it appears at the time to kill
mother as well as son.

Romances typically veer towards tragedy before contriving wondrously
comic resolutions. In *The Winter's Tale* it is striking that this shift is effected
in gendered terms, as the play turns in the fourth act towards the daughter
to whom Hermione gave birth while out of favour at court, and whom
Leontes banished as an infant to almost certain death. Miraculously, Perdita
is saved by a shepherd, and when the play lurches forward 16 years she is in
the full bloom of youth. Equally miraculously, she shines out amongst her
rustic companions, and has attracted the attention of Florizel, the son of

Leontes' former friend, Polixines. Perdita is associated here, conventionally
enough, with nature; however, she is characterized throughout by her dignity and wit, especially in her debate with Polixines about the respective
virtues of nature and art. Perdita at this point represents the play's hope for
regeneration, but yet again the violence of patriarchy must be overcome in
order to achieve this result, since Polixines is enraged by his son's inexplic-
able attraction to an apparent shepherdess. In flight, the young lovers return
to the court of Leontes, where the king has spent 16 years under the relentless tutelage of another woman, Paulina, who refuses to allow him to forget
his treatment of his wife.

The play's climax focuses on the restoration of the mother–daughter relationship which was so cruelly ruptured after Perdita's birth. When Paulina
reveals to Leontes and his daughter a 'statue' of Hermione, she is in fact presenting Hermione herself. The scene provides a stunning counterpoint to the
closing lines of *Romeo and Juliet*, in which the respective fathers promise to
commission golden statues of the lovers. Here, the female body is not perfectly monumental; indeed, Leontes comments as he views the 'statue',
'Hermione was not so much wrinkled, nothing / So aged as this seems'
(V.iii.28–9). This body is middle-aged, possibly past child-bearing, yet very
much alive. When the 'statue' is eventually revealed as Hermione, Leontes
struggles in vain to maintain control over an undeniably moving scene.
Curiously, though, while Leontes fixes his attention on his wife, she speaks
only to her daughter, asking, with simple maternal profundity, 'Tell me,
mine own, / Where hast thou been preserved?' (V.iii.124–5). While this
moment does not necessarily signal a rejection of Leontes, it powerfully
underlines the play's point that the codes by which he structured his family
are sterile and destructive. The play instead seeks new principles of affective
bonds, and looks towards women as a way of imagining them.

Notes

1 Roger Lockyer, *Buckingham: The Life and Political Career of George Villiers,
   First Duke of Buckingham 1592–1628* (London and New York, 1981), p. 42.
2 *Essays*, ed. John Pitcher (London, 1985), p. 88.
3 *Essays*, p. 89.
4 On the political functions of courtly love, see especially Catherine Bates,
   Rhetoric of Courtship in Elizabethan Language and Literature (Cambridge,
   1992); and Arthur Marotti, 'Love is not Love: Elizabethan Sonnet Sequences and
   the Social Order', *ELH*, 49 (1982), 396–428.
5 Lawrence Stone, *The Family, Sex and Marriage in England 1500–1800* (London,
   1979), pp. 82, 70.
6 Keith Wrightson, *English Society 1580–1680* (London, 1982), pp. 66–118.

7 See, for example, John R. Gillis, *For Better, For Worse: British Marriages, 1600 to the Present* (Oxford, 1985), pp. 11–54.

8 *The Diary of Roger Lowe*, ed. William L. Sasche (New Haven, 1938), p. 24; quoted in Gillis, *For Better, For Worse*, p. 40.

9 *The Faerie Queene*, I.vii.7; *Paradise Lost*, IX.1009–13.

10 *Essays*, p. 88.

11 Cf. Cleopatra's uses of the word, at II.v.78 and IV.xvi.65.

12 Catherine Belsey, *The Subject of Tragedy: Identity and Difference in Renaissance Drama* (London, 1985), p. 184.

13 *Of Domesticall Duties*, pp. 185–6.

14 Cf. Karen Newman, *Fashioning Femininity and Renaissance Drama* (Chicago and London, 1991), pp. 15–31.

15 See further Jean E. Howard, *The Stage and Social Struggle in Early Modern England* (London and New York, 1994), pp. 123–4.

16 Stephanie Hodgson-Wright, 'Introduction' to her edition of *The Tragedy of Mariam* (Peterborough, Ontario, 2000), p. 22.

17 See Alan Bray, *Homosexuality in Renaissance England* (London, 1982).

18 See Valerie Traub, *The Renaissance of Lesbianism in Early Modern England* (Cambridge, 2002).

19 Bruce R. Smith, *Homosexual Desire in Shakespeare's England: A Cultural Poetics* (Chicago and London, 1991).

20 *Shakespearean Negotiations: The Circulation of Social Energy in Renaissance England* (Oxford, 1988), p. 93.

21 Catherine Belsey, 'Disrupting Sexual Difference: Meaning and Gender in the Comedies', in *Alternative Shakespeares*, ed. John Drakakis (London and New York, 1985), p. 188.

22 Paul Hammond, *Figuring Sex Between Men from Shakespeare to Rochester* (Oxford, 2002), p. 14.

23 Roger Sales, *Christopher Marlowe* (Basingstoke, 1991), p. 42.

24 Smith, *Homosexual Desire in Shakespeare's England*, p. 215.

25 *Of Domesticall Duties*, pp. 209–10; cf. the marriage service in the Book of Common Prayer, available electronically at <http://justus.anglican.org/resources/bcp/BCP_1549.htm>.

26 See esp. Gillis, *For Better, For Worse*, pp. 37–43; Wrightson, *English Society*, pp. 70–1.

27 Wrightson, *English Society*, p. 68.

28 These views are most clearly represented by Stone, in *The Family, Sex and Marriage*, pp. 69–89.

29 *Of Domesticall Duties*, pp. 271–3.

30 Wrightson, *English Society*, p. 91.

31 Catherine Belsey, *John Milton: Language, Gender, Power* (Oxford, 1988), p. 55.

32 Anthony Low, *The Reinvention of Love: Poetry, Politics and Culture from Sidney to Milton* (Cambridge, 1993).

33 See Paul Griffiths, *Youth and Authority: Formative Experiences in England* (Oxford, 1996).

34 Griffiths, *Youth and Authority*, p. 27.

35 We might well compare here the way men idealize dead women in the early scenes of *The Revenger's Tragedy*.

36 Cf. especially the interpretations of this play by: Coppèlia Kahn, 'Coming of Age in Verona', *Modern Language Studies*, 8 (1978), 171–93; and Kiernan Ryan, '*Romeo and Juliet*: The Language of Tragedy', in *The Taming of the Text: Explorations in Language, Literature and Culture*, ed. Willie van Peer (London and New York, 1989), pp. 106–21.

37 Wrightson, *English Society*, p. 105.
38 Stone, *The Family, Sex and Marriage in England*, pp. 83–4.
39 *Ben Jonson: The Complete Poems*, ed. George Parfitt (Harmondsworth, 1975), p. 48.
40 This quote is from the quarto version of the text, at xxiv.299–303. *The Norton Shakespeare* usefully prints both the quarto and the quite different folio version, as well as a conflation of the two.
41 On these issues, see especially Carol Thomas Neely, *Broken Nuptials in Shakespeare's Plays* (New Haven and London, 1985), pp. 166–209.

|4|

Society: the problem of order

'An Exhortation, Concerning Good Order and Obedience, to Rulers and Magistrates' (an extract from which is this chapter's document; see pp. 151–2), was published as part of a volume titled *Certain Sermons appointed by the Queen's Majesty*. Based on a text prepared in the early years of English Protestantism, and repackaged to mark the accession of Elizabeth I, the book is a bold effort to disseminate social and moral doctrine sanctioned by the state Church. As proclaimed on the title page, the sermons were intended to be read in churches 'every Sunday', 'for the better understanding of the simple people'. Listening to the 'Exhortation, Concerning Good Order and Obedience', the 'simple people' heard a familiar yet intimidating outline of a profoundly hierarchical society. Just as the sun, moon and stars observe God's order, the sermon declares, so every person has a fixed and preordained role to fulfil: 'Some are in high degree, some in low, some kings and princes, some inferiors and subjects, priests and laymen, masters and servants, fathers and children, husbands and wives, rich and poor.' They also heard, if they listened carefully, notes of intense anxiety, stimulated by the threat of *dis*order: 'For where there is no right order, there reigneth all abuse, carnal liberty, enormity, sin, and Babylonical confusion.' If the prevailing structures of authority are overthrown, 'no man shall ride or go by the highway unrobbed, no man shall sleep in his own house or bed unkilled, no man shall keep his wife, children and possessions in quietness'. Quite simply, it concludes, 'all things shall be common'.

That last phrase is so telling because it underlines the sermon's status as ideology. With a dogmatism that now seems breathtaking, it sets out a scheme of ideas which rationalizes and justifies England's social and political hierarchies. It depicts a structure founded on inequality, and committed above all to an order of property. But while this might be accepted as a statement of a dominant Elizabethan ideology, its proponents were consistently troubled by a sense that it did not quite fit with the complex realities of English society, and were haunted further by a shadowy awareness of alternative views. Just a few decades earlier, Sir Thomas More had toyed with ideas of common property in his *Utopia*, while among the 'simple people' themselves strains of radicalism are evident in the periodic riots and rebellions which punctuate the medieval and early modern periods. One sardonic couplet, which can be traced back to the Peasants' Revolt of 1381, epitomizes the challenge: 'When Adam delved and Eve span / Who was then the gentleman?'[1] The provocative suggestion raised by this rhetorical question is that social distinctions, which the dominant ideology is so determined to present as essentially natural, may rather be seen as products of human culture. Such a perspective exposes that ideology as a brutal trick, designed to keep the common people in a condition of compliant subservience.

On at least one occasion, in the anonymous play *The Life and Death of Jacke Straw*, that subversive couplet was brought onto the Renaissance stage.[2] While this by no means suggests that Renaissance drama fomented rebellion, it provides another valuable reminder of the dialogic nature of this literary form. Whereas the sermon is monologic, presenting a coherent and authoritative lesson to its audience, a play by its very nature mobilizes a range of different voices, perspectives and discourses. With this in mind, in this chapter we will begin by exploring some of the ways in which Renaissance playwrights respond to prevailing theories of social order, and equally to the unavoidable realities of disorder. The subsequent section will look more closely at London, as a site in which orthodox models of order seemed especially precarious, and as a focus of interest for an increasing number of playwrights. And the final section will consider the status and dramatic representation of individuals and groups on the margins of society. As becomes apparent in the remarkable representation of Elizabeth Sawyer in *The Witch of Edmonton* (by William Rowley, Thomas Dekker and John Ford), the way in which a community stigmatizes those on its margins reflects as much on that community as it does on the individual herself.

4.1 Order and disorder

In the latter decades of the sixteenth century, a number of writers sought to define the social order in England. Though unrealistically neat, and doubtless motivated in part by an anxiety that lines of distinction were becoming unnervingly blurred, such efforts usefully expand upon the bold outlines of the 'Exhortation'. William Harrison's 'Description of England', for instance, claims that the English 'divide our people commonly into four sorts, as gentlemen, citizens or burgesses, yeomen, and artificers or labourers'. The underlying assumption here is that each person may be classified, and therefore slotted into an immutable place in the social order. Distinctions are founded partly on economic status and partly on political authority. Hence gentlemen own land, yeomen have an annual income of £6, and citizens 'are of some likely substance to bear office' within a city. The 'fourth and last sort of people', meanwhile, 'have neither voice nor authority in the commonwealth', and 'are to be ruled and not to rule other'.[3] Excluded altogether are women and children, since Harrison assumes that their positions are effectively defined by the men who are responsible for them. Apart from widows – whose anomalous social status, as a tax-collector remarks in *Thomas of Woodstock*, makes them a kind of 'hermaphrodite' (III.ii.160) – women are almost universally accepted as subservient members of patriarchal households.

Most of Renaissance drama seems to fall comfortably into line with this ideology of fixed social distinctions. Characters are defined by their social ranks and economic roles, and are shown to be content with their positions, while (as we have seen in Chapter 3) marriages across lines of social degree are rare. Yet, even when plays are overtly conservative, some playwrights equally invite audiences to question the origins and justifications of difference. Shakespeare's *As You Like It*, for instance, draws our attention to the fact that the aristocrats have a qualitatively different relation to their environment by virtue of their economic power. For the shepherds, the Forest of Arden is a place of employment, on the land of a 'master . . . of churlish disposition'; for Rosalind and Celia, by contrast, it is a site of opportunity, which they can purchase with the sole purpose of 'wast[ing]' their time on it (II.iv.75, 90).[4] There are unquestionable differences between the characters of different degree in this play, and the comic ending conventionally couples like with like. Nonetheless, for one remarkable moment we are invited to wonder whether these differences are products of human culture rather than the effect of divinely ordained nature.

The structure of social hierarchy is theoretically held together by a network of personalized bonds between individuals of different social degree.[5] Though essentially relations shaped by power, the dominant social theory insisted that those in a subordinate position should respect and defer to those above them, and that those of superior status should accept a responsibility for those beneath them. (For obvious reasons, historians refer to these as 'vertical' bonds, as opposed to the 'horizontal' bonds more characteristic of a modern class-based social structure.) Social and economic relations were therefore fundamentally moralized – as becomes apparent in a prayer 'For Landlords', published in another volume sponsored by the state, for use in churches across the nation. The prayer states that landowners should not 'take unreasonable ... incomes after the manner of covetous worldlings', but should ensure that their tenants will be able 'honestly to live, to nourish their family, and to relieve the poor'.[6] The purpose of landowning, therefore, is not the maximization of profits, but rather the nurturing of community.

The unit which best realized these values, according to many writers, was the rural manorial estate. Although landholding practices could differ greatly from place to place and time to time, the 'typical' manorial estate was controlled by a single landlord, and included a range of farming house-holds, of varying sizes and incomes. For social commentators, this was held to be a 'little commonwealth' in itself, within which a landlord, tenants, labourers, servants, and all their respective families, might live together in a self-sustaining unit.[7] Ben Jonson contributes to the mythology of the man-orial estate in his poem 'To Penshurst', directed to the home of the Sidney family. In its central scene, tenants and labourers joyously converge on the house for a meal, each bearing 'An emblem of themselves, in plum, or pear' – a line which at once conflates their lives with the estate's produce, and deftly suppresses their economic relationship with the landlord.[8] On stage, Philip Massinger's comedy, *A New Way to Pay Old Debts*, similarly pre-sents an ideal English landlord, Lord Lovell, who steadfastly refuses to treat his land merely as an economic resource. For him, the manor brings respon-sibilities as well as riches.

Yet both Jonson's poem and Massinger's play contrast the ideal with its antithesis. In *A New Way to Pay Old Debts*, Lovell is set against Sir Giles Overreach, who tries to apply to the countryside his ruthlessly exploitative values. His failure is predictable enough; this is a play with a comfortable moral framework. Nonetheless, the play and poem alike admit that the con-servative ideal is besieged by forces of change. A rapidly growing population in England – which rose from a little over 3 million in 1551 to 5 million in 1641 – put intense strains on the nation's resources.[9] Partly as a result of these pressures, the prices of basic commodities soared, making life increas-ingly hard for those at the lower end of the social scale. Crucially, these changing conditions encouraged new economic practices, such as the devel-opment of trade and small industries. And in the countryside, the model of the manorial estate was undermined by a movement towards enclosure, which involved the abolition of common rights over land, placing it instead 'completely under the power of one owner to do with as he pleased'.[10] Though always controversial, enclosure typified the newly individualistic and mercantile values which were becoming apparent in the period.[11] Thomas Tusser, the yeoman-farmer responsible for *Five Hundred Points of*

Good Husbandry, which became the biggest-selling book of poetry in the reign of Elizabeth I, articulated the appeal of enclosure in his cry, 'Again what a joy is it known, / When men may be bold of their own!'[12] Such a statement presents a striking rebuff to the discourses of moral economy outlined above.

Renaissance drama commonly responds to these social and ideological tensions by creating narratives that affirm traditional values. In the late Elizabethan *A Knacke to Knowe a Knave*, Piers Ploughman complains directly to the king about the rapacious practices of 'Walter the husbandman', who mysteriously finds the money to purchase 'whole Lordships' (sig. E3r). The king duly endorses Piers as 'one of the best members in a common wealth' (sig. E3v), and authorizes the appropriate punishments and rewards. Later plays, such as *A New Way to Pay Old Debts*, and Jonson's *The Devil is an Ass*, depict more sophisticated practices of economic individualism. In the latter, the gullible country gentleman Fitzdottrel is conned by the fraudulent entrepreneur Meercraft, who sets forth fantastic visions of fen-drainage and 'winged ploughs' (II.iii.47). Such texts seek to control initiatives of innovation and individualism by rendering them ridiculous; indeed even the name of the villain in *A New Way to Pay Old Debts*, Sir Giles *Overreach*, sets him in a neat moral framework. But despite such acts of comic wish-fulfilment, the facts of change were unavoidable. Even Harrison accepted that merchants 'often change estate with gentlemen, as gentlemen do with them, by a mutual conversion of one into the other'.[13] Christopher Marlowe's sceptical reworking of a morality play model in *The Jew of Malta* is equally worldly, giving his audience a comic usurer undone by his greed, yet situating him within an entire society governed by amoral principles of self-interest. As one character frankly states, 'The wind that bloweth all the world' is 'Desire of gold' (III.v.3–4).

Those disadvantaged by social change were periodically moved to express their concerns in riots and rebellions. Many of these were in fact conservative in nature; in enclosure riots, for example, hedges which had been planted to mark newly enclosed land were uprooted, the rioters impelled by a desire to reassert traditional models of landholding and to remind landlords of their social responsibilities. Yet such protests could equally become vehicles for the propagation of more radical ideas. If the traditional ideology was no longer working, and the poor were being left increasingly unsupported by those above them on the social scale, then perhaps the entire structure was faulty. In the 1596 Oxfordshire Rising, one man was quoted as proclaiming that 'it would never be merry til some of the gentlemen were knocked down'.[14] Fascinatingly, Shakespeare's audience heard an almost identical cry in the theatre just a year or two earlier, when one of Jack Cade's rebels in *2 Henry VI* says that 'it was never merry world in England since gentlemen came up' (IV.ii.6–7). In presenting a scene from history, Shakespeare is exploring simultaneously the popular politics of his own day. Most critics agree that his staging of Cade's rebellion is unsympathetic; indeed, his bumbling rebels seem almost to require the firm hand of authority. But it is not altogether clear that such fragments of a truly radical political discourse can be so easily contained, especially once aired in the public theatres of London.[15] Even the inept rebels in *The Tempest* are capable of seeing beyond the mind-forged manacles of conservative ideology, as they sing: 'Flout 'em and cout 'em, / And scout 'em and flout 'em. / *Thought is free*' (III.ii.116–18; my italics).[16]

It is also worth considering the way in which the rebels of *The Tempest* combine insurrection with festivity, as they celebrate their pact with a song. Although this can appear foolish on stage – as though they are only ever *playing* at rebellion – it in fact accords closely with documented patterns of riot and rebellion. Moments of licensed popular festivity, such as the annual carnival celebrations on Shrove Tuesday, always carried the potential for insurrection. They were times of large popular gathering, when the people might take an opportunity to reflect on structures of social inequality. London's civic authorities were haunted especially by memories of the 'Ill May Day' of 1517, when apprentices responded to social stresses by attacking foreigners in the city. In the 1590s, when the collaborative play *Sir Thomas More* reached the desk of the censor, he was sufficiently uneasy about a scene involving Ill May Day that he instructed the players to delete it.[17]

In order to appreciate the significance of such incidents, both in actuality and on the stage, it is worth attending to theories of the 'carnivalesque', based on the work of the Russian theorist Mikhail Bakhtin. Bakhtinian theory approaches carnival less as an event than as a concept. Bakhtin argues that the carnival represents both a populist utopian vision of the world seen from below and a festive critique of the 'high' culture.[18] It involves, in other words, a popular wisdom which threatens to subvert that of the dominant culture: a wisdom which is visibly enacted in moments of festivity, but which is always present among the people. It not only underpins practices of social protest, but also enables radical visions of revolutionary change. Critics of Bakhtin often point out that the authorities *allowed* certain festive occasions, since they were widely believed to serve as a kind of safety-valve for the release of social pressures. Festive energy, that is, could be released yet contained. But while this argument can be supported by a weight of evidence from social history, it does not negate Bakhtin's perception about less tangible forces within popular culture. Furthermore, his theory directs the

attention of literary critics to certain festive uses of language, which might
be seen further to disrupt discourses of authority. Practices of punning and
wordplay, for instance, enable a plural and comic view of the world, and
may provide a weapon with which to challenge, or destabilize, conservative
codes of thought.

On the Renaissance stage, we might well think of Shakespeare's Falstaff
as an embodiment of the carnivalesque. Although he is a gentleman by
birth, Falstaff is figured in both *1 Henry IV* and *2 Henry IV* as a spokesman
of popular culture, and is associated throughout with commoners. For
Prince Henry, Falstaff represents an utterly different way of perceiving the
world and fashioning his own role within it than that presented by his
father, King Henry IV. In Falstaff's view of the world, even the fundamental
aristocratic codes of 'honour', which were used to justify lines of social difference, may be exploded in a virtuoso performance of wordplay:

> Can honour set-to a leg? No. Or an arm? No. Or take away the grief
> of a wound? No. Honour hath no skill in surgery, then? No. What is
> honour? A word. What is in that word 'honour'? What is that 'hon-
> our'? Air.
>
> (*1 Henry IV*, V.i.130–4)

As opposed to this fundamentally materialistic perception of the world,
Prince Henry instead comes to believe in the course of these plays that the
order of words is interconnected with social and political order. Words *must*
mean something, or else the system will collapse, bringing the very concept
of kingship with it. He also learns, not coincidentally, to reject Falstaff and
all that he represents. The carnivalesque challenge is thus contained, but not
without a significant cost, as registered in the sense of loss felt by audiences
at the banishment of Falstaff. His perspective may not be for the pragmatist
or the powerful, but its provocatively subversive edge resonates through the
plays in which he appears.

One of Shakespeare's most extensive engagements with popular politics
occurs in a play which is not set in England, but is informed throughout by
English issues and events. *Coriolanus* in fact begins with a scene of popular
insurrection in Rome – a scene which may in part have been inspired by the
English Midlands Rising of 1607. In the play, the Roman citizens riot for
want of food, and the wily politician Menenius pacifies them by rehearsing
a social model familiar to the English commoners. He tells them a fable
about 'a time when all the body's members, / Rebelled against the belly',
claiming that it was merely 'idle and unactive . . . never bearing / Like labour
with the rest' (I.i.85–90). The belly responds in a 'deliberate' manner,

arguing that it is 'the storehouse and the shop / Of the whole body', and pointing out that it distributes nutrition carefully throughout the whole (I.i.117–23). Menenius then turns to the rioters:

> The senators of Rome are this good belly,
> And you the mutinous members. For examine
> Their counsels and their cares, digest things rightly
> Touching the weal o'th'common, you shall find
> No public benefit which you receive
> But it proceeds or comes from them to you,
> And no way from yourselves.
>
> (I.i.137–43)

What he offers is the model of the 'body politic', which was a common vehicle through which conservative ideology mystified social difference in early modern England. Each member of the body politic has a function, and each function is dependent upon all the others. It is attractive enough – though more so if one identifies oneself with the belly or the head rather than, say, the 'great toe' that Menenius perceives in front of him (I.i.144). The fact that the citizens meekly succumb to Menenius's fable seems merely to underline their inherent inferiority.

But the play as a whole resists such simplistic solutions to social disharmony. Indeed, it circles endlessly, and by no means conclusively, around questions of social and political structure. At its centre stands Coriolanus himself, a man whose incomparable military valour seems to claim for him a place in Rome's ruling elite, but who cannot bring himself to beg the plebeians for their support. And then there are the plebeians themselves, on whom Menenius does not have the last word. As was the case in many processes of selection for English parliamentary seats, the populace in Rome are given the right to assent to the elevation of any candidate put before them.[19] Although Coriolanus heaps scorn on this process, the other elite characters do not. As Sicinius says, 'Sir, the people / Must have their voices' (II.ii.136–7). In due course, the facts of Roman history reinforce this statement, as Coriolanus is banished from Rome after rejecting its one element of political populism, and is then murdered in exile. Indeed, according to historical narratives that would have been familiar to many of Shakespeare's contemporaries, in the aftermath of the uprising staged at the outset of *Coriolanus* the plebeians were granted the right to elect their own representatives.[20] Significantly, then, the play's confrontation between a hero with delusions of self-sufficiency and a populace desperate only to be heard, is set within a context of nascent republicanism in Rome.

Coriolanus despises the people. He refers to them dismissively as 'The beast / With many heads', and sees them as the 'musty superfluity' of the state, fit only to be consumed in the heat of war (IV.i.1–2; I.i.217). At times they seem themselves to accord with these representations. After all, their riot is not founded on any substantive point of political principle, while it is clear that the mere sight of Coriolanus's war-wounds would be enough to gain their assent to his selection for the position of consul. One citizen even supports Coriolanus's denigration of the people as the 'manyheaded multitude':

> We have been called so of many, not that our heads are some brown, some black, some abram, some bald, but that our wits are so diversely coloured; and truly I think if all our wits were to issue out of one skull, they would fly east, west, north, south, and their consent of one direct way should be at once to all the points o'th compass.
>
> (II.iii.16–21)

But while the text hardly idealizes the people, nor does it dismiss their right to a voice in the nation. The play's politics are thus not as forthright as those of William Harrison, who (as we have seen) dismissed the bulk of England's populace to the 'fourth and last sort of people', who 'are to be ruled and not to rule other'. Like Shakespeare's English contemporaries, this play is alert to the complexities of social instability and political tension.

4.2 Staging the city: London

London was the most significant manifestation of social and economic change in England, and also one of the most important forces motivating such change. Its population grew very rapidly: from 60,000 in the 1520s to 200,000 in 1600, and on to 575,000 by 1700.[21] In this period it became an increasingly important commercial centre, as England emerged for the first time ever as a major economic and political force in Europe. The population was also highly mobile. The majority of its inhabitants had been born elsewhere, and it has been estimated that in the period between 1580 and 1650 one person in eight of all those surviving to adulthood in provincial England would become a Londoner at some point in his or her life.[22] Contemporary ballads trace the comic tribulations of people encountering the baffling new environment for the first time.[23] James I was less sanguine; he voiced a nightmarish vision in which 'all the country is gotten into London; so as with time, England will only be London, and the whole country be left waste', and he made several efforts to force country gentlemen residing in the city to return to their estates.[24] As James appreciated all too well, London was an environment which challenged many traditional assumptions of social order, and which therefore threatened to undermine some of the nation's prevailing myths of social order.

Crucially, ideas of locality and community, which we have seen to be central within conservative discourses of social order, did not hold their shape in London. Although the Elizabethan John Stow tried hard to depict an orderly network of neighbourhoods in his *Survey of London*, the city was in fact changing rapidly around him. His isolated praise for one landowning couple who never raised their rents only serves to highlight the prevalence of economic upheaval throughout the city, as old theories about individuals being linked by bonds of deference and responsibility were increasingly displaced.[25] Instead, London fostered unnervingly individualistic patterns of social and economic relations. Although this shift was neither simple nor immediate, there is no question that preexistent notions of community and personal obligations were not conducive to success in this environment, and that modern principles of self-interest and contractual obligation were increasingly informing social relations. Jonson imagines the consequences of this in his creation for *The Alchemist* of the character Face. Though employed as a servant in an apparently traditional gentry household, Face takes advantage of his master's absence from town, and stages an elaborate series of confidence tricks. Common to all these tricks is a theatrical manipulation of identities. As signalled by his enigmatic name, Face evades any effort by those around him to pin any identity or meaning upon him; rather, he stands as a quintessential product of the environment he inhabits, and he merges back into that environment at the end of the play, notably unpunished.

As the example of Face signals, London is appreciated in this period as a space of consumption and competition. The Elizabethan poet Isabella Whitney wrote a poem in the form of a will, which memorializes the city in which she has spent her life, navigating its streets and suburbs by identifying the different goods that each one supplies. Cheapside furnishes gold and jewels, Watling Street affords woollens, the Steelyard is stocked with wines, and so on.[26] As a statement of an individual positioning herself in relation to her world, the poem presents a striking contrast to Jonson's celebration of a self-sustaining rural community in 'To Penshurst'. Cultural historians have helped us to explain this change by identifying the emergence in London at this time of a *market culture*.[27] This term highlights the uncertainty of social and economic relations, at a time when traditional ideals of moral economy were being eroded, but nobody was sure what would replace them. This is an era, we should remember, in between the classic phases of feudalism and capitalism in England. Further, the idea of market culture directs our attention to the new ways in which individuals were perceiving and shaping social and economic relations. In a market culture, identity is no longer derived exclusively from one's inherited status, but instead from one's success – as producer and commodity – in the market.

Plays staged within this period at once explore and help to define these new conditions of opportunity and instability. As we have seen already, Dekker's *The Shoemaker's Holiday* is one of the most optimistic of London comedies, representing the staggering financial gains of the shoemaker Simon Eyre as a kind of miracle. Eyre simply stumbles into a fortune, purchasing a ship's rich cargo for a pittance. Although his transaction involves him impersonating a man of greater status, and although we are also dimly aware of a 'merchant owner' who has invested heavily in the ship and will now lose his investment, the play nonetheless depicts Eyre's gain as a kind of windfall (vii.17). It is attributable not so much to the market as to the 'love' Eyre has inspired in the disguised gentleman Lacy (vii.19). Like modern representations of lottery winners, Eyre's success thus seems to hurt nobody, and his sensational rise leaves the basic hierarchical structures of his society unchanged. Yet even this romance of the city is not without reminders of the precarious nature of life for many other Londoners. When the journeyman-shoemaker Ralph is conscripted into the army, his wife simply disappears into the metropolis, and is subsequently tempted for financial reasons by the offer of marriage made by the gentleman Hammon. Ralph returns and order is restored, but in the meantime Dekker invites his audience to feel the very real pressures on a woman who is considerably less fortunate than the play's protagonist.

While optimism survives on the Jacobean stage – as evidenced, for example, by the rosily moralistic conclusion of *Eastward Ho*, written by George Chapman and others – city comedies generally become more sceptical about the strength of virtue in a mercantile world. These plays trace the paths of losers as well as winners, and their pervasive satire leaves little room for *The Shoemaker's Holiday*'s romance wish-fulfilment, as they depict the workings of a grotesque machinery of self-interest in London's market culture. The action of such texts typically centres on a competition for a finite resource, such as the wealth brought to town by a frivolous young gentleman, or the money to be obtained by the man who wins the hand of an heiress. Within this milieu, traditional notions of social difference effectively collapse; instead, the writers of city comedy 'discovered in urban life a degree of arbitrariness, interchange, and mobility that undermined the possibility of identifying moral integrity with any portion of the existing social body'.[28] All people are reduced to the level of economic competitors, and anybody may rise at the expense of anybody else.

In Jonson's city comedies, Katharine Eisaman Maus identifies a common underlying model, of a world containing 'a predetermined quantity of substance, a quantity not subject to increase'.[29] Modern proponents of capitalism will argue that it allows money to generate more money; Jonson, by contrast, represents any one person's gain as another's loss. Those who suggest otherwise are inevitably con-men. In *The Devil is an Ass*, Meercraft claims:

> Sir, money's a whore, a bawd, a drudge,
> Fit to run out on errands. Let her go.
> *Via pecunia*! When she's run and gone,
> And fled and dead, then will I fetch her again
> With aqua-vitae out of an old hogshead!
>
> (II.i.1–5)

The point of Jonson's satire is that this discourse of investment and gain is used to cheat a fool out of his money. In all of Meercraft's schemes, nothing is actually produced, and nobody other than he stands to gain.

Within this environment, almost every item or experience is transformed into a commodity, with its own identifiable value. Hence rural estates, which we have seen idealized as sites of stable community and moral economy, become mere objects of mercantile desire. This competition for land – which promises to transform a citizen into a gentleman – is often represented on stage by tussles over legal documents. A character in Massinger's *The City-Madam*, for instance, dreams of 'A manor bound fast in a skin of parchment, / The wax continuing hard, the acres melting' (III.iii.36–7). He has, predictably, no interest whatsoever in the society sustained by his desired manor. Similarly, the meaning of money itself is revised, as playwrights grapple with ongoing debates about usury (lending money at a rate of interest).[30] Money-lending had no legitimate role in a moral economy, since money was conceived as 'a standard of value' rather than 'a thing of value'.[31] To 'trade nothing but money' – like the usurer in *Eastward Ho* (II.ii.107–8) – smacked of fraud and idleness. As one Elizabethan critic of usury wrote: 'money was not first devised for this end, to be merchandise, but to be a measure and a beam betwixt man and man, for the buying and selling of wares'.[32] Money, he recognizes, was becoming 'merchandise' – another commodity in the marketplace.

Shakespeare deals with this debate in his Elizabethan romantic comedy *The Merchant of Venice*, by drawing a clear distinction between the attitudes of the Jewish money-lender and the Christian merchant. For the Christian, Antonio, money should be loaned freely between friends, whereas for Shylock, trading in money becomes a basic means of support. It is hard to avoid concluding that this play endorses a stigmatization of the Jew, in a manner which invites an audience to attribute disturbing manifestations of economic change to a difference in religion. Money-lending is thus a non-Christian evil, and it is appropriate not only that Shylock should reveal his competitive desires as essentially murderous, but equally that he should be defeated by Portia's New Testament doctrine of 'mercy'. Yet we might also notice the way in which Shylock is constructed from the beginning as an outcast and an enemy, and is thereby effectively forced to rely upon contractual obligations rather than codes of 'friendship'. He has no choice but to live by the rules of the market. City comedies, written in subsequent years, are more rigorous in developing a mercantile logic, offering no alternative to the sort of isolated and competitive individualism that in Shakespeare's play is given a name and a religion.

Consequently, while Antonio's pound of flesh is revealed to be beyond the reach of the market, in the period's more savage satires no aspect of human life escapes. Affective relations are routinely subordinated to market values, as men and women alike hunt for lucrative marriages, and members of the younger generation seek to wheedle money out of the older generation. In Jonson's *Epicene*, Dauphine sees no use for his uncle once he has been tricked out of his wealth, and thus makes no effort even to pretend that family ties may have a meaning beyond the pecuniary: 'Now you may go in and rest, be as private as you will, sir. I'll not trouble you till you trouble me with your funeral, which I care not how soon it come' (V.iv.212–14). Family bonds, typically endorsed at the end of a comedy through marriage, are here utterly without value once a legal contract has been sealed. At the lower end of the social scale, characters such as Pompey and Mistress Overdone in Shakespeare's *Measure for Measure* survive by accepting the value that the marketplace fixes to female sexuality. When asked whether being a bawd is a 'lawful trade', Pompey's cynical answer epitomizes the amoral pragmatism of the mercantile opportunist: 'If the law would allow it, sir' (II.i.201–2).

But to suggest that city comedies might be read as treatises on the process of commodification in a market culture would be to diminish their power as literary texts. In a play such as *Measure for Measure*, and especially in Jonson's *Bartholomew Fair* (to which we will now turn), much of the text's dynamism is derived from a tension between a satiric condemnation and a comic celebration of humanity. In *Bartholomew Fair*, which is one of the most complex and intriguing of all city comedies, the central location, an annual fair erected in the heart of the city, is a site of both festivity and trade. As with many city comedies, readers are consequently posed the question of whether it is 'a foul play or a fair one – a dark indictment of human irrationality and moral decay or a celebration of the rejuvenating energies of folly and festival disorder'.[33]

There is certainly a vibrant comic energy throughout Jonson's play, derived in part from the sheer multitude of characters, and in part from the understated sense of community binding the various inhabitants of the fair. The booth operated by the massive 'pig-woman', Ursula, stands as its centre. This not only provides roast pig, but also serves as 'a tavern, a brothel, a public lavatory and a bank for stolen goods'. It has been interpreted as an image of 'the seedy metropolis in microcosm', and in this respect its capacity to level social distinctions and explode moral pretensions is critical.[34] Indeed, this site typifies the way in which the play as a whole offers elements of a carnivalesque critique of high culture, as the audience observes various myths of authority being eroded by the forces of festivity. At one point, the play's three principal figures of authority – the Justice of Peace, Adam Overdo, the religious zealot, Zeal-of-the-land Busy, and the tutor, Humphrey Wasp – are all placed in the stocks. Their respective discourses of order, Jonson suggests, have in turn been rendered ineffectual by the irrepressible energies of the fair.

But the incisive nature of Jonson's satire consistently mitigates against the comic momentum. This is a world in which human lives are routinely translated into economic values, and all efforts to pretend otherwise are exposed as mere cant. We observed in Chapter 3 the way in which Grace Wellborn is forced to accommodate herself to the rules of the marketplace in order to make for herself a marriage that will not be completely ruinous.[35] Win Littlewit and Mistress Overdo, though both already married, are similarly debased once they are drawn into Ursula's booth. Tellingly, the horse-trader Knockem deploys a discourse of the market to entice Win into prostitution:

> Is't not pity my delicate dark chestnut here – with the fine lean head, large forehead, round eyes, even mouth, sharp ears, long neck, thin crest, close withers, plain back, deep sides, short fillets, and full flanks; with a round belly, a plump buttock, large thighs, knit knees, straight legs, short pasterns, smooth hoofs, and short heels – should lead a dull honest woman's life, that might live the life of a lady?
>
> (IV.v.20–7)

Knockem's detached tone and commercial motivation are revealing indices of the process of commodification we are invited to observe. Indeed, *Bartholomew Fair* works throughout to expose the operation and consequences of an environment founded upon the marketeer's cry of 'What do you lack?' (II.ii.30). And while there is something comfortingly communal about Overdo's concluding invitation, that all the characters should come 'home with me to my house, to supper', this remains to the end a peculiarly atomized community (V.vi.118–19). Individuals are economic agents first, and neighbours second.

4.3 Figures on the margins

Those at the bottom of the social scale were in an anomalous position. When employed in recognized tasks they were commonly celebrated as forming the very foundation of society. In the mid-sixteenth-century play *Gentylnes and Nobylyte* (probably by John Heywood), for instance, the Ploughman boldly tells the Knight and Merchant that 'every thing whereby ye do live / I nourish it and to you both do give' (ll. 307–8). But those people just a step beneath such labourers, often rendered poor and outcast through no fault of their own, were a more troubling presence. In the terminology of the day, these were 'masterless men' – people, that is, who simply did not fit into the orthodox model of a society structured around vertical bonds of deference and responsibility.[36] Since their numbers increased throughout the period 1560–1640, and their existence stimulated considerable debate among moralists and law-makers, it will be worthwhile to conclude this chapter by considering their status on the stage. In certain crucial instances, the representation of marginal figures in Renaissance plays exposes irresolvable tensions at the heart of orthodox social discourse.

Attitudes towards the marginal veered erratically between paternalism and fear. For the mid-Tudor social critic Robert Crowley, who wrote a series of moralizing poems addressed to people of different social degrees, beggars had a duty to accept their fate:

> Yea though thou shouldst perish for food,
> Yet bear thy cross patiently:
> For the end shall turn to thy good,
> Though thou lie in the streets and die.[37]

As practical advice, this is clearly ridiculous, even offensive. It is important to recognize, however, that Crowley was otherwise a sincere and passionate defender of the disadvantaged; he just had no way to incorporate the displaced into his governing social model, so he resorted to codes of charity. It is also fair to say that the other extreme in the debate over policy on poverty and vagrancy was hardly any better. Social critics and legislators united in vitriolic attacks on 'unsufferable swarms of rogues and vagabonds in every street, highway, and place'.[38] In Cornwall, the Elizabethan gentleman

Richard Carew dismissed the poor as 'vermin', who maintain 'idleness, drunkenness, theft, lechery, blasphemy, atheism, and, in a word, all impiety'.[39] Corporal punishment and forced labour were sanctioned by the government's poor laws, while some parishes went to great lengths to exclude from their midst individuals who might pose demands on their resources of charity. Unmarried women on the verge of childbirth might thus be transported across a parish border, to leave the baby to weigh on the conscience of another community.[40]

Certain literary texts from this period control anxieties about marginal individuals by fixing them within predominantly comic models. In pamphlets on rogues and coney-catchers, which proliferated in the latter decades of the sixteenth century, orthodox moralism gives way to delight in the facility of the villain.[41] Thus Dekker, who combined pamphleteering with playwriting, and was never far from poverty himself, admires the resourcefulness of con-men on horseback, whose 'business is weighty, their journeys many, their expenses great, their inns everywhere, their lands nowhere'.[42] On the stage, the early Elizabethan audience of *Common Conditions* was invited to laugh at the three tinkers Shift, Drift and Unthrift. In the reign of James I, Shakespeare created the rogue Autolycus, for *The Winter's Tale*. Despite being a vagrant and a thief, Autolycus is absorbed into the celebratory pastoral mood of the play's long fourth act, his crimes rendered as clownish stage-tricks. Importantly, he also declares a residual allegiance to the prince Florizel, whom he has once served. When he follows the central characters to Sicilia at the end of Act IV, he states his fortuitously twinned desires to pursue 'gold, and a means to do the Prince my master good' (IV.iv.803–4). This is a sanitized image of the masterless man, presenting no threat to orthodox models of social order.

Cultural anxieties about the marginal are felt more urgently in plays concerned with the city. The world of the transient fair-people in *Bartholomew Fair*, though not without its own values, consistently resists the knowledge and authority of the state: this is Jonson's effort to imagine a kind of underworld functioning within his native city. *Measure for Measure* uses a similar plot-structure to Jonson's play, as a disguised authority-figure (here, the Duke of Vienna) seeks to eradicate the vice that has proliferated under his nose. Although Shakespeare's Vincentio is an altogether more sophisticated individual than Jonson's bumbling Adam Overdo, his fantasy of surveillance and control is not necessarily any more successful. In *Measure for Measure* the specific concern is with immorality and sexual licentiousness in the suburbs – areas of the city which are created very much in the image of the suburbs of London, which caused James I to worry early in his reign about a 'great confluence

... of excessive numbers of idle, indigent, dissolute and dangerous persons'.[43] Vincentio worries that his laws have not been enforced with sufficient strength, and that as a result 'Liberty plucks Justice by the nose', and the state has lost 'all decorum' (I.iii.29–31).

Yet *Measure for Measure* is concerned to demonstrate that such fantasies are sterile and oppressive, and to examine by contrast the unquenchable demands of liberty. Although focused specifically on sexual liberty, this is in fact a remarkably incisive political play, and the irrepressible marginal characters do much to expose the central ideological confrontations.[44] At the play's end, while a clutch of marriages is achieved, the various prostitutes, pimps and petty criminals remain, significantly, at liberty. And we might do well to consider the treatment of the unrepentant murderer Barnardine – the only serious felon in the play – who declares defiantly that he is too drunk to be hanged. In the final scene, in a gesture that accords more with comic laws than with the effort to reassert order in Vienna, the Duke pardons him. Barnardine's response to this miracle of justice is unclear; however, it would be entirely consistent with his character to suggest that he should leave the stage with a mere shrug. Barnardine remains to the end masterless and intransigent. His very presence on the stage therefore undermines not only Vincentio's myth of control, but also the prevailing English discourses of social order.

In *The Witch of Edmonton*, a play loosely based on a news-pamphlet narrating a witchcraft trial, attention is focused on a single marginal figure within a rural community. Although the existence and nature of witchcraft were widely debated in this period, James I was one notable believer, and accusations were commonly raised in court.[45] Strikingly, however, *The Witch of Edmonton* offers an alternative, social explanation of witchcraft. The play introduces the old and isolated Elizabeth Sawyer gathering sticks for her fire. She asks:

> And why on me? Why should the envious world
> Throw all their scandalous malice upon me?
> 'Cause I am poor, deformed and ignorant,
> And like a bow buckled and bent together
> By some more strong in mischiefs than myself,
> Must I for that be made a common sink
> For all the filth and rubbish of men's tongues
> To fall and run into? Some call me witch,
> And, being ignorant of myself, they go
> About to teach me how to be one, urging

> That my bad tongue, by their bad usage made so,
> Forspeaks their cattle, doth bewitch their corn,
> Themselves, their servants and their babes at nurse.
> This they enforce upon me, and in part
> Make me to credit it.
>
> (II.i.1–15)

As a study in the social construction of identity, this is unparalleled in Renaissance drama. Sawyer argues that because of her marginal existence she has been stigmatized as a witch, and thereby invoked as a way of explaining the farmers' problems with their 'cattle' and 'corn'. This process has become so pervasive that she is left with virtually no other way of conceiving of herself; as she says, she is 'in part' prompted to 'credit' the accusations.

Almost immediately, however, the play complicates matters. The devil appears to Elizabeth, in the form of a dog, and she signs away her soul in exchange for the true powers of a witch. We might, of course, choose to interpret this as an easy act of comic vilification, providing a popular audience with an image of witchcraft that accords entirely with their nightmares. But there is much more to the play than this. Notably, Sawyer sustains throughout a cogent social critique, which reminds us of wider processes of corruption. At her trial, she declares:

> A witch! Who is not?
> Hold not that universal name in scorn then.
> What are your painted things in princes' courts,
> Upon whose eyelids lust sits, blowing fires
> To burn men's souls in sensual hot desires,
> Upon whose naked paps a lecher's thought
> Acts sin in fouler shapes than can be wrought?
>
> (IV.i.116–22)

Her crimes, she suggests, are no worse than those of women who incite moral depravity at court, or of city-wives whose excessive consumerist desires cause them to waste in one year 'what scarce twenty win' (IV.i.128–31). And the play itself affords ample evidence of corruption, as the second plot unfolds a tale of illicit sex, bigamy and murder among the middling and upper levels of society in Edmonton. Sawyer's arguments are therefore vital to an understanding of this remarkably subtle play. As she claims, her society sustains its myths of order and justice in part through the stigmatization and victimization of individuals on its margins.

Notes

1 Albert B. Friedman, '"When Adam Delved ...": Contexts of an Historic Proverb', in *The Learned and the Lewed: Studies in Chaucer and Medieval Literature*, ed. Larry D. Benson (Cambridge, Mass., 1974), pp. 213–30.
2 See Annabel Patterson, *Shakespeare and the Popular Voice* (London, 1989), p. 46.
3 Harrison's text was first published in Holinshed's *Chronicles of England, Scotland and Ireland* (1587), Shakespeare's principal source for his history plays. I quote from *The Description of England*, ed. Georges Edelen (Ithaca, 1968), pp. 94, 118.
4 Elliot Krieger, *A Marxist Study of Shakespeare's Comedies* (London, 1979), pp. 91–4.
5 See Keith Wrightson, *English Society 1580–1680* (London, 1982), pp. 57–61.
6 *A Prymmer or boke of private prayer ... auctorysed and set fourth by the Kinges majestie* (1553), sig. P5r.
7 John Norden, *The Surveyors Dialogue* (1610), p. 27.
8 *Ben Jonson: The Complete Poems*, ed. George Parfitt (Harmondsworth, 1975), p. 96.
9 E. A. Wrigley and R. S. Schofield, *The Population History of England 1541–1871: A Reconstruction* (London, 1981), pp. 208–9.
10 J. R. Wordie, 'The Chronology of English Enclosure, 1500–1914', *Economic History Review*, second series, 36 (1983), 484.
11 See further Andrew McRae, *God Speed the Plough: The Representation of Agrarian England, 1500–1660* (Cambridge, 1996), pp. 135–228.
12 *Five Hundred Points of Good Husbandry*, ed. Geoffrey Grigson (Oxford, 1984), p. 138.
13 *Description of England*, p. 115.
14 Wrightson, *English Society*, p. 150.
15 This critical debate is well represented by: Richard Helgerson, *Forms of Nationhood: The Elizabethan Writing of England* (Chicago and London, 1992), pp. 195–245; and Patterson, *Shakespeare and the Popular Voice*, pp. 32–51.
16 The phrase 'mind-forged manacles' is from William Blake's poem 'London' (*William Blake: The Complete Poems*, ed. Alicia Ostriker (Harmondsworth, 1977), p. 128).
17 Helgerson, *Forms of Nationhood*, p. 210.
18 Mikhail Bakhtin, *Rabelais and his World*, trans. Helene Iswolsky (Cambridge, Mass., 1968); and see also Peter Stallybrass and Allon White, *The Politics and Poetics of Transgression* (Ithaca, 1986).
19 Patterson, *Shakespeare and the Popular Voice*, p. 128.
20 Katharine Eisaman Maus, 'Introduction to *Coriolanus*', in *The Norton Shakespeare*, p. 2786.
21 C. G. A. Clay, *Economic Expansion and Social Change: England 1500–1700*, 2 vols (Cambridge, 1984), 1.170.
22 Jeremy Boulton, 'Neighbourhood and Migration in Early Modern London', in *Migration and Society in Early Modern England*, ed. Peter Clark and David Souden (London, 1987), pp. 107–49.
23 For example, see 'A Clown's Journey to See London, in Somerset Dialect', Bodleian Library, Ashmole MS 36, 37, fols. 112r–113r.
24 King James VI and I, 'Speech in Star Chamber, 1616', in *Political Writings*, ed. J. P. Sommerville (Cambridge, 1994), p. 226. On James's policy, see Felicity Heal, 'The Crown, the Gentry and London: The Enforcement of Proclamation,

1596–1640', in *Law and Government Under the Tudors: Essays Presented to Sir Geoffrey Elton*, ed. Claire Cross *et al.* (Cambridge, 1988), pp. 211–26.

25 *A Survey of London*, ed. Charles Lethbridge Kingsford, 2 vols (Oxford, 1908), 1.151.

26 'The Manner of Her Will, and What She Left to London and to All Those in It, at Her Departing', in *Women Poets of the Renaissance*, ed. Marion Wynne-Davies (New York, 1999), pp. 2–10.

27 See especially Douglas Bruster, *Drama and the Market in the Age of Shakespeare* (Cambridge, 1992); and Jean-Christophe Agnew, *Worlds Apart: The Market and the Theater in Anglo-American Thought, 1550–1750* (Cambridge, 1986).

28 Lawrence Manley, *Literature and Culture in Early Modern London* (Cambridge, 1995), p. 452.

29 Katherine Eisaman Maus, 'Satiric and Ideal Economies in the Jonsonian Imagination', *English Literary Renaissance*, 19 (1989), 44.

30 See Norman Jones, *God and the Moneylenders: Usury and the Law in Early Modern England* (Oxford, 1989).

31 Agnew, *Worlds Apart*, p. 71.

32 Thomas Wilson, *Discourse Upon Usury* (1572); quoted in Agnew, *Worlds Apart*, p. 71.

33 Leah S. Marcus, *The Politics of Mirth: Jonson, Herrick, Milton, Marvell, and the Defense of Old Holiday Pastimes* (Chicago and London, 1986), p. 38.

34 Neil Rhodes, *Elizabethan Grotesque* (London, 1980), p. 142.

35 See above, pp. 56–7.

36 See A. L. Beier, *Masterless Men: The Vagrancy Problem in England 1560–1640* (London, 1985).

37 *The Voyce of the laste trumpet . . . callynge al the estates of menne to the right path of theyr vocation* (1549), sig. A3r.

38 *Stuart Royal Proclamations*, ed. James F. Larkin and Paul L. Hughes, 2 vols (Oxford, 1973–83), 2.185.

39 *The Survey of Cornwall* (Redruth, 2000), pp. 78–9.

40 A. L. Beier, *The Problem of the Poor in Tudor and Early Stuart England* (London and New York, 1983).

41 Cf. *Rogues, Vagabonds, and Sturdy Beggars: A New Gallery of Tudor and Early Stuart Rogue Literature*, ed. Arthur F. Kinney (Amherst, 1990), p. 158.

42 *Lanthorn and Candle-light* (1609); in *The Non-Dramatic Works*, ed. Alexander B. Grosart, 5 vols (New York, 1963), 3.250.

43 *Stuart Royal Proclamations*, 1.47.

44 See further Jonathan Dollimore, 'Transgression and Surveillance in *Measure for Measure*', in *Political Shakespeare: Essays in Cultural Materialism*, ed. Jonathan Dollimore and Alan Sinfield (Manchester, 1994), pp. 72–87.

45 See J. A. Sharpe, *Instruments of Darkness: Witchcraft in England, 1550–1750* (London, 1996); and Diane Purkiss, *The Witch in History: Early Modern and Twentieth-Century Representations* (London, 1996).

|5|

Staging religion: the meaning of thunder

The document for this chapter is an extract from John Foxe's *Acts and Monuments of these latter and perilous days* (1563) (see pp. 153–5). This capacious book, which became known as the *Book of Martyrs*, is a patchwork of accounts of Christian persecution and martyrdom in England. It was also an extremely effective ideological tool. Published after three decades of violent and divisive religious turmoil, Foxe's text sets England's fledgling Protestant Church within a broader pattern of conflict. It surveys 1,500 years of Church history, shaping a narrative of 'unrelenting warfare between the false church, visible, commanding and apparently flourishing, and the true church, depressed almost out of sight'.[1] Hence the suffering of Protestants during the reign of the Catholic queen, Mary (1553–8), which Foxe documents with such care, is given a clear meaning. Page after page attests to the belief that God is shaping events, and is forging a righteous nation out of a history of struggle. This perception is never more resonantly presented than in the words Foxe attributes to Bishop Hugh Latimer, bound to a stake in Oxford along with Bishop Nicholas Ridley, as flames began to lick their legs: 'We shall this day light such a candle by God's grace in England, as (I trust) shall never be put out.'

Foxe's narrative is richly dramatic, from the detail of Ridley giving away 'some napkins, some nutmegs, and races [roots] of ginger' before his execution, through to the description of his agonies when the fire burns too poorly to kill him. Yet drama itself was to become a problem for the Protestant Church. In the reign of Edward VI (1547–53), and again in the first half of the reign of Elizabeth, a new body of religious and moral drama was used for both 'propagandistic and didactic purposes'.[2] Such plays employed popular festive traditions in order to promote religious ideas that were new and unsettling. By the time that the public playhouses were established in London, however, the Church was notably wary about the relation between religion and the stage. In Chapter 1 we encountered the puritan Phillip Stubbes, who assembled a plethora of moral and theological arguments against the theatre. Although his position represents one extreme in an ongoing debate, the Church hierarchy listened to such arguments and steadily withdrew support for religious drama, sponsoring instead legislation which restricted the dramatic representation of religious narratives and issues. A 1606 Act prevented players even from speaking 'the holy name of God or of Christ Jesus, or of the Holy Ghost or of the Trinity'.[3]

These restrictions presented significant challenges for the new London playwrights. Nothing was more fundamental to English culture than Christianity, and despite understandable popular confusion following the doctrinal seesawing of the mid-sixteenth century, only a small minority of people ever challenged or rejected the Church. Under such conditions, it would be absurd to expect dramatists to expunge religion from their work; religion was too profoundly intertwined even with issues we would now consider entirely secular, such as politics, the family or social order. It provided, in a sense, the filter through which people understood their world. But playwrights had to find new ways of addressing religious concerns, even if this meant having characters refer to pagan gods where once they would have invoked the Christian deity. This context creates challenges in turn for readers of Renaissance drama, and in this chapter we will confront some of these. Firstly, we will outline some of the key cultural changes effected by the Reformation, and ask how playwrights engaged with the project of defining the Protestant nation. Secondly, we will examine the emergence of divergent religious opinions and groups, and will suggest that playwrights not only responded to evidence of division but also helped to give shape to different types. And thirdly, we will explore some of the ways in which Renaissance plays stage arguments about the authority of God. As we shall see, in some tragedies the doctrine of providence – which posits God's constant and meaningful intervention in human affairs – collides with radical strains of scepticism.

5.1 The Reformation and English religious culture

It is worth thinking about the Protestant Reformation in England as a process rather than an event. Admittedly, there were some key moments: Henry VIII's break with Rome in the 1534 Act of Supremacy; the short-lived period of Protestant radicalism in the reign of Edward VI; and the consolidation of Protestantism in the years following the accession of Elizabeth I. But struggles continued throughout the period, over the central doctrines of

Protestantism, the structure of the state Church, and the authorized practices of worship. On the ground, moreover, change could be a complex and uncertain process. Shakespeare's bumbling priests, Sir Oliver Martext in *As You Like It* and Nathaniel in *Love's Labour's Lost*, are comic representations of a common enough type of ill-educated clergyman, who did precious little to support the massive project of re-education required for the Reformation to succeed. And evidence of religious beliefs at lower levels of society confirms the magnitude of the problem. Although church attendance was compulsory, some clearly slipped through the net of enforcement; Thomas Dekker's canny Londoner Firk, in *The Shoemaker's Holiday*, boldly declares, 'I never go to church' (xvi.117). Others remained outwardly committed, but grappled in vain with the finer points of Protestant theology. One Elizabethan man, questioned on his death-bed, stated that his soul 'was a great bone in his body', and expected that after death, 'if he had done well he should be put into a pleasant meadow'.[4]

This man's mind stumbled on the intellectual demands of Protestantism. Medieval Catholicism had educated largely through images – from the vivid paintings that commonly adorned the interiors of churches, to the lively mystery plays, based on biblical narratives, that were regularly staged in towns across the country. By contrast, Protestantism was largely a religion of the written word. Protestant reformers rejected the vast array of visual imagery produced by the Catholic Church, and as a result much of England's greatest religious art was simply destroyed, in waves of passionate iconoclasm. Pictures on church walls were white-washed, often to be replaced by the words of the ten commandments, or other equally austere biblical texts. Religious publishing boomed. Foxe's *Book of Martyrs* was one of several thousand Protestant texts brought to the press in our period, including sermons, theological discourses, godly manuals and ballads. And above all else was the Bible, made available in English translation for the first time by Protestant reformers in the sixteenth century. As one seventeenth-century man declared: 'The Bible, the Bible only I say is the religion of Protestants.'[5] In Thomas Heywood's *If You Know Not Me, You Know Nobody, Part I*, a play based on Foxe's narratives, Queen Elizabeth's closing speech is devoted to this 'Jewel', which she declares to be 'for ever ... free' to her people (ll. 1582, 1586).

The potent Reformation image of a reader alone with a Bible, directly encountering the word of God, also highlights the extent to which Protestantism undermined existing notions of Christian community. Medieval Catholicism was a religion geared towards reinforcing local bonds. Religious ceremonies symbolically bound communities together, while the Catholic belief that good works could earn a person's salvation underpinned vital social traditions of charity and hospitality. Clergymen played a pivotal role in communities, since they were perceived to intercede between individuals and God, as they routinely heard confessions and granted absolution. Protestantism, by contrast, radically reoriented these relationships. Although the clergy continued to claim a monopoly on the business of biblical interpretation, the vernacular translation exposed this most unstable of texts to intense scrutiny. It is worth remembering that virtually all of the novel social and religious arguments of the period were made by people who sincerely believed they had biblical authority for their positions; in Christopher Hill's memorable image, the English Bible at this time was 'a huge bran-tub from which anything might be drawn'.[6] Moreover, orthodox Protestant doctrine placed responsibility for maintaining a relationship with God firmly on the individual, insisting at once that the clergy had no special powers of intercession, and that good works had no effect on the destiny of one's soul. As we have seen already in Chapter 2, the Protestant reformer Martin Luther argued that salvation was achieved by faith alone. And according to John Calvin, whose doctrine was widely embraced by the English Church until the 1630s, salvation was a matter of predestination, and could not be affected in any way by any person. The individual was either marked from birth as one of the elect, or was damned for ever.[7]

The impact of these shifts was so widespread, and so pervasive throughout Renaissance culture, that at this point it is worth isolating an example, by considering the dramatic functions of ghosts. To a considerable extent, medieval Catholicism was a religion carried out by the living on behalf of the dead. Since most souls were thought to go to purgatory, and since the Catholic Church taught that prayers and even payments of money could accelerate a soul's passage onward to heaven, the Christian community was by no means restricted to the living. Many monasteries, in fact, were maintained with the principal function of praying for souls of the dead, and many monks did very little else. Ghosts, within popular medieval belief, were fitted into this view of human life. They were generally accepted as real, and explained as being souls from purgatory, set loose in order to make contact with people who were still alive. The Reformation, however, eradicated at a stroke connections between the living and the dead, as Protestant theology dismissed the very existence of purgatory and insisted that God's judgements are absolute and immutable. As a character in John Marston's *The Fawn* reminds his companion, 'you may not pray for the dead. 'Tis indifferent to them what you say' (II.i.306–7). And if purgatory did not exist, ghosts could not exist; so whenever a ghost appears on the Renaissance stage, we might legitimately begin by asking just where it might have come from.

Some writers, such as Thomas Kyd in *The Spanish Tragedy*, are more indebted to classical traditions than Christian models, as they figure ghosts emerging from an underworld governed by pagan deities such as Revenge. By comparison, Shakespeare's ghosts assume more complex functions. Stephen Greenblatt has written an entire book trying to come to terms with the Ghost in *Hamlet*.[8] In what is otherwise such a rigorously innovative exploration of selfhood, the ghost of old Hamlet seems anomalous; its repeated injunction to 'remember me', meanwhile, is subtly different from the more common demand of stage-ghosts for bloody revenge. In other Shakespearean plays, such as *Macbeth* or *Richard III*, ghosts seem as much aligned with Protestant theories of conscience as with the Catholic doctrine of purgatory. Interestingly, nobody but Macbeth sees the ghost of Banquo, which so unmans him at his banquet. Similarly, the procession of ghosts that appears to Richard III in his sleep might almost be interpreted as emanations of a conscience which is finally asserting itself within the corrupt king. 'O coward conscience,' he exclaims when he wakes, 'how dost thou afflict me?' (V.v.133). A stage presence with a long classical and native heritage, the ghost thus becomes a vehicle through which Shakespeare negotiates his way between old and new religious doctrines, creating as a result subtle suggestions of interiority within his disturbingly heroic villains.

The ghosts in each of these plays also alert the audience to historical narratives, which we are invited to see as being shaped by the hand of God. Banquo directs our attention to a genealogical line ending in James I (IV.i.126–40); the ghosts in *Richard III* prefigure the providential emergence of the Earl of Richmond, who in the final scenes will purge the kingdom of its evil monarch and establish the Tudor line on the throne. But while such incidents may gesture towards the establishment of a Protestant nation, few playwrights directly represent on stage the struggles of the Reformation. For Christopher Marlowe, the 1572 St Bartholomew's Day Massacre of Protestants in France was just far enough away – geographically and temporally – to be the subject of his early 1590s' play, *The Massacre at Paris*. Closer to home, the risks of involvement in religious controversy were too great. As a result, perhaps the most notable ways in which writers engage with religious conflict is through non-realistic modes of representation. The poet Edmund Spenser carved one important path, using allegory in *The Faerie Queene* (Book I) to figure the English nation's quest to identify the true religion. When turning to drama of the period, although the use of allegory and symbolism is not always familiar to us, it pays to be alert to its potential significance, whether in particular images or in sustained narratives.

Dekker's early Jacobean play, *The Whore of Babylon*, provides an opportunity to consider these methods more closely. Dekker's play takes few risks; instead it presents a thoroughly orthodox narrative of English Protestantism's apocalyptic trials under the reign of Elizabeth. As the list of characters declares, the queen herself is figured in Spenserian fashion as 'Titania the Faerie Queene', while the Empress of Babylon stands for 'Rome'. The Empress – or 'whore', an image drawn from the Book of Revelation – is aided in her campaign to dethrone Elizabeth by the kings of France, Spain and the Holy Roman Empire, and also by a variety of Catholic clergymen and disaffected scholars. In the course of the play, Dekker alludes to various historical plots against Elizabeth's life, and he concludes with the event which sealed her place in Protestant mythology, the defeat of the Spanish Armada in 1588. The underlying allegorical structure is clarified from the opening dumb-show – by the early seventeenth century, a dated but still recognizable dramatic device – in which the sleeping figure of Truth wakes at the accession of Titania, and replaces her black robes with white. Finally, 'certain grave learned men, that had been banished, are presented to Titania, who shows to them the book, which they receive with great signs of gladness' (ll. 49–51). Dekker's England, like that of Foxe, will be founded on the Bible.

Dekker's greatest problem is that Elizabeth's supposed perfection is almost beyond representation. According to the prevailing national mythology, she was pure and unchanging – and these qualities leave a playwright little scope for the fashioning of character. In this respect the play's allegory and realism sit in uneasy tension, which Dekker resolves in part by focusing more on the forces of evil, who are altogether more theatrical. As the Empress instructs one plotter:

> Have change of hairs, of eyebrows, halt with soldiers,
> Be shaven and be old women, take all shapes
> To escape taking.
>
> (III.i.162–4)

Dekker also creates the figure of Plain-Dealing, who is derived from the dramatic tradition of sixteenth-century morality plays. Plain-Dealing, who 'dare[s] / Not be a slave to greatness' (I.i.236–7), acts as a moral touchstone, as he shifts his allegiance at the outset from the Empress to Titania, yet relentlessly identifies hidden corruption within Titania's state. Allegory merges here with satire, a form more familiar to Dekker and his audience, especially from city comedies. Arguably, however, Plain-Dealing's satiric function also problematizes the play's distinctions between good and evil, Protestant and Catholic. While the allegorical logic posits absolute difference, the satiric logic suggests a more complicated situation, as it reflects upon a nation riven by ongoing tensions and unsuppressed vices. Titania's realm is simply not as pure as it initially appears to be.

Dekker's play thus demonstrates the difficulties of translating English Reformation ideology onto the stage. There is all too little room to combine the dominant myth of an apocalyptic struggle between good and evil with the Renaissance theatre's new strategies of characterization. Titania can quite simply never be allowed to assume the complexity of King Lear. We might even suggest, in agreement with Jean Howard's interpretation of the play, that Dekker is trapped into the paradoxical position of writing a play which is predominantly anti-theatrical.[9] As we move on to consider plays that are more familiar to us, it is worth remembering that *The Whore of Babylon* was staged in direct competition to the classics of Shakespeare and Jonson. Dekker's text represents a genuine effort to stage religion in a forthright and nationalistic manner; others, though, would find more subtle methods.

5.2 Religious identities

As a result of the Reformation, being a Christian was no longer a straightforward matter. John Donne, who was raised a Catholic but died at the heart of the English Church as Dean of St Paul's, struggled harder than most with this fact. In his 'Satire III' he finds inadequacy and corruption in all the different religious types he sees around him, and opts instead for a rigorous and intensely personal pursuit of truth:

> To adore, or scorn an image, or protest,
> May all be bad; doubt wisely, in strange way
> To stand inquiring right, is not to stray;
> To sleep, or run wrong is.[10]

As we have already seen, playwrights were somewhat more constrained in their representations of religious difference than Donne is in his poem, since presenting Catholicism on stage as a viable choice was simply not possible. Nonetheless, the theatre was an ideal forum in which to explore the characteristics of different religious types, from Catholics through to Puritans. As such, playwrights were helping to make sense of religious differences, and reflecting in the process on the orthodoxies of the English Church.

Catholics provided easy targets. Early Reformation plays, many of which were written by reforming clergymen, commonly lampooned Catholics. This model, endorsed by Foxe's *Book of Martyrs*, finds its way onto the

Renaissance stage in *If You Know Not Me, You Know Nobody, Part I*, which isolates the mid-sixteenth-century Catholic bishop Stephen Gardiner as the central villain. Tragedies set in continental Catholic countries often extend this tradition. As we will see in Chapter 6, English playwrights were concerned about the relation between politics and morality in their own country; their common focus on Catholic contexts, however, gave them a way of managing or deflecting this anxiety, as they associate political skulduggery with a despised religious code. In John Webster's plays, for example, senior figures in the Catholic Church are represented as manipulative politicians, undermined by personal ambitions and physical desires. The Cardinal in *The White Devil* thus inhabits a corrupt courtly world, and his eventual election as pope is a triumph of politics rather than piety. Justice here is notably partial; as Vittoria states sarcastically to the Cardinal and others when she is on trial for whoredom, 'I fain would know if you have your salvation / By patent, that you proceed thus' (III.ii.276–7). Salvation, as Webster's audience had been taught from the pulpit, is not a matter of courtly decrees or royal 'patent', but rather of an individual's relationship with God. Although Vittoria is hardly pure herself, she deftly undermines the Cardinal's claims to moral authority on the basis of his clerical position.

But it would be a mistake to assume that a Catholic in a Renaissance play is necessarily evil, since skilled playwrights often use Catholic figures and contexts in order to explore more fundamental questions about religion. In *Measure for Measure*, the Duke assumes a disguise as a friar; however, Shakespeare has no apparent interest here in attacking Catholicism. To take another example, the Friar in *Romeo and Juliet* offers an insightful image of the relation between a clergyman and his local society, which seems equally applicable to a Protestant world. Although his efforts to use the marriage of Romeo and Juliet to effect a reconciliation between the feuding families ultimately fail, this could hardly be attributed to his Catholicism, but rather exposes more basic tensions between religious morality and secular motivations. Or, to return to Webster, the grotesque Cardinal in *The Duchess of Malfi* is juxtaposed against his sister, the Duchess, whose religion is altogether more complex. The Cardinal is scheming, lascivious and almost entirely lacking in moral values; he presents, in fact, a classic figure of Catholic stage-villainy. Consequently, as the play follows the Duchess herself, the audience is invited to consider how an individual should act when organized religion is controlled by essentially irreligious forces. Some critics find in the play 'a suggestion that [the Duchess's] cynicism about religion goes too far', citing 'her rhetorical question, after her private betrothal, "What can the Church force more?" (I.i.489)'.[11] But we might equally point to her attitude in the face of her assassins, as they prepare to strangle her:

> Pull, and pull strongly, for your able strength
> Must pull down heaven upon me. –
> Yet stay. Heaven gates are not so highly arched
> As princes' palaces; they that enter there
> Must go upon their knees.

(IV.ii.227–31)

While the first two lines of this speech bespeak the bravado and arrogance evident in her dismissal of Church marriage, she turns, after a short pause, in an entirely new direction. The humility and simple piety of the following lines reveal a woman marking out her own religious pathway, in a world which offers no reliable signposts.

In the era of Webster and Shakespeare, playwrights were also faced with the fact that the Protestant Church itself was by no means unified. Though initially defined by its oppositional status (from the verb, to *protest*), the parameters and practices of Protestantism became hotly contested in the decades after the initial Reformation. By the early seventeenth century, the English Church was as much troubled by internal dissensions as it was by external threats; and by the middle of that century, such ructions would be contributory causes of the English Civil War. We generally describe those who challenged or separated from the established Church as 'puritans'; however, it is worth noting that, in Shakespeare's lifetime, very few people were prepared to identify themselves in this way. These people were characterized rather by a more intense or zealous attitude to Protestantism, and a willingness to interpret the Bible in accordance with these attitudes. They believed that the Protestant Church had resisted the full implications of the Reformation, and they wished to continue the process of reform in the Church. Although some of them came to accept the term 'puritan', it in fact 'began life as a term of more or less vulgar abuse and continued as a weapon of increasingly sophisticated stigmatisation'.[12] It was therefore a way of differentiating people who considered themselves true Protestants, and who were striving for a place within the national Church. For, if someone is rendered comic, their threat is in part defused.

What makes the representation of puritans on the Renaissance stage so important is precisely the fact that the category was at the time mysterious and unstable. Playwrights thus contributed to the process of definition; they helped, that is, to give meaning and substance to the very category of 'puritan'. Patrick Collinson traces this process back to a number of jigs which were presented in the London playhouses in the 1590s. Probably sponsored by the government, these were intended as a way of countering the threat posed by a series of pamphlets attacking the Church authorities, published under the pseudonym Martin Marprelate. Although the scripts for jigs rarely survive, it seems that the stage-puritan at this time became an instantly recognizable type, characterized by 'outward piety (indicated by the white of the upturned eye), inner corruption, consisting of avarice, lust and sedition – in a word, hypocrisy incarnate'.[13] Therefore, when Shakespeare created the steward Malvolio for *Twelfth Night*, he was clarifying and reinforcing an existing stereotype. Described as 'a kind of puritan' (II.iii.125), Malvolio projects an image of intense moral rectitude, but reveals a hidden pride and ambition when he believes that his employer, Olivia, loves him.

Similarly, Jonson's Zeal-of-the-land Busy in *Bartholomew Fair* finds ways of rationalizing his obvious desire to visit the fair and eat roast pig, despite his puritanical opposition to all that it represents:

> Surely, it may be otherwise, but it is subject to construction – subject, and hath a face of offense with the weak, a great face, a foul face, but that face may have a veil put over it, and be shadowed, as it were. It may be eaten, and in the fair, I take it, in a booth, the tents of the wicked. The place is not much, not very much; we may be religious in the midst of the profane, so it be eaten with a reformed mouth, with sobriety and humbleness.
>
> (I.vi.69–76)

As Jonson's contemporary audience would have appreciated, Busy wrests biblical teachings into dangerously new shapes in order to suit his own desires. While the Psalms celebrate a religious ethic which shuns 'the tents of the wicked', and St Paul warns starkly against eating 'meats offered to idols' (Psalms 84.10; Acts 15.29), Busy still finds a way to the fair. Jonson underscores his satiric point in Busy's use of the words, 'The place is not much, not very much'. Busy argues that the puritan party can be in the fair without being affected by it; however, his obvious hypocrisy suggests otherwise, making a mockery of his notion of a 'reformed mouth'. After this moment, the degradation of the puritans in the following acts comically fulfils all the audience's expectations.

Specific religious sects were especially feared by the authorities, since they threatened to undermine the model of universal membership of a single Church. To withdraw from membership of a parish in order to identify with a more exclusive group of Christians was to challenge the fundamental role of the Church as a force of social and moral order. A sect, almost by definition, believed that it alone was righteous, and it alone was interpreting the Bible correctly. Interestingly, although sectarian activity does not appear to have been significant until the middle decades of the seventeenth century, dramatists nonetheless helped to galvanize images of the threat they posed. To take one example, a sect called the Family of Love definitely existed in some form, and was generally respectable socially; however, it was particularly annoying to the authorities because its members believed they had a moral right to lie about their allegiances.[14] Stage representations typically play on the potential connotations of the group's name. Like the parish, in orthodox ideology the family was one of the foundation-stones of social order; the Family of Love, however, is represented as eradicating the family's basic structures and values. Stage familists are thus routinely figured as sexually indiscriminate. Familists in Middleton's *A Mad World, My Masters* and Marston's *The Dutch Courtesan* are whores, while in Middleton's *The Family of Love* the sect's mysterious essence is finally revealed when a gallant infiltrates a meeting and encounters a scene of sexual debauchery. Familist meetings are thus 'revealed as consisting of random, anonymous, haphazard couplings', which subvert authorized meanings of both 'family' and 'love'.[15]

We can see, then, that satiric acts of stigmatization are an easy way of controlling anxieties about religious identities. The puritan is rendered ridiculous, and is thereby stripped of any real challenge he or she may pose to the beliefs held by others. But puritans were to some extent distinguishable only by the fact that they were more deeply troubled than others by the implications of Protestant theology. The Calvinist doctrine of election, in particular, provoked intense self-scrutiny and anxiety in some individuals, since it offered so little reassurance or guidance on the matter of salvation. Such people were neither extremists nor cranks; they were merely concerned with an issue which is more important to a Christian than any other. Playwrights appreciated this well enough, and some explored more subtly this basic tenet of the Protestant Church. Christopher Marlowe's *Doctor Faustus*, which follows a pre-existent narrative of a scholar who sells his soul to the devil, offers one of the most direct and interesting of such studies. Early in the play, Faustus considers the inscrutable power of the Protestant God:

> When all is done, divinity is best.
> Jerome's Bible, Faustus, view it well.
> [*He reads*] '*Stipendium peccati mors est.*' Ha!
> '*Stipendium,*' etc.
> 'The reward of sin is death.' That's hard.
> [*He reads*] '*Si peccasse negamus, fallimur,*
> *Et nulla est in nobis veritas.*'
> 'If we say that we have no sin,

> We deceive ourselves, and there's no truth in us.'
> Why then belike we must sin,
> And so consequently die.
> Ay, we must die an everlasting death.
> What doctrine call you this? *Che serà, serà*:
> 'What will be, shall be'?

(I.i.37–50)

As Alan Sinfield has noted, the biblical texts Faustus cites were used by Calvin and other Protestant reformers to justify the doctrine of election. Salvation is unfathomable: 'God chooses to save the elect despite their depravity; the others go to hell. Faustus' summary, "What will be, shall be," is doctrinally satisfactory.'[16]

Yet religion in *Doctor Faustus* is a more complicated matter than this summary might suggest, and much of the play's power derives from the way in which it juxtaposes different theological codes. Crucially, Faustus is shown actively choosing to sell his soul to the devil, and the Good Angel offers him ample opportunity throughout the play to change his mind and repent. Because of this, his end hardly seems predestined. Nonetheless, conflicting strands of a Calvinist doctrine continue throughout; as Sinfield suggests, the Good Angel tells Faustus 'what he ought to do but cannot', since he is marked from birth for damnation. The play, according to this view, explores the situation of a person trapped in a brutal narrative of predestination, making choices which only ever *seem* to be those of a free agent. 'In this view Faustus is not damned because he makes a pact with the Devil, he makes a pact with the Devil because he is damned.'[17] Certainly his final speech is doctrinally orthodox, in its acceptance of an 'enormous gulf between his sinful self and an angry God'.[18] The point is underlined in his short, factual clauses: 'The stars move still; time runs; the clock will strike; / The devil will come, and Faustus must be damned' (V.ii.72–3). A humanist discourse of heroic aspiration is here brought into collision with a conflicting discourse of religious determinism, and the play is so effective in part because it is so searchingly honest about the implications of this conflict.

5.3 The meaning of thunder

After Marlowe's early exploration of God's power, certain playwrights of the following generation more consistently scrutinized the doctrine of providence, which found the deity's hand directing all aspects of human life. As we have seen, Foxe identifies a providential design in the trials of early

English Protestants. Similarly, numerous poems and prose texts of the period outline narratives of individuals meeting with miraculous rewards and punishments, all directed by providence. For example, Thomas Beard's *The Theatre of God's Judgements* (1597) collects anecdotes of heavenly vengeance from biblical times through to the present, all designed to represent God as an implacable authority, directing human lives in a manner comparable to that of a dramatist. Not surprisingly, these stories provided source material for the human dramatists of the London playhouses; the plots of *Arden of Faversham* and *The Duchess of Malfi*, for example, are heavily indebted to Beard.[19] But plays are by nature more dialogic or interrogatory than Beard's text, and many playwrights were fascinated by current ideas which presented important challenges to the doctrine of providence. Consequently, although playwrights remained constrained by the censorship laws, in many tragedies they examine this basic Protestant tenet with a subtle yet incisive scepticism.

Challenges to the doctrine of providence came from several different sources. Firstly, increasing levels of knowledge about other cultures, garnered at once through travel and the study of ancient texts, prompted Western European Christians to accept that there were other, radically different, ways of perceiving the world. We will return to this issue in Chapter 7; here, though, we might simply note the uncertain significance of Islam in Marlowe's plays. While Moslems were normally perceived as representing a pagan threat to Christianity, it is curious that those in *The Jew of Malta* are perhaps the play's only truly consistent and trustworthy characters. Marlowe hardly has the knowledge or inclination to promote Islam; however, he does seem to use the very difference between this religion and Christianity as a way of questioning claims made by the latter to a unique possession of higher truths. Secondly, increasing knowledge of the natural world offered newly rational and scientific explanations for events that might otherwise be attributed to the hand of God. Comets, eclipses, droughts and diseases were among the occurrences under debate; as the seventeenth-century Italian astronomer Galileo Galilei discovered when he confronted outraged Church authorities with his argument that the earth orbits the sun, science could be a perilous business. And, thirdly, political theorists were positing the heretical notion that earthly power might be a matter of amoral manipulation, rather than being fixed within a model of providential design. Most notably, the Italian Niccolò Machiavelli argued that there was an art to the seizure and maintenance of power. Such matters, he suggested, had little to do with the will of God.

Renaissance playwrights regularly engage with these simmering debates about God's power. In medieval drama, God was a familiar presence on the stage, directing the course of human history just as he does in the Bible. Although the Reformation laws forbidding players to use even the name of God severed this vital dramatic tradition, some playwrights nevertheless managed to find ways around them. In Shakespeare's romance *Cymbeline*, for example, Jupiter sounds for all the world like the Old Testament God as he angrily reminds his doubters that there is a purpose to the play's muddle of conflict and suffering. He proclaims: 'Whom best I love, I cross, to make my gift, / The more delayed, delighted' (V.v.195–6). But such forthright declarations of a providential order are uncommon – especially beyond the genre of romance, which typically leans on intimations of divine intervention. The absence of God in other plays instead provides the opportunity for dramatists to explore explanatory models other than that of providence. Countless plays incorporate references to pagan concepts such as 'fortune', 'fate' or 'destiny'. Sometimes these ideas are roughly assimilated in the texts with an orthodox doctrine of providence, and thus present no real challenge to Christianity; sometimes they are proclaimed by characters who are clearly deluded about the ultimate authority of God; sometimes they are more mysterious, and present important challenges for an audience. How, for instance, are we to account for the multiple revolutions in Marlowe's *Edward II*? When resigning his crown, the king consoles himself with the words, 'what the heavens appoint, I must obey' (V.i.56); when Mortimer Junior subsequently falls, he blames 'Base Fortune', whose 'wheel' will make him 'tumble headlong down' (V.vi.59, 61). For the audience, it becomes difficult to see any clear purpose or structure whatsoever.

Another possibility, of course, is that the events of *Edward II* may all be attributable to clashes of human wills.[20] As much as Edward and Mortimer may seek comfort in the notion that they are being directed by forces beyond their control, the play unquestionably allows the audience to see each man as simply self-deluded. Neither has been crafty enough, and each looks for a way of rationalizing his failures. This possibility undermines the doctrine of providence, with all of its assumptions about the influence of God over human affairs, and it is thus not something that a playwright can afford to express too openly. Yet it always pays to be alert to such traces of scepticism, which may prompt fundamental reassessments of certain texts. When Bosola, in *The Duchess of Malfi*, states gloomily that 'We are merely the star's tennis balls, struck and banded / Which way please them' (V.iv.56–7), we might choose to interpret the play as making a statement about the inscrutable nature of providence. But we might equally argue that Bosola, in a moment of desperation, is clutching at straws in an effort to explain the violent consequences of the play's cycles of human conflict.[21]

And, as the play has made perfectly clear, Bosola's own amoral desire for power and material reward has played a pivotal part in those cycles.

One way of pursuing this complex issue a little further is to focus on the significance of thunder in Renaissance plays. The effect of thunder was easily produced – 'from the "roul'd bullet" on a sheet of metal, or a "tempestuous drum", as Jonson said' – and was commonly employed to signify divine intervention.[22] In *Cymbeline*, Jupiter's miraculous appearance is signalled with 'thunder and lightning', the deity 'throw[ing] a thunderbolt' and referring to himself simply as 'the thunderer' (V.v.187 sd, 189). The interests of producing a memorable spectacle merge conveniently here with those of figuring divine authority. Similarly, in *Macbeth* the enormity of the king's assassination is marked by unprecedentedly wild storms. The night of his death is appropriately described as 'unruly' (II.iii.50): the breach of a natural political order is counterpointed by instability in the heavens. God is angry; retribution will follow. Elsewhere, characters implore justice, or concede their own corruption, by invoking thunder. Flamineo, the Machiavellian schemer in *The White Devil*, meets his death with the couplet, 'Let no harsh flattering bells resound my knell, / Strike thunder, and strike loud to my farewell' (V.vi.275–6).

But while it clearly has a conventional meaning on the stage, thunder is by no means an uncontestable sign. In Cyril Tourneur's *The Atheist's Tragedy* the overreaching D'Amville mocks a companion who is troubled by the thunder and lightning that greet D'Amville's expressions of scepticism:

> What!
> Dost start at thunder? Credit my belief,
> 'Tis a mere effect of Nature.
> An exhalation hot and dry, involv'd
> Within a wat'ry vapour i'the middle
> Region of the air, whose coldness
> Congealing that thick moisture to a cloud,
> The angry exhalation shut within
> A prison of contrary quality,
> Strives to be free, and with the violent
> Eruption through the grossness of that cloud
> Makes this noise we hear.
>
> (II.iv.140–51)

While we might wish to question D'Amville's grasp of meteorology, the critical point is that he dares to offer a scientific explanation for what is otherwise accepted as a sign of divine disfavour. By comparison, King Lear is more circumspect, though profoundly doubtful, when he asks Edgar, 'What is the cause of thunder?' (III.iv.143). An earlier dramatic version of the Lear story, the chronicle play *King Leir*, provides the orthodox reply to this question: 'God's anger' (ll. 1633, 1739).[23] By contrast, Shakespeare leaves the question unanswered. His King's greatest insights in the storm are social rather than spiritual; it alerts him, all too feelingly, to the conditions of life endured by the 'houseless' and 'unfed' subjects he has hitherto ignored (III.iv.31). Responsibility rests with him rather than with God.

In *The Revenger's Tragedy*, probably written by Middleton (though sometimes attributed to Tourneur), the orthodox meaning of thunder is even more pointedly opened to question. Thunder figures on two occasions; however, in each case the revenger Vindice seems perversely in control of things. In the first, he comments sardonically on the corruption of another character:

> O, thou almighty Patience! 'Tis my wonder
> That such a fellow, impudent and wicked,
> Should not be cloven as he stood,
> Or with a secret wind burst open!
> Is there no thunder left, or is't kept up
> In stock for heavier vengeance? [*Thunder sounds*] There it goes!
>   (IV.ii.199–204)

And in the second, when the play's bloody conclusion is heralded by thunder, Vindice cries: 'Mark, thunder! / Dost know thy cue, thou big-voiced crier?' (V.iii.43–4). For an audience, there is something unavoidably disturbing about the image of the revenger successfully invoking God's thunder, and something belittlingly comic about his representation of the deity as a 'big-voiced crier' who speaks on 'cue'. As Jonathan Dollimore argues, 'such lines beg for a facetious Vindice, half turned towards the audience and deliberately directing its attention to the crudity of the stage convention involved'. A conventional sign of providence is thereby subverted by the play's metatheatrical form of 'black camp'. 'In effect,' Dollimore concludes, 'the conception of a heavenly, retributive justice is being reduced to a parody of stage effects.'[24]

The fear that *King Lear* explores so eloquently, and *The Revenger's Tragedy* holds at bay with its wit, is that of meaninglessness. Like many other texts from this period, these plays acknowledge the possibility that there is no god directing human events, and therefore no reason behind any particular instance of human suffering. Perhaps the Protestant martyrs, exhaustively lauded in Foxe's *Book of Martyrs*, died senselessly. Perhaps humans create religions in order to support existing structures of power; as Marlowe is alleged to have said (echoing Machiavelli), 'the beginning of religion was only to keep men in awe'.[25] And perhaps humans may instead determine their own histories, through the sheer exertion of will. This is certainly the position suggested by a succession of figures from Renaissance drama: Marlowe's Tamburlaine; Shakespeare's Coriolanus; Webster's Flamineo; Tourneur's D'Amville. Admittedly, almost all such characters meet violent ends; most spectacularly of all, D'Amville lifts an executioner's axe to kill his last remaining enemies, and dashes out his own brains by mistake. But these endings do not necessarily erase the ideological challenges that the characters pose, nor do they resolve the tensions and contradictions of the plays. As we shall see in the following chapter, Renaissance drama's subtle interrogation of power is extended further in its concentration on the central site of human authority, the court.

Notes

1 Patrick Collinson, *The Birthpangs of Protestant England: Religious and Cultural Change in the Sixteenth and Seventeenth Centuries* (Basingstoke, 1988), p. 12.

2 Collinson, *Birthpangs of Protestant England*, p. 102.

3 Quoted in Andrew Gurr, *The Shakespearean Stage 1574–1642*, 3rd edn (Cambridge, 1992), p. 54.

4 Quoted in Keith Thomas, *Religion and the Decline of Magic* (London, 1971), p. 194.

5 Quoted in Collinson, *Birthpangs of Protestant England*, p. 95.

6 Christopher Hill, *The English Bible and the Seventeenth-Century Revolution* (London, 1993), p. 5.

7 See above, pp. 25–6.

8 Stephen Greenblatt, *Hamlet in Purgatory* (Princeton and Oxford, 2001).

9 Jean E. Howard, *The Stage and Social Struggle in Early Modern England* (London and New York, 1994), pp. 49–57.

10 *John Donne: The Complete English Poems*, ed. A. J. Smith (London, 1986), p. 163 (ll. 76–9).

11 Julia Briggs, *This Stage-Play World: Texts and Contexts, 1580–1625* (Oxford, 1997), p. 165.

12 Patrick Collinson, 'A Comment: Concerning the Name Puritan', *Journal of Ecclesiastical History*, 31 (1980), 486.

13 Patrick Collinson, 'Ben Jonson's *Bartholomew Fair*: The Theatre Constructs Puritanism', in *The Theatrical City*, ed. David L. Smith *et al.* (Cambridge, 1995), p. 167; on the jig, see above, p. 13.

14 See Christopher Marsh, *The Family of Love in English Society, 1550–1630* (Cambridge, 1994).

15 Kristen Poole, *Radical Religion from Shakespeare to Milton: Figures of Nonconformity in Early Modern England* (Cambridge, 2000), p. 98.

16 Alan Sinfield, *Literature in Protestant England 1560–1660* (London and Canberra, 1983), p. 117.

17 Sinfield, *Literature in Protestant England*, pp. 118, 116.

18 John N. King, 'Religious Writing', in *The Cambridge Companion to English Literature 1500–1600*, ed. Arthur F. Kinney (Cambridge, 2000), p. 128.
19 Alexandra Walsham, *Providence in Early Modern England* (Oxford, 1999), p. 112.
20 On this issue, see especially Jonathan Dollimore, *Radical Tragedy: Religion, Ideology and Power in the Drama of Shakespeare and his Contemporaries*, 2nd edn (New York, 1989).
21 It is also worth considering the implications of the editorial decision, made by the editors of *English Renaissance Drama*, to indicate a singular 'star'. Webster's original text is not clear on this, and most other editors opt for a plural, 'stars".
22 Gurr, *The Shakespearean Stage*, p. 122.
23 Briggs, *This Stage-Play World*, p. 153.
24 Dollimore, *Radical Tragedy*, pp. 140, 149.
25 J. B. Steane, *Marlowe: A Critical Study* (Cambridge, 1970), pp. 363–4.

|6|

The court: issues of power

For students of early seventeenth-century politics and literature, King James VI and I is a marvellously forthcoming monarch. James knew no life other than that of a king; he was King of Scotland in 1567 at the age of 1, assumed the throne of England and moved to London after the death of Elizabeth I in 1603, and continued to rule both kingdoms until his death in 1625. Throughout his life, he not only involved himself closely in the processes of government, but also wrote widely about kingship and various contemporary issues. The document for this chapter (pp. 155–8) is an example of his work. Written in the early years of the 1620s, 'The Answer to the Libel called "The Commons' Tears"', responds angrily to those of his subjects who dared to question his methods of government and choice of counsellors. It represents an audacious effort by a reigning monarch to engage directly with his critics, as he forcefully reminds them of the unique and unassailable power of a king. He asserts that 'God above all men kings inspires', and argues that as a result of this status criticism is effectively futile. Subjects must rather accept the logic of divine-right absolutism, forgoing criticism in favour of a compliant awe: 'Hold you the public beaten way, / Wonder at kings, and them obey'.

James's poem vividly alerts us to the facts of historical difference. In this period, democracy was barely understood and widely feared, while parliaments bore little relation to those of the twenty-first century. Even the very category of 'politics', which is now so familiar to us as a way of conceiving of the machinations of power, did not exist in its modern form. In orthodox thought, as reflected in the writings of James, power simply could not be approached as a science; instead, it was necessarily mysterious, and centred firmly in the person of the monarch. This helps us to appreciate the significance of the court in Renaissance England. The court may be defined as the place where a monarch resides, the establishment and surroundings of a monarch, or the monarch with his ministers and counsellors as the ruling power in the state. In each case the existence of the court is determined by the presence of the monarch, and power is assumed to be a product of monarchy. As a result, in this structure there is little of our modern sense that power resides rather in institutions and bureaucracies; instead, it is access to the monarch, and personal relationships at court, that are critical in determining a subject's status and influence. For dramatists, therefore, the court becomes the obvious setting in which to examine power relations.

There were three different monarchs in England in our period, and consequently three different courts. The reign of Elizabeth (1558–1603) was followed by that of James (1603–25), and James was succeeded by his son, Charles (1625–49). Moreover, plays concerned with the court are often especially sensitive to their particular historical moments. The anxieties at court in the final years of the reign of Elizabeth, for example, inform numerous plays written at this time, and have prompted many critics to pursue close, topical interpretations.[1] Such approaches certainly accord with those of the censors, who were always on the lookout for possible allusions to contemporary figures. But while it would be impossible to deny the potential value of such investigations, the approach to historical context here is less narrowly focused. In accord with our practice throughout the book, we will consider in this chapter the ways in which plays articulate the debates and anxieties of the age. Given the strictures on political discourse, court-based plays ran certain risks; in many cases, however, they also provide complex studies of personal and ideological struggles. The theatre was thus a central forum for investigations into power, throughout decades in which James's authoritarian assumptions were increasingly challenged. By the 1640s, such challenges led to civil war.

6.1 Discourses of power: monarchs and machiavels

James was entirely in accord with orthodox political theory of his time when he asserted the divine right of kings.[2] According to this doctrine, a monarch is ordained by God and is answerable only to God. The monarch directly appoints all counsellors, judges and state officers, while parliament is called at the royal discretion and is considered merely as an advisory body. All power therefore resides in the monarch; as the brother of the French king laments in George Chapman's *Bussy D'Ambois*,

> There is no second place in numerous State
> That holds more than a cipher: in a King
> All places are contain'd.

>   (I.i.34–6)

This model effectively controls the parameters of political debate. While counsellors may disagree among themselves, the monarch's decisions are absolute and unchallengeable. Titania, Thomas Dekker's dramatic representation of Queen Elizabeth in *The Whore of Babylon*, reminds a petitioner that she may be 'counselled' by those around her at court, but not 'controlled' by them (I.ii.211). Consequently, whereas a modern system of political parties is based on an assumption of conflict, the divine-right model renders opposition to the crown virtually unthinkable. Countless figures in Renaissance plays thus face the same challenge as those who became increasingly disenchanted with the early Stuart monarchs: how can one express dissent without accepting the status of a rebel? This question became particularly pressing through the 1620s and 1630s, as each Stuart king clashed with his parliaments, and many people became worried about the excesses of courtly power. Indeed, even when they confronted the king's armies on the battlefields of the 1640s, many men earnestly believed that they were fighting merely to protect the king from evil counsellors, and only very few sought at this time to overthrow the structure of monarchy.

Counsellors themselves lived privileged yet precarious existences. In *Basilikon Doron*, a book of advice on statecraft written for his son, James devoted much attention to the selection and employment of counsellors. Since he must ultimately 'be answerable to God', James argued that the king should select only 'men of known wisdom, honesty, and good conscience'. While he advises a choice of 'men of the noblest blood that may be had', he acknowledges the tensions at court between those born into positions of authority and those rising through merit.[3] This was a central conflict throughout the period: under Elizabeth, William Cecil rose to the highest levels of state as a result of his unparalleled bureaucratic skills; under James, George Villiers developed an intimate personal relationship with the king, and was consequently elevated from origins in the gentry to become, as Duke of Buckingham, the most powerful statesman in the land. Such miraculous careers could hardly fail to arouse resentment among those who believed themselves to be better qualified for office on account of their 'noblest blood'.

This debate between birth and merit is staged in numerous plays, focusing attention on the qualities and motivations of characters such as Antonio in John Webster's *The Duchess of Malfi*, and Chapman's Bussy D'Ambois. As some of the more subtle political thinkers of the time perceived, such men were also exposed to considerable danger at times of stress. Francis Bacon suggested that those closest to monarchs may be forced to act as 'screens . . . in matters of danger and envy', and that 'there is less danger of them if they be of mean birth'.[4] Since a king is 'above the reach of his people', a counsellor will perforce be blamed for problems, and may in extreme cases 'be offered as a sacrifice to appease the multitude'.[5] Such was the fate of the Earl of Stafford, who was handed over for execution to an angry parliament in 1641, by a king desperate to avoid civil war. On stage, such is the fate of the successive court favourites of Christopher Marlowe's *Edward II*, while in *The Duchess of Malfi* one might argue that the Duchess is brought down because she has too closely intertwined the personal and the political. Once he is her husband, it is almost impossible for her to detach herself from Antonio.

As these examples demonstrate, theories of consensus at court did not prevent tensions, which could often have devastating results for the individuals involved. The challenge, however, was to manage those tensions. The influential manual, *The Book of the Courtier*, written by the Italian Baldassare Castiglione, proposed highly stylized modes of interaction at court as a means of masking rivalries and conflicts. In particular, he celebrated the quality of *sprezzatura*: the ability to disguise artful effort so that it seems natural. Partly as a result of his arguments, court life in the Renaissance was characterized by elaborate practices of personal display, and intricate codes of etiquette.[6] In their plays, dramatists not only mimic the visual splendour of the court, but also represent the backbiting of courtly life, as becomes evident especially in various scenes in which courtiers offer sardonic comments as their peers process across the stage. In the second scene of *The Duchess of Malfi*, for instance, Antonio looks through the magnificence of the court, interpreting for both Delio and the audience the underlying 'natures / Of some of your great courtiers' (I.i.83–4). In *Troilus and Cressida*, Shakespeare uses this model for comic effect, indicating Troilus's shameful lack of heroic qualities, and exposing more fundamentally the artifice at the heart of court life (I.ii). At times in this play, Shakespeare prompts his audience to question what there is to the courtier *apart from* a glorious exterior.

In the early decades of the seventeenth century, interpersonal tensions were increasingly situated within a context of factional confrontations. Factions were partly based on family connections, but were generally united by similar views on issues such as foreign policy and religion.[7] Here, therefore, was a vehicle for the expression of the age's emergent ideological confrontations; and here, also, was a manifestation of courtly conflict which seemed to require new explanatory models. Notably, many people in these decades were studying the works of the Roman historian Tacitus and the sixteenth-century Florentine Niccolò Machiavelli. Each man's ideas were responsible in part for the early development in England of an identifiably modern study of politics, which approached power relations as a science, divorced from notions of divine right and mysteries of state. Tacitus delineates political discord in Rome, focusing on a courtly milieu in which there is 'nothing simple and sincere, and no true fidelity even amongst friends'.[8] Machiavelli effectively banishes religion from the realm of politics, and argues that unethical means may be required by a person who wants to gain and hold on to power. What became known as 'reason of state' theory, which was informed by both Tacitus and Machiavelli, therefore rejected providence as an adequate explanation for political conflict. For many people, such attitudes were frighteningly subversive; by the late 1620s, according to one troubled commentator, 'Reason of State' had 'infected Europe like a contagious disease'.[9]

The challenge posed by these new theories is explored in numerous plays. As seen in Chapter 1, in the late sixteenth century popular perceptions of Machiavelli are conflated with the medieval dramatic figure of the Vice – and this produces Machevil, who introduces the action of Marlowe's *Jew of Malta*. By the early decades of the seventeenth century, the implications of these new political ideas were absorbed more thoroughly within English culture, and Marlowe's Machevil gives way to the more complex figure of the 'politician'. For one commentator, the politician 'cares little how great a rupture he make through God's sacred laws . . . to meet with his own advantage'.[10] Theatrical politicians are rarely presented as attractive or heroic, yet they commonly offer compelling insights into the nature of power. In Webster's *The White Devil*, for instance, Flamineo sustains a jaundiced commentary on the play's action. Of religion, he notes, 'oh, how it is commeddled with policy'; of ambitious courtiers, he states that, 'when knaves come to preferment, they rise as gallowses are raised i'th'Low Countries, one upon another's shoulders' (III.iii.37–8; II.i.318–20). For him, a courtier who is not a 'politician' is simply lacking in 'wit' (I.ii.49–50); and, despite his downfall, the action of the play provides considerable support for his view. Like the Machiavellian figures in numerous other Renaissance tragedies, Flamineo inhabits a world governed more by policy than providence.

Reason of state theory underpinned new attitudes towards history. Whereas the past had previously been approached in a search for 'a general source of wisdom and moral behaviour', Renaissance courtiers and writers were increasingly influenced by Machiavelli's more pragmatic view of history, 'as a guide to making tough decisions'.[11] A writer of a history play, therefore, was in a delicate position. Many of the earlier English history plays maintain a celebratory and nationalistic tenor, suggesting that the hand of God has directed the nation to its current happy state. At the end of

Shakespeare's *Richard III*, for instance, Richmond is figured unmistakably as an agent of providence. Such texts carefully shape and interpret the facts of history, so as to produce an acceptable narrative for a contemporary audience. Yet while Richard III might be moulded into the form of a stage villain – just one step away from the medieval Vice – a king who loses his grip on power simply through his own weakness presents greater challenges. This was one interpretation of the downfall of Richard II, which was charted in two significant Renaissance plays. The anonymously authored *Thomas of Woodstock* focuses mainly on Richard's poor counsellors, who emerge as foolish and self-interested. By comparison, Shakespeare's *Richard II* is more subtle, exploring the dilemma facing subjects who are genuinely troubled by the state of their country under inept leadership.

As noted in Chapter 1, supporters of the Earl of Essex's unsuccessful rebellion in 1601 sponsored a revival of *Richard II*, presumably in an attempt to garner support from the people of London. Poor kings, the play suggested to the rebels, may legitimately be replaced. But in many respects we might see this as an overly simplistic interpretation of a play which explores with considerable subtlety the intervention of humans into the mysteries of kingship. As his grip on power weakens, Richard invokes his divine right with increasing desperation. 'God omnipotent', he declares, 'Is mustering in his clouds on our behalf / Armies of pestilence', which will 'strike' his enemies and their descendants (III.iii.84–7). In the deposition scene, both Richard and the ascendant Bolingbroke (who will become King Henry IV) struggle to find a ceremonial form that will legitimize this trans-fer of authority. As he teases Bolingbroke with the crown – which is offered, withdrawn, and offered again – Richard opens to question the value of this object as a signifier of authority. It had, quite simply, defined him; without it, 'I must nothing be' (IV.i.191). For Bolingbroke, its significance is less clear. He is left in this scene clutching the crown and ordering his own coro-nation – an event which he hopes will legitimize his rule, yet one that the play does not stage.

Richard II thus destabilizes certain fundamental discourses of monarchical authority. The play represents a movement away from a society based on ceremony and feudal bonds, towards one based rather on pragmatism and opportunism. At the end, the authority of Bolingbroke is by no means assured, as he faces rebellion in Gloucestershire and tries to distance himself from the murder of the deposed Richard. Shakespeare subsequently develops the troubled character of this monarch through the two parts of *Henry IV*. Notably, while in *1 Henry IV* he is introduced planning a crusade to Jerusalem, as a way of marking himself as a godly warrior rather than a Machiavellian usurper, he dies late in *2 Henry IV* with that goal unfulfilled. Ironically, this monarch whose relationship with God has been so troublingly uncertain, makes it no further than a room in his own palace, known as 'Jerusalem' (IV.iii.362). As a study in history, Shakespeare's representation of this king therefore casts a sceptical eye across the orthodox myths of power, which James I was trying so hard to maintain a few decades later.

6.2 Speech and scandal: representing the court

In the early years of the reign of James I, John Marston wrote two plays in which dukes disguise themselves as commoners, and use their new status to expose corruption at court. He was not alone in using this model; writers including Dekker, Middleton and Shakespeare also wrote 'disguised ruler plays' in these years.[12] But Marston's plays, *The Malcontent* and *The Fawn*, are notable for their concentration on corruptions of language at court. His disguised rulers uncover courts that are cankered by speech-acts which have lost their truth-value. The language of the court is rather characterized by flattery and scandal, as various courtiers compete for preferment within a corrupt system. Those who are successful are those who can temporize: literally shaping their speech in accordance with the times. As one debased courtier declares in *The Malcontent*, ''Tis good run still with him that has most might; / I had rather stand with wrong than fall with right' (IV.v.92–3). In opposition to this ethos, his disguised dukes propound the values of free speech. In *The Fawn* Hercules states:

> Freeness, so't grow not to licentiousness,
> Is grateful to just states. Most spotless kingdom,
> And men, O happy born under good stars,
> Where what is honest you may freely think,
> Speak what you think, and write what you do speak.
>
> (I.ii.318–22)

A regime of free speech, Hercules suggests, not only liberates individuals from the dishonesty of temporizing, but also cleanses a kingdom in which nothing can any longer be taken at face value. The comic conclusions of Marston's plays powerfully enact this process of purification, as the dukes eventually reveal themselves and assert true standards of justice.

Because the duke himself proclaims the value of free speech in Marston's play, it is easy to overlook just how radical a vision he offers. The play suggests that the only cure to courtly dissimulation and temporizing is the freedom to speak, albeit with the critical qualification that it 'grow not to licentiousness'. As we have already seen, King James was less convinced. His

1620 'Proclamation Against Excess of Lavish and Licentious Speech of Matters of State', to which he refers in his grumpy poem against libellers, was notably equivocal about the borderline separating an allowable 'convenient freedom of speech' from overly 'bold censure'.[13] Like some of his more astute subjects, James appreciated that entirely free speech was not consistent with an absolutist regime. For the freedom to discuss all aspects of government posited a new model of political interaction, in which monarchs could no longer assert their rights to deal alone with mysteries of state. In effect, it turned passive subjects into active citizens.[14] Understandably, James insisted on censorship. In fact, until the 1640s it was illegal to print news about English politics, and even members of parliament were occasionally imprisoned for overstepping the hazy line between 'convenient freedom of speech' and 'bold censure'. Jonson's *The Staple of News* echoes James's policy, representing those who seek to circulate political news as involved not in acts of freedom and truth, but rather in a grotesque marketplace which distorts language and undermines order.

Partly because of the conditions of censorship, information had a special value at court. History plays, in particular, reflect these conditions: 'What news, I prithee?' Queen Margaret asks a messenger in *2 Henry VI* (III.ii.369); 'What fare? What news abroad?' Warwick demands immediately as he enters the action in *3 Henry VI* (II.i.95). Those without access to reliable information could resort to the thriving courtly sub-culture of gossip and scandal.[15] James's poem is specifically concerned with this, as he targets those who dared to attack his counsellors – in particular, the Duke of Buckingham – in the anonymous verse libels which proliferated at this time. These poems could be pointed and explicit, tempting the reader with the hint of illicit truths. One piece takes the form of a prayer, begging God to protect James from various threats posed by his favourite. It implores:

> From such a smooth and beardless chin
> As may provoke, or tempt to sin;
> From such a hand whose moist palm may
> My sovereign lead out of the way
>   [. . .]
> Bless my sovereign, and his feeling.[16]

James understandably interpreted such works as attacks on himself, and potentially on the entire system of monarchy. But for others, gossip and libel were unavoidable products of a censorship regime, and represented a vital form of popular political action. Certainly Barnabe Barnes's *The Devil's Charter*, which contains one of the most substantial representations of libelling afforded by Renaissance drama, suggests that libels are occasionally necessary in order to circumvent corrupt court officials. Other plays are more equivocal. For instance, when we hear in *The Duchess of Malfi* that 'paper bullets' have been spreading to 'the common people' the gossip that the Duchess is 'a strumpet', our reactions are inevitably divided (III.i.49, 24, 26). While the libels are certainly uncovering a hidden fact, their characterization of her position feels brutal and partisan; this culture of gossip is hardly serving the interests of truth and justice.

Webster's great tragedy also foregrounds one of the other products of court culture: the spy. In his opening speech, Antonio presents a vision of an ideal court, in which 'flatt'ring sycophants' and 'infamous persons' are banished, and 'a most provident council ... dare[s] freely / Inform' the king of 'the corruption of the times' (I.i.8–9, 17–18). But in Malfi this is no more than wishful thinking. Hence the rise of Bosola, who has in the past committed murder for the Duchess's brother, the corrupt Cardinal, and who now transforms himself into 'a very quaint invisible devil, in flesh: / An intelligencer' (I.i.262–3). Interestingly, the play generates a measure of sympathy for Bosola: partly because of his self-awareness; partly because of his ultimate discovery of a conscience; and partly also because of the underlying perception that he is no more than one symptom of a corrupt system. Bosola trades in news and rumour because the court affords him very few alternatives. Whereas Marston's court-based comedies offer good rulers purging their courts and reasserting order, Webster's tragedies are much more bleak in their appreciation of systemic failures. Such plays, though in very different ways, were therefore bringing to the stage central debates about the structure of courts and the nature of politics.

Perhaps the most insightful of all dramatic explorations of court culture is afforded by Jonson's *Sejanus*. Like many other dramatists in the early seventeenth century, Jonson turned his attention to Roman history, which afforded ample opportunities to explore the political ideas of Tacitus. *Sejanus* creates a world in which language has been transformed from an instrument of communication into a tool of self-interest. It is epitomized by Afer the orator:

> One that hath phrases, figures, and fine flowers
> To strew his rhetoric with, and doth make haste
> To get him note, or name, by any offer
> Where blood or gain be objects.
>
> (II.419–22)

At the other extreme, the works of the truth-telling historian, Cordus, are ordered to be burned; as Afer declares, 'It fits not such licentious things should live / T'upbraid the age' (IV.467–8). Truth, Jonson's satire suggests, has no place in this court. Moreover, throughout this intricately conceived play, characters are routinely spying on one another, and twisting the words of others in order to serve their own purposes. Jonson underlines the point with a wealth of imagery surrounding the word 'ear'. The emperor Tiberius appoints Macro 'To be our eye and ear' (III.681); Arruntius comments sardonically on those who surround Sejanus, hoping to come within 'ear- or tongue-reach' so that they can 'with a buzz / Flyblow his ears' (V.509–11). And in one of the play's most telling lines, the ear is translated into an actively malevolent agent, as Arruntius notes that 'Nothing hath privilege 'gainst the violent ear' (IV.311).

Sejanus has risen through this system to a position in which he is second only to Tiberius. Although he is not of especially noble birth, Sejanus has skilfully nurtured his relationship with the emperor, and ruthlessly suppressed those who have dared to oppose him. When it comes, his downfall seems sudden; however, it is foreshadowed in a pivotal scene in which Sejanus and Tiberius talk alone, and the favourite expresses his desire to marry Livia, the widow of the emperor's murdered son:

> *Sejanus*. The only gain, and which I count most fair
> Of all my fortunes, is that mighty Caesar
> Hath thought me worthy his alliance. Hence
> Begin my hopes.
> *Tiberius*.   H'mh?
>
> (III.512–15)

Tiberius's quizzical response is at least as significant as Sejanus's request. At this point Sejanus makes the fatal mistake of admitting his ambition; by contrast, Tiberius, sphinx-like, withholds a response. The point, which becomes clear in the final act, is that Tiberius is the better Machiavellian. For Machiavelli teaches that 'the ideal ruler should cultivate the art of acting and learn to be a master at feigning', and Tiberius in this play proves himself a master of dissimulation.[17] Even when he withdraws from Rome, teasing his subjects with hints of political ineptitude, he remains most firmly in control of both his state and his overreaching subject.

In the final act of *Sejanus*, certain supernatural events destabilize the mighty counsellor. Firstly, a statue of Sejanus sends forth smoke, 'black and dreadful', followed by a 'great and monstrous serpent' (V.30, 37); secondly, when Sejanus visits the temple of Fortune, the image of the goddess averts its head. For a Christian audience in Jonson's London, the suggestion here is clear: the hand of providence is finally exerting divine retribution on a man who has dared to say that 'religion' makes 'excellent fools ... of men'

(V.69–70). Consequently, when the Roman Senate is read a letter from Tiberius, which effectively invites the politicians and commoners to destroy Sejanus and his family, the audience is presented with a critical dilemma. Who caused the downfall: the gods, Tiberius, or a combination of both? Does Tiberius overcome the challenge presented by Sejanus because he is the divinely ordained sovereign, or rather because he is the better politician? Ultimately, the questions themselves are more important than any particular answer, since they identify a telling ideological faultline in the text. As we have observed in the conclusions of other Renaissance tragedies, the final act of *Sejanus* seems determined to resist the full implications of the Machiavellian logic it has otherwise explored. In Jonathan Dollimore's words, 'Act V involves a crude attempt to interpret history according to . . . providentialist justice'.[18]

In the decades after Jonson's play was first performed, critics of the English court had little doubt about the significance of *Sejanus*. The play was the first of several early seventeenth-century texts, in a range of genres, which retold the narrative of Sejanus's rise and fall, and sought to apply the lessons of his life to a contemporary context. When the Duke of Buckingham rose to extraordinary heights of power, one of his fiercest opponents in Parliament, Sir John Eliot, explored the parallel at length:

> He is bold. We had the experience lately and such a boldness, I dare boldly say, as is seldom heard of. He is secret in his purposes and more, that we have showed already. Is he a slanderer? Is he an accuser? I wish this parliament had not felt it . . . And for his pride and flattery, what man can judge the greater?[19]

King Charles got the point – commenting that 'He must intend me for Tiberius' – and sent Eliot to the Tower.[20] Jonson, who was still alive and closely concerned with political events, must surely have reflected on the way in which his play had contributed to the development of an anti-court discourse. Drama, as we shall see further in the following section, was never disengaged from the crises and confrontations of this era.

6.3 Imagining opposition

On 30 January 1649, King Charles was led onto a stage which had been erected outside the banqueting hall of the Palace of Whitehall, and beheaded. The act marked the culmination of the civil wars which had devastated the nation over the previous 7 years; however, it had never been stated as a goal of the parliamentary forces, and it shocked the majority of the population. Given the prevailing political discourses we have examined above, it is fair to say that for a great many people – including Charles himself – executing the king was quite literally unthinkable. In the decades preceding 1649, however, many people were dissatisfied with the king and court, and were struggling to find ways of expressing their dissent. Dramatists engaged with these struggles, producing plays which explore the contours of political conflict. In this final section, therefore, we will consider briefly some of the ways in which representations of courtly excess and corruption in drama may assume radical inflections, helping in the process to formulate new discourses of political opposition.

Renaissance tragedies often hinge on crises of justice at court. As we saw in Chapter 2, revenge tragedies typically focus attention on an individual whose access to justice is blocked. Hieronimo, in Thomas Kyd's *The Spanish Tragedy*, is a man who has devoted his life to legal service within the state, and is driven into insanity when his son is murdered by the king's nephew. Not only does the murderer thwart Hieronimo's efforts to beg for justice; more interestingly, Hieronimo seems almost incapable of putting into words his shocking realization of corruption at the heart of the court he serves. Later plays present courtroom scenes, in which those in positions of greatest authority directly interfere with the course of justice. In the second scene of *The Revenger's Tragedy*, the Duke's stepson jests with judges and lawyers as he faces a charge of rape. The Duke seems genuinely flustered: too corrupt to allow justice to take its course, but too inept a politician to see a way of intervening. He eventually chooses to defer the trial, and as a result succeeds only in angering those on both sides. In *The White Devil*, a church-court, headed by the future Pope Paul IV, tries Vittoria for whoredom. Although, by the standards of the time, the charges are not unjustified, the patent hypocrisy of her judges exposes the way in which Vittoria is being used as a scapegoat. There is therefore considerable moral force behind her cry, 'A rape, a rape', for the court has indeed 'ravished Justice, / Forced her to do your pleasure' (III.ii.278–80).

Evidence of corruption and scandal at the contemporary court further informed radical political discourses. In 1621, for instance, Francis Bacon, one of the senior legal figures in the nation, was impeached by parliament for accepting bribes. England's legal system, Bacon's critics argued, was in the thrall of a corrupt court and self-seeking courtiers. In the previous decade, the scandal surrounding Frances Howard was as salacious as the plot of any tragedy. Howard was married as a child to the Earl of Essex; however, as an adolescent she regretted the marriage, and wished instead to marry Robert Carr, who was then James's court favourite. In the course of a sensational court hearing – in which Howard accused Essex of impotence, and Essex countered with allegations of infidelity – the king exerted considerable pressure to produce a result allowing a divorce. Subsequently, both Howard and Carr were implicated in the poisoning of Sir Thomas Overbury, who had counselled Carr against the marriage. Howard and Carr evaded the death-penalty for murder, but were forced to retire from court in disgrace. Contemporary commentary on the case, including a wealth of vitriolic libels, presented it as a signal instance of courtly immorality. Professional playwrights could not afford to be so explicit, but nor could they be expected simply to ignore the implications of such a scandal.[21]

Critics of the early seventeenth-century court also focused their attention on its sheer excess. Led by kings who were uncomfortable when in direct contact with commoners, the early Stuart court was easily portrayed as self-absorbed and immoral, far removed from the concerns and standards of most English people. To many, the court masque epitomized this culture. Masques were elaborate and extortionately expensive theatrical productions, staged for one night only, which involved members of the court and employed song, dance, lavish costumes and settings. According to orthodox theory, they idealized and celebrated the power of the king.[22] According to critics, they were little more than occasions for debauchery and fawning. As one character comments in *The Maid's Tragedy* (by Francis Beaumont and John Fletcher), masques are 'tied to rules of flattery' (I.i.11); in the late 1620s, John Donne commented to a friend that 'to spend all my little stock of knowledge upon matter of delight, were the same error, as to spend a fortune upon masques and banqueting houses'.[23] When the puritan William Prynne was examined in the Star Chamber for his massive anti-theatrical volume, *Histrio-Mastix* (1633), the judges were disturbed particularly by his attacks on masques and plays at court. An entry in the index, 'women actors, notorious whores', was thought to refer to the queen, Henrietta Maria. Prynne, as a result, had his ears cropped.

Some dramatists made a very good living out of writing masques. Most notably, Ben Jonson took great pride in this literary form, which brought him into close proximity with the king. Setting such authors aside, however, we might do well to consider the ways in which dramatic representations of masques figure in plays produced for the public stage. At a time when masques were such prominent events at the English court, what was the cultural significance of masque-scenes in tragedies? And, more specifically, what might we make of recurrent scenes in which masques are used to cloak actual acts of violence? In *The Revenger's Tragedy*, for example, two opposing groups stage mock-masques with murderous intent, and the ensuing muddle of violence destroys most of the senior figures at court. Moreover, the confusion is enough to protect the revenger Vindice, who is undone only afterwards, when he unaccountably admits his villainy. One critical response to such a scene would be to see it merely as a superb theatrical spectacle, pandering to the tastes of a popular audience. Another, though, would be to highlight the way in which the play's representation of a masque subverts orthodox courtly discourses. By linking the masque so closely with courtly corruption, we might argue that such plays converge with the anti-court discourse that was taking shape in the reigns of James and Charles.

To conclude this section, it will be worth focusing on the work of a playwright who was particularly closely engaged with contemporary political debates, Thomas Middleton. In an influential study of Middleton, Margot Heinemann describes his work as 'oppositional', and links him to a political discourse that challenged the authority of the court.[24] While more recent historians have argued convincingly that the concept of 'opposition' is anachronistic in the 1620s, because there were at this time no clear lines of political confrontation, Heinemann's thesis cannot be dismissed so easily. Indeed, it is perhaps even more interesting if we modify it, and consider the way in which Middleton contributed to the *construction* – or *imagination* – of opposition.

As we have already seen, plays written throughout Middleton's career afford glimpses of a nascent oppositional perspective. The early Jacobean *Revenger's Tragedy*, which Middleton probably wrote, is one of the bleakest and most unsettling of all revenge tragedies. In the following decade, *The Witch* seems to allude to the scandal surrounding Frances Howard and the murder of Thomas Overbury; the play's modern editor interprets it as 'deliberate, particularised and dangerous satire', and argues that it was suppressed by the government.[25] Around the same time, in *Women Beware Women*, Middleton conceived perhaps the most elaborate of all mockmasques, in which most of the central characters suffer spectacularly symbolic deaths. And in the 1620s, he was responsible for one of the most notorious political allegories of the era, when *A Game at Chess* achieved a great run of success at the Globe before being closed by the censors. Although it ostensibly supports the government's policy of the day, *A Game at Chess* is challenging in its representation of politics and international relations as a game, and raises some pointed questions about the influence of the Spanish ambassador at the English court.

The Changeling, which was co-written with William Rowley, develops an especially incisive critique of power. Although it is not specifically set at a court – rather in a castle, owned by a nobleman with no distinct political status – the play clearly signals its relation to a contemporary English context, especially in its central narrative of a woman who is prepared to sponsor the murder of the man her father has arranged for her to marry. Middleton underlines the point with a couple of topical allusions to the trial of Howard – most notably in the scene in which Beatrice-Joanna undergoes a virginity test, which is a parodic version of the invasive investigation to which Howard was subjected. But the play's challenge to the court runs deeper than this echo of Jacobean scandal. Whereas many commentators on Howard blamed the whole sequence of events on female sexual excess, Middleton directs attention rather to the broader culture within which his female protagonist lives.

Crucially, he focuses on 'honour', a concept which underpinned individual identity and interpersonal interaction at the English court. As we saw in Chapter 4, other playwrights were equally prepared to interrogate codes of honour: for Shakespeare's Falstaff, it is no more than 'air' (*1 Henry IV*, V.i.134); for a character in *The Maid's Tragedy*, it 'bears us all / Headlong unto sin, and yet itself is nothing' (IV.ii.318–19). In *The Changeling*, characters are almost universally preoccupied with outward indices of status, such as the purportedly impregnable walls of Vermandero's castle, and Beatrice-Joanna's spotless reputation for chastity and obedience.[26] When De Flores, after committing murder for her, demands that she have sex with him, Beatrice-Joanna says, 'Let me go poor unto my bed with honor, / And I am rich in all things' (III.iv.158–9). De Flores, though, reveals this for what it is: evidence of a culture that prioritizes reputation over reality, and identifies a person's social status as the foundation of his or her authority. For him, this is no more than a trick of ideology. 'You must forget your parentage to me', he tells her; to him, she has lost her authority in the act of murder, and is translated instead into 'the deed's creature' (III.iv.136–7).

In the play's final scenes, Beatrice-Joanna's father, Vermandero, is left looking equally inadequate, as he seeks to assert his control over a mystifying sequence of violence. As the play's central figure of patriarchal authority, he assumes that he will be able to understand and control the disruptive forces within his castle; however, he falls surprisingly easily into identifying two innocent men as the villains. The play's grisly climax, in which De Flores stabs Beatrice-Joanna behind a closed door while the deluded figures of authority celebrate their apparent successes as investigators, leaves Vermandero isolated and confused. There has been corruption at the very heart of his court: a murder committed, in fact, in the hidden and secret passageways of his castle. Significantly, Vermandero and his son-in-law, Alsemero, attempt to deal with the revelation in a manner that is entirely in accord with the logic of their society, as they unite in condemnation of a disruptive woman. Alsemero declares a case of 'beauty changed / To ugly whoredom', and assures Vermandero that he still has 'a son's duty living' (V.iii.207–8, 227). Patriarchal authority can be re-established, while the corruption of female sexuality may be purged; as Beatrice-Joanna says to her father, she is 'that of your blood was taken from you / For your better health' (V.iii.159–60).

But *The Changeling*'s closing image of men binding together in the aftermath of calamity is far from satisfactory. For the play has opened to question the central values upon which they have based their authority; and, even at the very end, these two men seem determined to ignore the full implications of what has happened. Therefore, like a number of Middleton's other works, and like so much of Renaissance drama, this text contains an understated yet insistent strain of political radicalism. Although it does not confront the contemporary court with any coherent oppositional programme, it stages a striking challenge to the prevailing discourses of courtly authority. Such texts, it is fair to say, helped to make the confrontations of the 1640s thinkable.

Notes

1 See especially Leah S. Marcus, *Puzzling Shakespeare: Local Reading and its Discontents* (Berkeley, 1988).
2 See J. P. Sommerville, *Royalists and Patriots: Politics and Ideology in England 1603–1640* (London and New York, 1999), pp. 9–54.
3 King James VI and I, *Political Writings*, ed. Johann P. Sommerville (1994), p. 37.
4 *Essays*, ed. John Pitcher (London, 1985), pp. 173–4.
5 *A Letter of Advice Written by Sir Francis Bacon to the Duke of Buckingham, When he became Favourite to King James* (1661), p. 2.
6 See Daniel Javitch, *Poetry and Courtliness in Renaissance England* (Princeton, 1978).
7 Linda Levy Peck, *Court Patronage and Corruption in Early Stuart England* (London, 1990), pp. 53–6.
8 Quoted in Alan T. Bradford, 'Stuart Absolutism and the "Utility" of Tacitus', *Huntington Library Quarterly*, 46 (1983), 128.
9 Quoted in Bradford, 'Stuart Absolutism and the "Utility" of Tacitus', 136.
10 Nathanael Carpenter, *Achitophel, Or, The Picture of a Wicked Politician* (1629), p. 5.
11 D. R. Woolf, *The Idea of History in Early Stuart England: Erudition, Ideology, and 'The Light of Truth' from the Accession of James I to the Civil War* (Toronto, 1990), p. 144.
12 See further Leonard Tennenhouse, *Power on Display: The Politics of Shakespeare's Genres* (New York and London, 1986), p. 154.
13 *Stuart Royal Proclamations*, ed. James F. Larkin and Paul L. Hughes, 2 vols (Oxford, 1973–83), 1.495.
14 See Markku Peltonen, *Classical Humanism and Republicanism in English Political Thought 1570–1640* (Cambridge, 1995), pp. 1–17.

15 See Andrew McRae, *Literature, Satire and the Early Stuart State* (forthcoming, Cambridge, 2003), ch. 1.

16 Bodleian Library, Malone MS 23, p. 29. The poem is often attributed to William Drummond, and is printed in some editions of his work.

17 Richard Allen Cave, *Ben Jonson* (New York, 1991), p. 33.

18 Jonathan Dollimore, *Radical Tragedy: Religion, Ideology and Power in the Drama of Shakespeare and his Contemporaries*, 2nd edn (New York, 1989), p. 135.

19 *Proceedings in Parliament 1626*, ed. William B. Bidwell and Maija Jansson, 4 vols (New Haven and London, 1991–6), 1.223.

20 Quoted in Peter Burke, 'Tacitism', in *Tacitus*, ed. T. A. Dorey (London, 1969), p. 162.

21 On the cultural response to this scandal, see David Lindley, *The Trials of Frances Howard: Fact and Fiction at the Court of King James* (London and New York, 1993).

22 See Stephen Orgel, *The Jonsonian Masque* (Cambridge, Mass., 1965).

23 Quoted in Annabel Patterson, *Censorship and Interpretation: The Conditions of Writing and Reading in Early Modern England* (Madison, 1984), p. 113.

24 Margot Heinemann, *Puritanism and Theatre: Thomas Middleton and Opposition Drama under the Early Stuarts* (Cambridge, 1980).

25 Elizabeth Schafer, 'Introduction' to her edition of Middleton, *The Witch* (London, 1994).

26 Sara Eaton, 'Beatrice-Joanna and the Rhetoric of Love', in *Staging the Renaissance*, ed. Peter Stallybrass and David Kastan (London, 1991), p. 284.

|7|

Encountering otherness: race and colonialism

How might a nation respond to the shock of encountering radically different cultures? More specifically, how did Western European civilization in an
age of global exploration react to the discoveries of different races, different
societies and different ways of living? One extreme response is documented
in a report by an English merchant, John Sarracoll, whose fleet came upon
a West African village in 1586. Sarracoll describes with wonder the village's
architecture and design – 'the streets of it so intricate that it was difficult for
us to find the way out that we came in at' – and notes admiringly that 'in the
houses nor streets was so much dust to be found as would fill an egg shell'.
Then, almost as an afterthought, he adds: 'Our men at their departure set
the town on fire, and it burnt (for the most part of it) in a quarter of an
hour.'[1] Difference is thereby effaced – eradicated – with a gesture at once
casual and chilling. Another extreme is articulated by Michel de Montaigne,
in his essay 'Of the Cannibals', an extract from which is this chapter's
document (see pp. 158–60). Information about native societies in the New
World, perhaps based as much on fantasy as fact, prompts Montaigne to
reflect on the imperfections of his own society. He establishes a simple
dichotomy between art and nature, and asserts that the 'cannibals' are
governed purely by the 'laws of nature', living in a society without agricul-
ture, trade, crime or property. 'The very words that import lying, falsehood,
dissimulation, covetousness, envy, detraction, and pardon were never heard
of amongst them.'

While it would be absurd to suggest that Montaigne's reaction had any
significant influence on the history of European colonialism – which contains, of course, all too many instances of violence and destruction – he
alerts us to a vital early modern debate about cultural difference. His central
point is that ideas of 'barbarism' are not natural, but rather culturally constructed. Reviewing the society of the 'cannibals', he finds nothing 'that is

either barbarous or savage, unless men call that barbarism which is not common to them'. Face to face with evidence of otherness, Montaigne thus acknowledges the challenge of difference, and establishes a rudimentary dialogue between the old and new worlds. In English culture in the age of Shakespeare, this dialogue was gaining in clarity and intensity every year. Sir Thomas More's *Utopia*, published early in the sixteenth century, contrasts European civilization with the imaginary land of the Utopians. Subsequently, the appearance of people from different cultures in the streets of London, and the dissemination of travellers' narratives, added fresh impetus to discussions. In Renaissance drama, we find that playwrights were actively engaged in these debates, bringing to the stage not only the wonder of different cultures but also the processes of questioning which those cultures prompted.

In this chapter, then, we will explore Renaissance drama within the context of the emergent practices and discourses associated with European exploration and colonization. The first section will outline some facts about England's participation in the discoveries of the era, and will discuss the ways in which an awareness of difference prompted the English to reflect upon their own culture. The second section will focus on race, firstly outlining some details about the state's responses to cultural and religious differences, before examining representations of otherness on the stage. And the final section will consider colonialism, which remained for the English a new and risky enterprise, but prompted in literary texts some searching studies of power relations.

7.1 Travellers' tales

At the beginning of the seventeenth century, England was by no means sure about its place in the world. History plays of the late sixteenth century circle anxiously around narratives of civil war, thereby reminding their audiences of the fragility of nationhood. Against a backdrop of rising civil dissension, Shakespeare's John of Gaunt presents a powerful image of England as:

> This other Eden, demi-paradise,
> This fortress built by nature for herself
> Against infection and the hand of war.
>
> (*Richard II*, II.i.42–4)

And yet, as Shakespeare's play demonstrates, this image of insularity and coherence was never more than an ideal, besieged by the turbulent facts of history. Moreover, the notion of a 'sceptred isle' wilfully overlooks the fact that England was only one part of the island of Britain, which also encompasses Scotland and Wales. While the latter was governed from London, the former was an entirely separate country in the sixteenth century, and relations between Scotland and England remained fraught even after King James united the kingdoms in 1603. Looking beyond their island, the English also remained deeply divided about their international responsibilities. Some argued passionately for English involvement in Europe's wars of religion, and fretted about their nation's failure to establish a presence in the New World. Others stuck with John of Gaunt, and valued their seclusion.

In practical terms, England's level of engagement with other lands was relatively slight. Trade routes with Europe and parts of North Africa were quite well developed, and the influx of exotic commodities was helping to establish London as a major international commercial centre. Yet even these regions were mysterious to most people, and texts by travellers such as Thomas Coryat and Fynes Morrison traded on the novelty of their journeys in countries such as Italy and Turkey.[2] England also failed to assert itself as a military power, and kept its distance from most of the period's continental wars. Its greatest triumph of the sixteenth century, the defeat of the Spanish Armada, was a purely defensive engagement, and seemed to many a providential sign of the virtues of insularity. Moreover, English sailors seemed motivated more by pragmatism than the pursuit of glory, and their achievements as a result were sporadic and piecemeal. Indeed, it is fair to say that England's only truly significant rewards from the New World in this period were reaped by acts of piracy. Sir Francis Drake, best known for his circumnavigation of the globe from 1577 to 1580, made a fortune for himself and his queen by raiding Spanish settlements and seizing their ships at sea.

Within England, while people were increasingly curious about foreign lands, their sources of information ranged from the unreliable to the fantastic. Many continued to depend on miraculous tales derived from classical and medieval sources. Pliny's *History of the World*, translated from the Latin in 1601, describes the 'Blemmyi', who 'have no heads, but mouth and eyes both in their breast', and the 'anthropophagi, that feed of man's flesh'.[3] Similarly, *Mandeville's Travels*, though presented as an account of journeys undertaken by a medieval gentleman, combines geographical detail with tales of romance, natural history with wondrous exoticism, fact with fiction.[4] And many early modern explorers were only too happy to exploit expectations of marvels in the New World. American natives, despite Montaigne's respect for them, were repeatedly situated within this context, and were occasionally exhibited commercially in London, either dead or alive. Hence Trinculo's speculation when he finds the evidently 'monstrous'

Caliban in Shakespeare's *The Tempest*: 'Were I in England now, as once I was, and had but this fish painted, not a holiday-fool there but would give a piece of silver' (II.ii.26–8).

Trinculo's optimism aside, the benefits of plantations and trade were by no means clear. In the sixteenth century, statesmen were unconvinced about the wisdom of international trade, many fearing that their nation's staple commodities would be frittered away in exchange for mere trinkets.[5] Nonetheless, new routes were developing rapidly, and economic commentators were becoming freshly aware that trade could be a way of generating wealth. The leading propagandist for trade and exploration was the Elizabethan Richard Hakluyt, who compiled narratives of recent endeavours in his *Principal Navigations of the English Nation*. Hakluyt aimed at once to educate his fellow countrymen about their nation's place in the history of naval exploration, and to stimulate fresh waves of adventurers and travellers. He promoted a vision of national expansion through trade; as Richard Helgerson comments, Hakluyt situates his nation as an 'aggressive commercial entity', thriving within 'a vast network of markets offering unlimited commodities and vent'.[6] For readers at the end of the sixteenth century, his book proposed a very different idea of England to that posited by John of Gaunt in *Richard II*.

The different sides of these debates about travel are presented in a range of Renaissance plays. Many simply trade on a representation of exoticism; Christopher Marlowe's two parts of *Tamburlaine the Great*, for instance, provided wondrous spectacles of foreign lands for their Elizabethan audiences. Others focus more on the purported achievements of contemporary travellers. *The Travels of the Three English Brothers*, written by John Day and others, idealizes the journeys in Europe and the Middle East undertaken by members of the Sherley family. (In fact it is possible that the family to some extent sponsored the playwrights, with a view to garnering financial support for two of the brothers, who were at the time 'effectively marooned abroad'.[7]) In this play, any consideration of the brothers' pursuit of wealth is subordinated to a celebration of irresistible Protestant virtue. Though doubtless less lucrative, the spread of the English faith was more easily represented as heroic than a mere scramble for gain.

In *The Travels of the Three English Brothers*, the playwrights use the simple yet decent Sophy of Persia, the most powerful political figure in the play, as a kind of moral touchstone. Although he oscillates between trusting his own judgement and listening to his evil counsellors, he is besotted from the outset by Sir Anthony Sherley; as he declares, 'But God or Christian, or whate'er he be, / I wish to be no other but as he' (i.78–9). After a series of trials, Anthony's brother Robert marries the Sophy's niece, and proclaims his intention to establish Christianity in Persia:

> This present day I have an infant born
> Who, though descended from the emperor's niece,
> A pagan, I'll baptise in Christian faith;
> Confute their ignorance, heaven assisting me,
> That mine own soul this comfort may partake:
> Sherley in Persia did the first Christian make.
>
> (xiii.50–5)

This vision of cultural conquest is in many respects analogous to the more violent scene narrated by John Sarracoll, quoted at the beginning of this chapter. Indeed, the play imagines the ill-defined religion of the Persians simply collapsing before the potency and virtue of the English. This is colonialism by stealth, offering a deceptively forceful endorsement of the achievements of English expansionism.

More commonly, though, playwrights mocked this sort of naive propaganda. Ben Jonson, as we saw in Chapter 4, was deeply suspicious of wealth-generating schemes, and consistently valorizes ideals of stability and order. Even in a poem celebrating the travels of his friend William Roe, he focuses on the mercantile adventurer's 'return' to his 'home', and makes no mention of his quest for financial 'returns'.[8] In his plays, travellers are invariably fools. For instance, in *Volpone* the English couple in Venice, Sir Politic Would-be and Fine Madam Would-be, provide occasion for satire on the English obsession with news, and are the butt for some of the play's practical jokes. In *Eastward Ho*, which Jonson co-wrote with George Chapman and John Marston, a shambolic expedition to the New World is inexplicably shipwrecked on the Thames. Drunk and foolish, Sir Petronel Flash is determined to believe that his party has at least reached France, and comically wanders the streets of the Isle of Dogs accosting English gentlemen in French.

The underlying argument of such satire is clarified in *The Antipodes*, written by the man who considered himself Jonson's theatrical heir, Richard Brome. Here, a doctor sets out to cure Peregrine of his obsession with miraculous tales of travel derived from *Mandeville's Travels*. Peregrine talks

> of monsters,
> Pygmies and giants, apes and elephants,
> Griffins and crocodiles, men upon women,
> And women upon men.
>
> (I.i.178–81)

The Doctor drugs Peregrine, convinces him that he has been transported to the antipodes while asleep, then employs actors to depict for him a world turned upside down. Though the satire is crude, and concerned more with contemporary England than the New World, Brome's audience can hardly miss the point that Peregrine's fanciful ideas of foreign marvels are causing him to neglect his duties at home. What the play figures as truly 'monstrous' is the way that Peregrine's wife is herself being driven slowly mad, after 3 years of an unconsummated marriage (I.i.204). Like so much of Jonson's own work, Brome's play endorses family over foreignness, and home over travel.

7.2 Race

George Peele's Elizabethan play, *The Battle of Alcazar*, offered one of the period's most cosmopolitan dramatic spectacles. The play brings to the stage an incident from recent history, in which the Portugese king, Sebastian, was fatally lured into a struggle in North Africa between the usurping Muly Mahamet and his uncle Abdelmelec. The action sprawls across the region, and is complicated further by a sub-plot involving a Catholic Englishman leading a papal army intended for the overthrow of English rule in Ireland. Throughout this murky study of international politics, while no character is marked as especially heroic, the text hinges on the confrontation between Muly Mahamet and Abdelmelec. The former is positioned as the villain, and his corruption is signalled in part by his racial status; he is 'the barbarous Moor', 'Black in his look, and bloody in his deeds' (I.6, 16). Abdelmelec is also a pagan, but uses a god-fearing discourse familiar to a Christian audience, and is not so clearly defined on stage by his colour. In its treatment of race, therefore, the play seems somewhat confused. While one Moor seems almost to be represented as corrupt *because* of his colour, the other is good regardless of it; and while 'blackness' of skin and mind are at times all too easily equated, the heroic Abdelmelec positively shines in comparison with the opportunistic Portugese king and the traitorous Englishman.

The challenges that confront us when reading Peele's play become familiar as we look more broadly at Renaissance drama, which often seems frustratingly inconsistent in its treatment of racial difference. In our study of such texts, while it would be foolish to overlook the influence of overt racism, it would be equally foolish to assume that race will always mean the same thing, from one text to another. As we see in numerous plays from the period – and perhaps most notably of all in Shakespeare's *Othello* – racial difference is not *necessarily* equated with depravity and corruption, but it can almost always be *made to mean* such things. Racist discourses, that is, are always available to characters on the Renaissance stage, though they are not always used in consistent ways.

Orthodox English social and political discourse of the early modern period assumed racial and religious homogeneity. Being English, in other words, meant being white and Protestant. Of course, this was always something of a myth; as Daniel Defoe reminded his early eighteenth-century readers, the notion of 'The True-Born Englishman' is a convenient fiction, since so many different waves of invaders and immigrants have contributed to the constitution of 'That Het'regeneous Thing'.[9] Yet on the Renaissance stage, cultural similarity was assumed, and even the Welsh and the Scots were sufficiently strange to warrant attention. The Welsh in Shakespeare's *1 Henry IV*, for instance, threaten English civilization. The play begins with the Earl of Westmorland lamenting the 'beastly' treatment of English corpses by Welsh women, while Mortimer's subsequent devotion to a woman who only speaks Welsh signals to the audience his dereliction of duty (I.i.44–5; III.i).[10] Scots became increasingly prominent in English society and literature alike after the accession of James I, when many of the king's fellow countrymen followed him south and assumed the same rights as the English; however, they were still commonly viewed as foreigners, and treated with suspicion. In particular, John Day's play *The Isle of Gulls* attracted the attention of the censors for its satire on Scotsmen at court.

Immigrants from beyond Britain, known generically as 'strangers', were valuable to the economy, often introducing important new skills. In general they were also absorbed successfully into society, just as the household of Simon Eyre embraces a supposed Dutch shoemaker in Thomas Dekker's *The Shoemaker's Holiday*. Yet strangers, like all others who were noticeably different, could also be a focus of resentment in difficult times. The 'Ill May Day' riots of 1517, dramatized in *Sir Thomas More* (by Anthony Munday and others), were directed specifically against London's population of strangers. Those groups which were also set apart on religious grounds, meanwhile, stimulated heightened anxieties. Jews, though officially expelled from England in 1290, existed nonetheless in small communities. They were expected either to wear a yellow cross to signal their status as aliens, or – as many did – to at least pretend to observe Christianity. Throughout Europe, Jews were generally forbidden to hold property, and as a result many concentrated their energies on trade and moneylending. In these roles, Jews were often blamed for confusing processes of economic change, as the economies of Western European countries shifted towards capitalism. As we have seen already in Chapter 4, Shakespeare explores this process of scape-goating in *The Merchant of Venice*. Indeed, Shylock powerfully confronts anti-Semitic discourse with the evidence of a common humanity, as he asks: 'Hath not a Jew eyes? Hath not a Jew hands, organs, dimensions, senses, affections, passions? (III.i.49–51).

Those who bore a mark of difference in the colour of their skin were positioned in still more precarious positions. Blackness was at this time mysterious enough to command attention and demand explanation; and while a writer such as Montaigne may have been able to approach racial difference in a spirit of cultural relativism, most others saw it rather as a deviation from a God-given norm. Some commentators traced the origin of blackness back to one of Noah's sons, Cham, who defied his father's prohibition of sex on the ark. According to this theory, God made Cham's son and all his descendants 'black and loathsome, that it might remain a spectacle of disobedience to all the world'.[11] Blackness is thus established as an inescapable sign of transgression, lustfulness and moral inferiority. Other writers expanded this stereotype, associating blackness further with characteristics such as jealousy, passion and gullibility. According to one, Moors' 'wits are but mean, and they are so credulous, that they will believe matters impossible, which are told them'; for another, blackness was simply a 'natural infection of the blood'.[12] Divergence from a pale skin-colour is thereby associated with powerful early modern discourses of the monstrous: identified, in other words, with all things that deviate from a supposed order of nature.

Black people themselves were not unknown in London, though they were certainly rare enough to be noticeable. Some North African trading agents lived in England, while Londoners in 1600 witnessed the splendour of an official Moroccan ambassadorial visit to England. Other blacks lived in less enviable conditions, as slaves, long-term servants, entertainers or prostitutes. Although England was not heavily involved in the nascent African slave-trade, its position was at best neutral on the morality of slavery; when Queen Elizabeth heard about the slave-trading of the adventurer John Hawkins, she initially pronounced his activities 'detestable', but eventually granted him a coat of arms, featuring an African 'bound and captive'.[13] Furthermore, in 1601 the blacks in England were targeted in a royal proclamation, which stated:

> Whereas the Queen's majesty, tendering the good and welfare of her own natural subjects, greatly distressed in these hard times of dearth, is highly discontented to understand the great number of Negroes and blackamoors ... who are fostered ... here, to the great annoyance of

her own liege people . . . hath given a special commandment that the said people shall be with all speed avoided and discharged out of this her majesty's realms.[14]

The move smacks of populism, and even desperation, as the ageing queen blames a powerless and numerically inconsequential minority group for the nation's ills. As in the Ill May Day riots, and as in Peele's dramatic representation of Muly Mahamet, difference is brought to people's attention, and made to matter.

Racist discourse is mobilized similarly in a range of Renaissance plays. The slave Ithamore, in Marlowe's *The Jew of Malta*, is a pantomime villain to match his master, the Jew Barabas. In Shakespeare's *Titus Andronicus*, Aaron the Moor, who becomes the lover of Empress Tamora, is figured as villainous and socially transgressive. When Tamora gives birth to a 'blackamoor child', the Nurse pronounces the popular interpretation:

> A joyless, dismal, black, and sorrowful issue.
> Here is the babe, as loathsome as a toad
> Amongst the fair-faced breeders of our clime.
>
> (IV.ii.66–8)

Although Aaron challenges her stigmatizing definition, the play offers little support for his position. Similarly, in John Webster's *The White Devil*, a play founded on imagery of black and white, the servant Zanche seems to carry a mark of sin on her face. She thus counterpoints the play's central 'white devil', her mistress Vittoria. While both participate in 'the black deed' of murder, and while the play insists that Vittoria's 'honour' is ineradicably 'stained', those around Zanche position her more straightforwardly as a pure force of evil (V.iii.251, IV.ii.108). For one observer, she is 'the infernal': a spirit of darkness (V.iii.217).

The fear haunting so many of these representations is that of miscegenation: the sexual mixing of different races. In *The Travels of the Three English Brothers*, the Sophy of Persia puts the case against miscegenation, when he initially fears that his niece will marry an Englishman:

> The princely lioness disdains to mate
> But with a lion; time and experience shows
> That eagles scorn to build or bill with crows.
>
> (xi.53–5)

In this instance, the discourse of racial difference is eventually overcome, and the Sophy learns to appreciate just how lucky he is that his heir will be half-English and a Christian. Similarly, in *The Island Princess*, by Francis

Beaumont and John Fletcher, Western virtue simply overwhelms the pagan women; as one jubilant man suggests to his lover at the end, 'If thou wilt give me leave I'll get thee with Christian, / The best way to convert thee' (V.i). But such representations take the form of romance wish-fulfilment, which effaces anxieties about cultural mixing as easily as the men's religion effaces that of their partners. As we have seen in *Titus Andronicus*, other representations are considerably less sanguine, especially when it is the man rather than the woman who is of a different race.

This is precisely the situation depicted in *Othello*. In the play's opening scene, Brabanzio is informed of his daughter's surreptitious marriage to a Moor by Iago's provocative cries from beneath his window:

> 'Swounds, sir, you're robbed. For shame, put on your gown.
> Your heart is burst, you have lost half your soul.
> Even now, now, very now, an old black ram
> Is tupping your white ewe. Arise, arise!
> Awake the snorting citizens with the bell,
> Or else the devil will make a grandsire of you.
>
> (I.i.86–91)

The speech is a masterful patchwork of racist discourse. Othello's blackness is figured on the one hand as evidence of a devilish spiritual depravity, which will mix Brabanzio's blood with that of 'the devil', and on the other hand as a force that will devalue his family, just as a flock of sheep is devalued if a black ram gains access to a white ewe. Shakespeare's play, though, is more complex in its treatment of race than Iago's language would suggest. This is a play in which almost all the principal characters struggle to maintain their reputations, in the face of a range of slanderous accusations. At one point, troubled by Iago's suggestions that Desdemona has been unfaithful to him, Othello gazes into his wife's face and asks, 'Was this the fair paper, this most goodly book, / Made to write "whore" upon?' (IV.ii.73–4). While he fantasizes about a mark of waywardness that will be legible, the problem Othello faces himself is that he bears an ineradicable mark of difference. The play's central question is what that mark might mean.

Othello does not initially shrink from the fact of racial difference. Indeed, when giving the court a narrative of his courtship of Desdemona, he seems almost prepared to exploit his exoticism:

> Her father loved me, oft invited me,
> Still questioned me the story of my life
> From year to year, the battles, sieges, fortunes

That I have passed.
I ran it through even from my boyish days
To th' very moment that he bade me tell it,
Wherein I spoke of most disastrous chances,
Of moving accidents by flood and field,
Of hair-breadth scapes i'th' imminent deadly breach,
Of being taken by the insolent foe
And sold to slavery, of my redemption thence,
And portance in my travellers' history,
Wherein of antres vast and deserts idle,
Rough quarries, rocks, and hills whose heads touch heaven,
It was my hint to speak. Such was my process,
And of the cannibals that each other eat,
The Anthropophagi, and men whose heads
Do grow beneath their shoulders. These things to hear
Would Desdemona seriously incline
             [. . .]
                 My story being done,
She gave me for my pains a world of kisses.
She swore in faith 'twas strange, 'twas passing strange,
'Twas pitiful, 'twas wondrous pitiful.
She wished she had not heard it, yet she wished
That heaven had made her such a man.

                                       (I.iii.127–62)

In this speech, Othello at once invokes and distances himself from certain racial stereotypes. At times he seems like an English traveller, looking with wonder at the cannibals and the Anthropophagi; at other times he becomes himself the object that Western travellers hunted, to sell into 'slavery'. In Venice he is emphatically alien – in Roderigo's evocative phrase, 'an extravagant and wheeling stranger / Of here and everywhere' (I.i.137–8) – yet he accepts this status and attempts to define its significance. He has risen in Venice through his power over men on the battlefield, and he now cements his place in the hierarchy by conquering the daughter of a senator by wielding power over language. 'This', he says, 'only is the witchcraft I have used' (I.iii.167).

But if Othello is initially capable of countering accusations that his racial difference is an essential sign of corruption, he cannot prevent others from constructing him as monstrous. Iago's goal, in his relentless assault on Othello's identity, is not only to convince others, but also to remould the perceptions of the man himself. In the pivotal scene in which Iago incites

Othello into a fury of doubt about his wife's constancy, he suggests to him that Desdemona requires greater surveillance because of an inherent (racial) difference:

> *Othello*: I do not think but Desdemona's honest.
> *Iago*: Long live she so, and long live you to think so!
> *Othello*: And yet how nature, erring from itself –
> *Iago*: Ay, there's the point; as, to be bold with you,
> Not to affect many proposèd matches
> Of her own clime, complexion, and degree,
> Whereto we see in all things nature tends.
> Foh, one may smell in such a will most rank,
> Foul disproportions, thoughts unnatural!
>
> (III.iii.230–8)

The power to define the boundaries of the 'natural' is the power to define ideology. Here, it is not clear what Othello is beginning to say about 'nature' when Iago interjects; however, Iago seizes the opportunity to make a point about race. For him, 'all things in nature' tend towards racial conformity in desire, while instances of non-conformity are dismissed as 'Foul disproportions'. Although Othello does not immediately respond, in his subsequent soliloquy he considers his blackness as one possible reason why Desdemona's affection may have waned (III.iii.267). He is not certain about it, but Iago has nevertheless successfully implanted racist codes into his mind – manipulating, in the process, the very category of monstrosity.

Othello's murder of Desdemona seems to be Iago's crowning achievement. When Othello appreciates what he has done, and looks remorsefully upon his wife's corpse, he turns upon himself a telling language of vilification:

> O cursèd, cursèd slave!
> Whip me, ye devils,
> From the possession of this heavenly sight.
> Blow me about in winds, roast me in sulphur,
> Wash me in steep-down gulfs of liquid fire!
>
> (V.ii.283–7)

Othello here invokes vivid imagery of damnation, positioning himself with the 'devils' in contrast to Desdemona's 'heavenly' status in death. More significantly, the man who claims at the play's outset that he has once experienced slavery now dredges up the most degrading epithet he can imagine: 'O cursèd, cursèd slave!' But Shakespeare again problematizes the inclination to identify skin-colour with monstrosity. Importantly, the final scenes show Othello's terms of self-abuse to be malleable, and not necessarily bound to racial difference. For those seeking to impose justice after the murder, Iago is instead the play's principal 'notorious villain' and 'damnèd slave' (V.ii.246, 250). The white Iago, even more than Othello, is equated at the close with monstrous villainy.

Finally, *Othello* seems more concerned with the processes through which identities are moulded than with questions about inherent racial characteristics. Although this issue remains a point of critical contention, I would argue that *Othello* is not a racist play, but rather a study in the ways in which racist discourses and stereotypes may be deployed for particular purposes. Potentially, this makes it a politically radical text, which denaturalizes rather than endorses racism.

7.3 Colonialism

The British Empire was largely a nineteenth-century invention. In the age of Shakespeare, as we have already seen, concerns about internal cohesion considerably outweighed those about external expansion. Indeed, 'Britain' itself was more an aspiration – promoted especially by King James – than a reality. Nonetheless, Spanish involvement in the New World stretched right back to the end of the fifteenth century, and as a result people in England were increasingly becoming aware of the potential value of colonialism. Early proponents stressed the intertwined economic, religious and political benefits. For one, a plantation in Virginia promised to expand the queen's 'honor, revenues, and . . . power', while also promoting 'the glory of God by planting of religion among those infidels'.[15] But the actual progress of English colonialism was considerably less glorious than this rhetoric might suggest, and the literature of our period is informed as much by a spirit of sceptical enquiry as it is by expansionist fervour.[16] Writers were openly exploring the possibilities and pitfalls of colonialism, and debating its moral and religious foundations.

Despite the claims of its supporters, colonization was not an easy route to wealth and glory in the early modern period. England's first colony in Virginia was established in 1584, but collapsed 2 years later when the colonists returned home. Another was founded in 1587, but this time the settlers disappeared without trace. In the early decades of the seventeenth century, the Virginia Company maintained the profile of colonization schemes; Michael Drayton's 1606 'Ode. To the Virginian Voyage', heralds one of its early expeditions, eulogizing the 'brave heroic minds' of the travellers.[17] Yet the first successful settlement was not established until 1620,

when the *Mayflower* landed in Massachusetts, and for the duration of our
period England's engagement with the Americas was more a matter of grim
farce than epic achievement. Meanwhile, the more urgent colonial encounters were closer to home, in Ireland, where England struggled to maintain
political control throughout the sixteenth and seventeenth centuries. Some
English settlers in Ireland amassed considerable fortunes, and the plantations at Munster (established in 1585) and Ulster (1609) seemed to offer
ways of imposing English values upon the face of the land. But these were
uneasy ventures, and the native Irish population staged a series of revolts
throughout the period. A *View of the Present State of Ireland*, written in the
late sixteenth century by the poet and Irish settler Edmund Spenser, insists
on the savagery of the native population and seeks to justify the use of brutal force to maintain English rule. Unlike Montaigne, Spenser found little
cause to reflect on cultural constructions of barbarism.

Other writers, less immediately involved in the messy realities of colonial
encounters, peddled seductive fantasies. Sir Walter Raleigh's *Discovery of
Guiana* (1596), tells of a land where gold awaits for the taking, and where
settlers will encounter natural abundance:

> There is no country which yieldeth more pleasure to the inhabitants,
> either for these common delights of hunting, hawking, fishing, fowling
> and the rest, than *Guiana* doth. It hath so many plains, clear rivers,
> abundance of pheasants, partridges, quails, rails, cranes, herons, and
> all other fowl; deer of all sorts, porks, hares, lions, tigers, leopards and
> diverse other sort of beasts.[18]

The land Raleigh sketches, as much from his imagination as his explorations, is a version of paradise, in which nature caters to every human
desire. It is also worth noting that his discourse of exploitation is distinctly
gendered, as he goes on to proclaim that 'Guiana is a country that hath yet
her maidenhead'. Discourse of colonialism is replete with such claims,
which turn a rapacious male gaze upon a purportedly untouched and fertile
land. John Donne, writing around the same time as Raleigh, notoriously
turns this trope inside out, addressing his lover in the enraptured language
of a New World explorer: 'O my America, my new found land, / My kingdom, safeliest when with one man manned'.[19] In plays concerned with
exploration, such as *The Travels of the Three English Brothers* and *The
Island Princess*, this conjunction of sexual and colonial discourses helps us
to appreciate the special significance of female natives, pliable to the desires
of Western males.

These textual strategies alert us, once again, to the power of language.
Debates over colonialism were in part debates over how distant lands and

mysterious peoples might be brought into discourse, and thus positioned in relation to the colonizing power. Theorists of colonialism, such as Edward Said, have suggested that colonizers typically respond to the challenge of encounters with otherness by insisting upon an absolute difference between the dominating and dominated cultures.[20] As noted in relation to Spenser, people in such positions can hardly afford the relativism of Montaigne; if their projects of conquest are to succeed, they must be convinced themselves of the value, or even necessity, of their rule. Tensions arise, though, at moments when the strict lines of difference are revealed as uncertain or artificial, and when colonial power is manifested as propelled by merely material concerns. At such moments, ideology becomes visible as ideology, and may effectively be demystified. This is the effect achieved in the most subtle of all Renaissance stagings of a colonial encounter, Shakespeare's *The Tempest*.

The issue of colonialism is foregrounded in the second scene of *The Tempest*, when Caliban declares to Prospero: 'This island's mine, by Sycorax my mother, / Which thou tak'st from me' (I.ii.334–5). While it is true that the play's island seems to be in the Mediterranean rather than the New World, and while Prospero hardly speaks the acquisitive language of Raleigh, this speech nonetheless establishes the relationship between Prospero and Caliban as that of colonizer and colonized. The point is underscored by Caliban's name, which is an anagram of 'cannibal', and thus recalls Montaigne's essay on the confrontation between old and new worlds. Moreover, the play presents the relationship in a particularly confronting manner, because according to medieval concepts of natural law, unoccupied land belonged to the first people to lay claim to it and establish settlement on it. These ideas were a recurrent problem for colonizers in the New World, who were all too well aware of the existence of established settlements. They prompted various convoluted ceremonies of possession, and in some parts of the world (such as Australia) would lead settlers to make the absurd claim that the land had not been settled at all.

In *The Tempest*, Caliban's forthright challenge forces Prospero to justify his rule. His legitimation relies heavily on assertions of Caliban's otherness; he claims that Caliban has resisted all the educative efforts of Western culture, and as a result requires to be placed in a position of servitude. According to Prospero, Caliban is 'A devil, a born devil, on whose nature / Nurture can never stick' (IV.i.188–9). Interestingly, one of the first modern texts on grammar, published in the year of Christopher Columbus's famous voyage to America, 1492, stated that 'language is the perfect instrument of empire'.[21] The underlying assumption here is that natives are essentially without their own culture, and will absorb that of the colonizing power as

they learn that power's language. Western language, in other words, will
help to fix in place colonial hierarchies and values. In *The Tempest*, it is
therefore appropriate that Prospero's power should be symbolized by his
books; however, it is equally striking that Caliban himself produces some of
the best verse of the play, especially in his lyrical responses to the island's
extraordinary blend of nature and the supernatural:

> Sometimes a thousand twangling instruments
> Will hum about mine ears, and sometimes voices
> That if I then had waked after long sleep
> Will make me sleep again; and then in dreaming
> The clouds methought would open and show riches
> Ready to drop upon me, that when I waked
> I cried to dream again.
>
> (III.ii.132–8)

Significantly, these lines use the colonizer's own language to posit very different attitudes towards the island. Whereas Prospero pragmatically
manipulates supernatural forces, Caliban responds with an intense aesthetic
appreciation; and whereas Prospero stands for values of reason and order,
Caliban 'cries' for a world of dreams. Although Caliban is undoubtedly less
powerful, and unquestionably different, he is not necessarily the lesser being
of Prospero's assertions.

The value of language is clarified in an exchange between Caliban and
Miranda:

> *Miranda*:   Abhorrèd slave,
> Which any print of goodness wilt not take,
> Being capable of all ill! I pitied thee,
> Took pains to make thee speak, taught thee each hour
> One thing or other. When thou didst not, savage,
> Know thine own meaning, but wouldst gabble like
> A thing most brutish, I endowed thy purposes
> With words that made them known.
>   [. . .]
> *Caliban*: You taught me language, and my profit on't
> Is I know how to curse. The red plague rid you
> For learning me your language!
>
> (I.ii.354–68)

In accordance with her father's colonial discourse, Miranda envisages the
educative project as imprinting culture onto the crude natural form of the
native. Before she came to the island, Caliban did not even 'Know thine own

meaning' – a phrase which not only suggests his incapacity to speak sensibly, but also implies that his very existence was meaningless without the imposed authority of Prospero and his daughter. Caliban's retort, as Stephen Greenblatt notes, 'might be taken as self-indictment: even with the gift of language, his nature is so debased that he can only learn to curse'. But there is more to the lines than this, as Caliban exposes Prospero's language as an instrument of power, and therefore 'achieves for an instant an absolute if intolerably bitter moral victory'.[22] At this moment, he recognizes that the colonizer's language will only ever define him as subordinate, and he forcefully rejects such meanings.

Caliban's argument is not dissimilar to that made by Montaigne, in his essay 'Of Cannibals'. Like Montaigne, Shakespeare appreciates that barbarism is a cultural construction; in the course of the play it is in fact exposed as a weapon, wielded by Prospero to legitimize his seizure of power on the island and his enslavement of its existing inhabitant. While Shakespeare's text does not present an argument, in the manner of Montaigne's essay, it subtly explores the contours of the struggle between colonizer and colonized. Like so many of the plays we have considered in this book, *The Tempest* brings to the public stage a crucial contemporary debate, and does not assume that the individual with more power is necessarily right.

Notes

1 Quoted in Stephen Greenblatt, *Renaissance Self-Fashioning: From More to Shakespeare* (Chicago and London, 1980), p. 193.
2 See *Coryat's Crudities* (1611), and Morrison's *Itinerary* (1617).
3 Quoted in E. A. J. Honigmann, 'Introduction' to his edition of Shakespeare, *Othello* (Walton-on-Thames, 1997), p. 5.
4 See Stephen Greenblatt, *Marvelous Possessions: The Wonder of the New World* (Oxford, 1991), pp. 27–51.
5 See C. G. A. Clay, *Economic Expansion and Social Change: England 1500–1700*, 2 vols (Cambridge, 1984), 2.206–13.
6 Richard Helgerson, *Forms of Nationhood: The Elizabethan Writing of England* (Chicago and London, 1992), p. 171.
7 Anthony Parr, 'Introduction' to his edition of *Three Renaissance Travel Plays* (Manchester and New York, 1995), pp. 8–9.
8 *Ben Jonson: The Complete Poems*, ed. George Parfitt (Harmondsworth, 1975), p. 84.
9 *The True-Born Englishman: A Satire*, 1.280; in *British Literature 1640–1789: An Anthology*, ed. Robert Demaria, Jr., 2nd edn (Oxford, 2001), pp. 308–21.
10 As many of Shakespeare's contemporaries would have known, the Welsh women were reputed to have cut off the genitals of dead English soldiers, 'and put one part thereof into the mouths of every dead man, in such sort that the cullions

hung down to their chins; and not so contented, they did cut off their noses and thrust them into their tails' (Raphael Holinshed, *Chronicles* (1587); quoted in Jean E. Howard and Phyllis Rackin, *Engendering a Nation: A Feminist Account of Shakespeare's English Histories* (London and New York, 1997), p. 171).

11 Richard Hakluyt, *The Principal Navigations Voyages Traffiques and Discoveries of the English Nation* (Glasgow, 1904), 7.263–4.

12 Quoted in Virginia Mason Vaughan, *'Othello': A Contextual History* (Cambridge, 1994), pp. 68, 54.

13 Julia Briggs, *This Stage-Play World: Texts and Contexts, 1580–1625* (Oxford, 1997), p. 87.

14 *Tudor Royal Proclamations*, ed. Paul L. Hughes and James F. Larkin, 3 vols (New Haven and London, 1964–9), 3.221.

15 Quoted in Helgerson, *Forms of Nationhood*, p. 167.

16 See Andrew Fitzmaurice, *Humanism and America: An Intellectual History of English Colonisation, 1500–1625* (Cambridge, 2003).

17 Drayton's poem is printed in *The Norton Anthology of English Literature*, 6th edn, ed. M. H. Abrams *et al.*, 2 vols (New York and London, 1993), 1.1056–7.

18 Extract printed in *The English Renaissance: An Anthology of Sources and Documents*, ed. Kate Aughterson (London and New York, 1998), p. 518.

19 'Elegy 19. To His Mistress Going to Bed', ll. 27–8; in *John Donne: The Complete English Poems*, ed. A. J. Smith (London, 1986), p. 125.

20 See especially Edward Said, *Orientalism* (London, 1978).

21 Antonio de Nebrija, quoted in Stephen J. Greenblatt, *Learning to Curse: Essays in Early Modern Culture* (New York and London, 1990), p. 17.

22 Greenblatt, *Learning to Curse*, p. 25.

Epilogue
A word about endings

For Renaissance audiences, the endings of plays were comfortingly predictable: generally speaking, comedies end with marriages, while tragedies end with deaths. And yet, as we have observed countless times throughout this book, endings may raise as many questions as they answer. To return to Shakespeare's *Twelfth Night*, we will recall the way in which certain characters may be excluded from otherwise joyous comic endings. Malvolio bitterly withdraws from the festivities, while the sea-captain Antonio watches silently as Sebastian, the man to whom he has devoted himself, brashly announces his marriage to Olivia. To return to *Romeo and Juliet*, we may reflect on the way in which tragedies are often brought to a close by frustratingly imperceptive characters. Two old men reacting to the deaths of their only offspring by erecting gold statues seems simply to miss the point of this play, so closely focused as it is on youthful desire and a rejection of family hierarchies. And to return to Ben Jonson's *Epicene*, we might note that playwrights occasionally delight in frustrating an audience's expectations. In this unconventional comedy's final scene, not only is the central marriage revealed as a sham because the 'bride' was a boy in disguise, but Dauphine looks forward to a funeral as he cruelly mocks his ageing uncle with thoughts of his death.

In instances such as these, conclusion is not the same as closure. Plays conclude because they must; and they conclude in accordance with generic conventions because authors are always constrained in various ways by unwritten laws of genre. But 'closure' signifies a conclusion that is aesthetically or ideologically satisfying: one that leaves no unanswered questions or unresolved anxieties. A strong sense of closure, that is, suggests a world in which problems can be fixed and conflicts reconciled. By contrast, we have been drawn to plays that seem in various ways to resist closure. Such texts have proved so fascinating in part because, as much as the authors may wish to provide neat and conventional endings, the central conflicts cannot be so easily resolved. As we have discovered, Renaissance plays typically engage themselves in controversies, bringing to the stage vital contemporary debates. Problematic conclusions, therefore, may be interesting precisely because they signal to us debates that unquestionably remain open, on stage as in contemporary life.

One final example will help us to grasp this closing point. In John Webster's *The Duchess of Malfi*, the common human desire to draw neat conclusions out of more complex sets of circumstances is underscored by the way characters recurrently reflect on events. For example, before he kills the Duchess, Bosola tells her that 'Glories, like glow-worms, afar off shine bright, / But, looked to near, have neither heat nor light'; and considering his own likely downfall later in the play, he comments, 'We value not desert nor Christian breath / When we know black deeds must be cured with death' (IV.ii.140–1; V.iv.42–3). Remarks of this kind are known as *sententiae*: short and pithy statements of conventional wisdom.[1] In context, however, they commonly seem either flawed or inadequate, since the play itself reveals human desires and conflicts to be far more uncertain and fraught than the sententiae seem capable of acknowledging. Indeed, this play looks sceptically upon efforts to identify overarching principles of justice or providential order. Its events seem propelled rather by essentially human forces; as Bosola tells the Cardinal, 'when thou killed'st thy sister, / Thou took'st from Justice her most equal balance, / And left her naught but her sword' (V.v.48–50). This point is figured dramatically in the notorious shapelessness of the final act, in which no character seems to exert any control, and no plans work out in the way intended.[2]

Order is ostensibly restored only in the final moments, when Delio returns to the stage with the surviving son of the Duchess and Antonio. He declares,

> Let us make noble use
> Of this great ruin, and join all our force
> To establish this young hopeful gentleman
> In 's mother's right. These wretched eminent things
> Leave no more fame behind 'em than should one
> Fall in a frost and leave his print in snow;
> As soon as the sun shines, it ever melts
> Both form and matter. I have ever thought
> Nature doth nothing so great for great men
> As when she's pleased to make them lords of truth.
> Integrity of life is fame's best friend,
> Which nobly, beyond death, shall crown the end.
>
> (V.v.128–39)

This is not altogether unconvincing. The image of a footprint in the snow extends the play's recurrent imagery of memory and memorialization, while the focus on 'integrity' recalls the Duchess's heroic resolution in the face of death. Yet the very fact that it is Delio delivering these lines draws our attention to flaws in the argument, since he is himself by no means a man of perfect judgement and integrity. Earlier in the play, he interpreted Antonio's 'love' for the Duchess as mere 'ambition', and also sought to participate in the sexually debased culture of the court by soliciting the Cardinal's mistress, Julia (II.iv.80–1, 73–4). Nor can the boy carry the weight of expectation that Delio places on his shoulders, for several reasons. Firstly, he is too young to be capable of ruling alone, and will therefore have to rely on the support of men such as Delio. Secondly, his claim to power is unconvincing, since the Duchess has an older son from her first marriage (who is mentioned but not seen in the play). Thirdly, the sight of the boy may prompt the audience to recall his father's dying request: 'let my son fly the courts of princes' (V.iv.75). And fourthly, the horoscope Antonio procured at the boy's birth predicted for him a 'short life' and 'violent death' (II.iii.61, 63). Despite Delio's efforts, therefore, the play itself asserts a counter-argument. Ultimately, there is little reason to suppose that the boy, any more than any other person, will be capable of establishing in Malfi a government based on virtue.

Moreover, although the boy has an undeniable symbolic value, he never speaks for himself, and therefore never takes shape as a convincing and authoritative character. As we have seen before, silence matters on stage. At the end of Shakespeare's *Measure for Measure*, Isabella fails to respond to the Duke's proposal of marriage. At the end of *Othello*, Iago dismisses questions about the motives of his villainy: 'What you know, you know. / From this time forth I never will speak word' (V.ii.309–10). Not only do these characters refuse to comply with the ideological trick of closure, they also draw attention to unresolved tensions and questions. For readers of Renaissance drama, situating the plays within their contexts will help us to appreciate the ways in which such questions inform their respective texts. We will learn that plays, like the debates they stage, are not so easily closed.

Notes

1 See further Kate McLuskie, 'Drama and Sexual Politics: The Case of Webster's Duchess', in *Drama, Sex and Politics*, ed. James Redmond (Cambridge, 1985), pp. 81–2.
2 Michael Neill, *Issues of Death: Mortality and Identity in English Renaissance Tragedy* (Oxford, 1997), p. 330.

Documents

1 From Philip Stubbes, *The Anatomy of Abuses* (1583)

[T]here is no mischief which these plays maintain not. For do they not nourish idleness? And *otia dant vitia*, idleness is the mother of vice. Do they not draw the people from hearing the word of God, from godly lectures and sermons? For you shall have them flock thither, thick and threefold, when the church of God shall be bare and empty; and those that will never come at sermons will flow thither apace. The reason is, for that the number of Christ his elect is but few, and the number of the reprobate is many; the way that leadeth to life is narrow, and few tread that path; the way that leadeth to death is broad, and many find it. This sheweth they are not of God, who refuse to hear his word (for he that is of God heareth God his word, saith our saviour Christ) but of the devil, whose exercises they go to visit.

Do they not maintain bawdry, insinuate foolery, and renew the remembrance of heathen idolatry? Do they not induce whoredom and uncleanness? Nay, are they not rather plain devourers of maidenly virginity and chastity? For proof whereof, but mark the flocking and running to theatres and curtains, daily and hourly, night and day, time and tide, to see plays and interludes; where such wanton gestures, such bawdy speeches, such laughing and fleering, such kissing and bussing, such clipping and culling, such winking and glancing of wanton eyes, and the like, is used, as is wonderful to behold. Then, these goodly pageants being done, every mate sorts to his mate, every one brings another homeward of their way very friendly, and in their secret conclaves (covertly) they play the Sodomites, or worse. And these be the fruits of plays and interludes for the most part.

And whereas you say there are good examples to be learned in them, truly so there are: if you will learn to deceive; if you will learn to play the hypocrite, to cog, lie and falsify; if you will learn to jest, laugh and fleer, to grin, to nod and mow; if you will learn to play the Vice, to swear, tear and blaspheme both heaven and earth; if you will learn to become a bawd, unclean, and to devirginate maids, to deflower honest wives; if you will learn to murder, flay, kill, pick, steal, rob and rove; if you will learn to rebel against princes, to commit treasons, to consume treasures, to practise idleness, to sing and talk of bawdy love and venery; if you will learn to deride, scoff, mock and flout, to flatter and smooth; if you will learn to play the whoremaster, the glutton, the drunkard, or incestuous person; if you will learn to become proud, haughty and arrogant; and, finally, if you will learn to contemn God and all his laws, to care neither for heaven nor hell, and to commit all kind of sin and mischief, you need to go to no other school, for all these good examples you may see painted before your eyes in interludes and plays. Wherefore that man who giveth money for the maintenance of them must needs incur the damage of *premunire*, that is, eternal damnation, except they repent. For the apostle biddeth us beware, lest we communicate with other men's sins; and this their doing, is not only to communicate with other men's sins, and maintain evil to the destruction of themselves and many others, but also a maintaining of a great sort of idle lubbers, and buzzing drones, to suck up and devour the good honey, whereupon the poor bees should live.

Therefore I beseech all players and founders of plays and interludes, in the bowels of Jesus Christ, as they tender the salvation of their souls, and others', to leave off that cursed kind of life, and give themselves to such honest exercises and godly mysteries as God hath commanded them in His word to get their livings withal. For who will call him a wise man, that playeth the part of a fool or a Vice? Who can call him a Christian, who playeth the part of a devil, the sworn enemy of Christ? Who can call him a just man, that playeth the part of a dissembling hypocrite? And, to be brief, who can call him a straight-dealing man, who playeth a cozener's trick? And so of all the rest.

Away therefore with this so infamous art! For go they never so brave, yet are they counted and taken but for beggars. And is it not true? Live they not upon begging of every one that comes? Are they not taken by the laws of the realm for rogues and vagabonds? I speak of such as travail the counties with plays and interludes, making an occupation of it, and ought so to be punished if they had their deserts. But hoping they will be warned now at the last, I will say no more of them, beseeching them to consider what a fearful thing it is to fall into the hands of God, and to provoke his wrath and heavy displeasure against themselves and others; which the Lord of His mercy turn from us!

2 From *Haec Vir; or, The Womanish Man* (1620)

Haec Vir: Most redoubted and worthy sir (for less than a knight I cannot take you), you are most happily given unto my embrace.

Hic Mulier: Is she mad or doth she mock me? Most rare and excellent lady, I am the servant of your virtues and desire to be employed in your service.

Haec Vir: Pity of patience, what doth he behold in me, to take me for a woman? Valiant and magnanimous sir, I shall desire to build the tower of my fortune upon no stronger foundation than the benefit of your grace and favour.

Hic Mulier: Oh, proud ever to be your servant.

Haec Vir: No, the servant of your servant.

Hic Mulier: The tithe of your friendship, good lady, is above my merit.

Haec Vir: You make me rich beyond expression. But, fair knight, the truth is I am a man and desire but the obligation of your friendship.

Hic Mulier: It is ready to be sealed and delivered to your use. Yet I would have you understand I am a woman.

Haec Vir: Are you a woman?

Hic Mulier: Are you a man? Oh Juno Lucina, help me!

Haec Vir: Yes, I am.

Hic Mulier: Your name, most tender piece of masculine.

Haec Vir: Haec Vir, no stranger either in court, city, or country. But what is yours, most courageous counterfeit of Hercules and his distaff?

Hic Mulier: Near akin to your goodness, and compounded of fully as false Latin. The world calls me Hic Mulier.

Haec Vir: What, Hic Mulier, the Man-Woman? She that like an alarm-bell at midnight hath raised the whole kingdom in arms against her? Good, let me stand and take a full survey, both of thee and all thy dependants.

Hic Mulier: Do freely and, when thou hast daubed me over with the worst colours thy malice can grind, then give me leave to answer for myself, and I will say thou art an accuser just and indifferent.

[*Haec Vir outlines arguments against women who present themselves as men*]

Hic Mulier: Well then, to the purpose. First, you say I am base, in being a slave to novelty. What slavery can there be in freedom of election, or what baseness to crown my delights with those pleasures which are most suitable to mine affections? Bondage or slavery is a restraint from those actions which the mind of its own accord doth most willingly desire, to perform the intents and purposes of another's disposition, and that not by mansuetude or sweetness of entreaty, but by the force of authority and strength of compulsion. Now for me to follow change according to the limitation of mine own will and pleasure, there cannot be a greater freedom. Nor do I in my delight of change otherwise than as the whole world doth, or as becometh a daughter of the world to do. For what is the world but a very shop or warehouse of change? Sometimes winter, sometimes summer; day and night; they hold sometimes riches, sometimes poverty; sometimes health, sometimes sickness; now pleasure, now anguish; now honour, then contempt; and, to conclude, there is nothing but change, which doth surround and mix with all our fortunes. And will you have poor woman such a fixed star that she shall not so much as move or twinkle in her own sphere? That were true slavery indeed and a baseness beyond the chains of the worst servitude!

[...]

But you will say it is not change but novelty from which you deter us, a thing that doth avert the good and erect the evil, prefer the faithless and confound desert, that with the change of opinions breeds the change of states, and with continual alterations thrusts headlong forward both ruin and subversion. Alas, soft sir, what can you christen by that imagined title, when the words of a wise man are, 'That was done, is but done again; all things do change, and under the cope of heaven there is no new thing.' So that whatsoever we do or imitate, it is neither slavish, base, nor a breeder of novelty.

Next, you condemn me of unnaturalness in forsaking my creation and contemning custom. How do I forsake my creation, that do all the rights and offices due to my creation? I was created free, born free, and live free; what lets me then so to spin out my time that I may die free?

To alter creation were to walk on my hands with my heels upward, to feed myself with my feet, or to forsake the sweet sound of sweet words for the hissing noise of the serpent. But I walk with a face erect, with a body clothed, with a mind busied, and with a heart full of reasonable and devout cogitations, only offensive in attire, inasmuch as it is a stranger to the curiosity of the present times and an enemy to custom. Are we then bound by the flatterers of time or the dependants on custom? Oh miserable servitude, chained only to baseness and folly, for than custom nothing is more absurd, nothing more foolish.

3 From William Gouge, *Of Domesticall Duties* (1622)

Of equality of estate and condition betwixt those that are to be married together.

Some equality in outward estate and wealth is also befitting the parties that are to be married together, lest the disparity therein (especially if it be over-great) make the one insult over the other more than is meet: for if a man of great wealth be married to a poor woman, he will think to make her as his maidservant, and expect that she should carry herself towards him so as beseemeth not a yokefellow and a bedfellow: so as such an one may rather be said to be brought under bondage, than marriage. And if a rich woman marry a poor man, she will look to be the master, and to rule him: so as the order which God hath established will be clean perverted, and the honour of marriage laid in the dust. For where no order is, there can be no honour.

The like may be said of outward condition, that therein also there be some equality: that princes, nobles, and gentlemen marry such as are of their own rank, and the meaner sort such as are of their degree. Note what sort of wives Abraham, Isaac, and Jacob married, and it will appear that they had respect to this parity. Disparity in condition as well as in estate, is a means to make men and women swell and insult above that which is meet: yea and to twit one another in the teeth with their former estate and condition.

Contrary on the one side are the practices of such as affect to marry above their own estate and degree: thinking by such marriages to advance themselves. This is the only thing which many seek after in seeking wives and husbands; whereby it cometh to pass that they oft meet with the worst matches, and make their marriage a kind of bondage unto them. Great portions make many women proud, dainty, lavish, idle, and careless; a man were much better, even for help of his own outward estate, to marry a prudent, sober, thrifty, careful, diligent wife, though with a small portion, than such an one. A proud back, a dainty tooth, and a lavish hand will soon consume a great portion; *but a wise woman buildeth her house*; and *a virtuous woman is a crown to her husband*.[1] Many wives also that are married to very rich husbands, are more stinted and pinched in their allowance, than such as are married to men of meaner estate. It is not the means which a

---

1   Gouge quotes from Proverbs 14.1 and 12.4.

man hath, but his mind and disposition that maketh him free and bountiful to his wife.

Contrary are the marriages which men of great authority and ability make with mean women, yea their own maids many times, and those of the lowest rank, their kitchen-maids; and which women of noble blood, and great estate make with their serving-men. Do they not herein bewray [i.e. reveal] much baseness of mind, and violence of lust?

If it be said that such marriages are not simply unlawful, the rule of the civil law giveth a good answer, *always in marriages not only what is lawful, but what is honest and meet, is to be considered.*

[. . .]

Of that mutual liking which must pass betwixt marriageable persons before they be married.

Having showed what persons are fit to be joined in marriage, it remaineth to show after what manner they are to be joined.

There are in scripture three steps or degrees commended unto us by which marriageable parties are in order to proceed unto marriage.

1. A mutual liking.
2. An actual contract.
3. A public solemnization of marriage.

The first liking is sometimes on the parents' or other friends' part, and then by them made known to the party to be married, as the friends of Rebecca, liking the offer of Isaac which was made by Abraham's servant, made it known to Rebecca herself.[2] Sometimes again the first liking is on the party's part that is to be married: and then if that party be under the government of parents, the matter must be moved to them, before there be any further proceeding therein, as Samson who seeing and liking a daughter of the Philistines, told his father and his mother thereof.[3] Yea though the party be not under the government of any, yea it is very meet that counsel be taken of wise and understanding friends: that in a matter so weighty as marriage is, there may be the advice of more heads than one, for the preventing of such mischiefs as through rashness might fall out. After a liking is thus taken by one party of a meet mate, that liking must be moved to the other party

---

2   Gouge cites Genesis 24.58.
3   Gouge cites Judges 14.2.

so liked, to know whether there be a reciprocal affection of one towards another. Thus Samson went and talked with that woman whom he liked to be his wife.[4] If at first there be a good liking mutually and thoroughly settled in both their hearts of one another, love is like to continue in them forever, as things which are well glued, and settled before they be shaken up and down, will never be severed asunder; but if they be joined together without glue, or shaken while the glue is moist, they cannot remain firm.

Mutual love and good liking of each other is as glue.

Let the parties to be married be herein well settled before they come to meet with trials through cohabitation, and that love will not easily be loosened by any trials.

Contrary is the adulterous and brutish practice of such as so soon as they cast their eye on any whom they like, never advise or consult about a right and due proceeding unto marriage, but instantly with all the eagerness and speed they can, like brute beasts, seek to have their desire and lust satisfied. Though to keep themselves free from the penalty of the laws under which they live, they procure means to be married, yet they declare a lustful and adulterous mind. And their practice is too like to the practice of the Benjamites, who catched wives from the daughters of Shiloh as they were dancing: or else to the practice of the old world, which so grieved the Spirit of God, that it repented him that he had made man, and thereupon he was moved to bring a general deluge on the whole world. Their practice was this, that *they took them wives of all that they chose:*[5] that is, they rashly and suddenly married whomsoever they liked, without any consideration of their condition.

1 From 'An Exhortation, Concerning Good Order and Obedience, to Rulers and Magistrates' (1559)

Almighty God hath created and appointed all things, in heaven, earth and waters, in a most excellent and perfect order. In heaven, he hath appointed distinct or several orders and states of archangels and angels. In earth he hath assigned and appointed kings, princes, with other governors under them, all in good and necessary order. The water above is kept and raineth down in due time and season. The sun, moon, stars, rainbow, thunder, lightning, clouds, and all birds of the air, do keep their order. The earth, trees, seeds, plants, herbs, corn, grass, and all manner of beasts, keep themselves

4   Gouge cites Judges 14.7.
5   Gouge cites Genesis 6.2.

in their order. All the parts of the whole year, as winter, summer, months, nights and days, continue in their order. All kinds of fishes in the sea, rivers, and waters, with all fountains, springs, yea, the seas themselves, keep their comely course and order. And man himself also hath all his parts, both within and without, as soul, heart, mind, memory, understanding, reason, speech, with all and singular corporal members of his body, in a profitable, necessary, and pleasant order. Every degree of people in their vocation, calling, and office hath appointed to them, their duty and order. Some are in high degree, some in low, some kings and princes, some inferiors and subjects, priests and laymen, masters and servants, fathers and children, husbands and wives, rich and poor, and everyone have need of other: so that in all things is to be lauded and praised the goodly order of God, without the which, no house, no city, no commonwealth can continue and endure or last. For where there is no right order, there reigneth all abuse, carnal liberty, enormity, sin, and Babylonical confusion. Take away kings, princes, rulers, magistrates, judges, and such estates of God's order, no man shall ride or go by the highway unrobbed, no man shall sleep in his own house or bed unkilled, no man shall keep his wife, children and possessions in quietness: all things shall be common, and there must needs follow all mischief and utter destruction both of souls, bodies, goods and commonwealths. But blessed be God that we in this realm of England feel not the horrible calamities, miseries, and wretchedness, which all they undoubtedly feel and suffer, that lack this godly order, and praised be God that we know the great excellent benefit of God showed towards us in this behalf. God hath sent us his high gift, our most dear sovereign lady Queen Elizabeth, with godly, wise and honourable council, with other superiors and inferiors in a beautiful order and goodly. Wherefore let us subjects do our bounden duties, giving hearty thanks to God, and praying for the preservation of this godly order. Let us all obey even from the bottom of our hearts, all their godly proceedings, laws, statutes, proclamations, and injunctions, with all other godly orders. Let us consider the scriptures of the holy ghost, which persuade and command us all obediently to be subject: first and chiefly, to the queen's majesty, supreme head, over all, and next, to her honourable council, and to all other noble men, magistrates and officers, which by God's goodness be placed and ordered: for almighty God is the only author and provider of this forenamed state and order, as it is written of God, in the book of Proverbs: through me kings do reign: through me councillors make just laws: through me do princes bear rule, and all judges of the earth execute judgement, I am loving to them that love me.[6]

6　See Proverbs 8.14–15.

5 From John Foxe, *Acts and Monuments of these latter and perilous days* (1583 edn)[7]

Upon the north side of the town, in the ditch over against Balliol College, the place of execution was appointed ... and when everything was in a readiness, the prisoners were brought forth by the mayor and the bailiffs.

Master Ridley had a fair black gown furred ... such as he was wont to wear being bishop, and a tippet of velvet furred likewise about his neck, a velvet nightcap upon his head, and a corner cap upon the same, going in a pair of slippers to the stake.

After him came Master Latimer in a poor Bristol frieze frock all worn, with his buttoned cap, and a kerchief on his head, all ready to the fire, a new long shroud hanging over his hose down to the feet, which at the first sight stirred men's hearts to rue upon them, beholding on the one side, the honour they sometime had, on the other the calamity whereunto they were fallen ...

Then Master Ridley looking back, espied Master Latimer coming after. Unto whom he said: 'Oh, be ye there?'

'Yea,' said Master Latimer, 'have after, as fast as I can follow.'

So he following a pretty way off, at length they came both to the stake, one after the other, where first Doctor Ridley entering the place, marvelous earnestly holding up both his hands, looked towards heaven; then shortly after espying Master Latimer, with a wondrous cheerful look, ran to him, embraced, and kissed him, and as they that stood near reported, comforted him, saying: 'Be of good heart brother, for God will either assuage the fury of the flame, or else strengthen us to abide it.'. . .

Incontinently they were commanded to make them ready, which they with all meekness obeyed. Master Ridley took his gown and his tippet, and gave it to his brother-in-law ... He gave away besides diverse other small things to gentlemen standing by ... as to Sir Henry Lee he gave a new groat, and to diverse of my Lord Williams' gentlemen, some napkins, some nutmegs, and races of ginger, his dial and such other things as he had about him. Some plucked the points of his hose. Happy was he that might get any rag of him.

Master Latimer gave nothing, but very quietly suffered his keeper to pull off his hose, and his other array, which to look unto was very simple. And being stripped unto his shroud, he seemed as comely a person to them that were there present, as one should lightly see. And whereas in his clothes, he

---

7   The martyrdom of Latimer and Ridley.

appeared a withered and crooked silly old man, he now stood bolt upright, as comely a father as one might lightly behold . . .

Then the smith took a chain of iron, and brought the same about both Doctor Ridley's and Master Latimer's middles. And as he was knocking in a staple, Doctor Ridley took the chain in his hand and shaked the same, for it did gird in his belly, and looking aside to the smith, said: 'Good fellow, knock it in hard, for the flesh will have his course'. Then his brother did bring him gunpowder in a bag, and would have tied the same about his neck. Master Ridley asked what it was. His brother said, 'Gunpowder'. Then said he, 'I take it to be sent of God, therefore I will receive it, as sent of him'. . .

Then brought they a faggot kindled with fire, and laid the same down at Doctor Ridley's feet. To whom Master Latimer spake in this manner: 'Be of good comfort Master Ridley, and play the man. We shall this day light such a candle by God's grace in England, as (I trust) shall never be put out.'

And so the fire being given unto them, when Doctor Ridley saw the fire flaming up toward him, he cried with a wonderful loud voice . . . 'Lord, Lord, receive my spirit'. Master Latimer crying as vehemently on the other side, 'Oh Father of heaven, receive my soul'; who received the flame as it were embracing of it. After, as he had stroked his face with his hands, and (as it were) bathed them a little in the fire, he soon died (as it appeared) with very little pain or none . . .

But Master Ridley, by reason of the evil making of the fire unto him . . . the fire burned first beneath, being kept down by the wood. Which when he felt, he desired them for Christ's sake to let the fire come unto him. Which when his brother-in-law heard, but not well understood, intending to rid him out of his pain . . . heaped faggots upon him, so that he clean covered him, which made the fire more vehement beneath, that it burned clean all his nether parts, before it once touched the upper, and that made him leap up and down under the faggots, and often desire them to let the fire come unto him, saying, 'I cannot burn' . . . Yet in all this torment he forgot not to call unto God still, having in his mouth, 'Lord, have mercy upon me', intermeddling this cry, 'Let the fire come unto me, I cannot burn'. In which pains he laboured till one of the standers-by with his bill pulled off the faggots above, and where he saw the fire flame up, he wrested himself unto that side. And when the flame touched the gunpowder, he was seen stir no more . . .

Some say that before he was like to fall from the stake, he desired them to hold him to it with their bills. Howsoever it was, surely it moved hundreds to tears, in beholding the horrible sight . . . But who so considered their preferments in time past, the places of honour that they sometime occupied in this commonwealth, the favour they were in with their princes, and the opinion of learning they had, could not choose but sorrow with tears, to see so great dignity, honour and estimation, so necessary members sometime accounted, so many godly virtues, the study of so many years, such excellent learning, to be put into the fire, and consumed in one moment. Well, dead they are, and the reward of this world, they have already.

6 From King James VI and I, 'The Answer to the Libel Called "The Commons' Tears"' (c. 1621)

O stay your tears you who complain,
Cry not as babes do, all in vain.
Purblind people why do you prate,
Too shallow for the depth of state.
You cannot judge what's truly mine,
Who see no further than the rine.
Kings walk the heavenly Milky Way,
But you by by-paths gad astray.
God and kings do pace together,
But vulgar wander light as feather.
I should be sorry you should see
My actions before they be
Brought to the full of my desires;
God above all men kings inspires.
Hold you the public beaten way,
Wonder at kings, and them obey,
For under God they are to choose
What rights to take, and what refuse;
Whereto if you will not consent,
Yet hold your peace least you repent,
And be corrected for your pride,
That kings' designs dare thus deride,
Which your king's breast shall never pierce.
Religion is the right of kings,
As they best know what good it brings,
Whereto you must submit your deeds,
Or be pulled up like stubborn weeds.
Kings ever use their instruments,
Of whom they judge by their events:
The good they cherish, and advance,

And many things may come by chance.
Content yourselves with such as I
Shall take near me, and place on high;
The men you named served in their time,
And so may mine as clear of crime.
And seasons have their proper intents,
And bring forth several events,
Whereof the choice do rest in kings,
Who punish, and reward them brings.
O what a calling were a king,
If he might give, or take no thing,
But such as you should to him bring.
Such were a king but in a play,
If he might bear no better sway.
And then were you in worser case,
If so to keep your ancient face.
Your face would soon outface his might,
If so you would abridge his right.
Alas, fond men, play not with kings,
With lions' claws or serpents' stings:
They kill even by their sharp aspect,
The proudest mind they can deject;
Make wretched the most mighty man,
Though he doth mutter what he can.
Your censures are in hurrying sound,
That rise as vapours from the ground.
I know when I shall be most fit,
With whom to fill, and empty it.
The parliament I will appoint,
When I see things more out of joint;
Then will I set all wry things straight,
And not upon your pleasure wait;
Where if you speak as wise men should,
If not, by me you shall be schooled.
Was ever king called to account,
Or ever mind so high dar'st mount,
As for to know the cause and reason,
As to appoint the means and season
When kings should ask their subjects' aid.
Kings cannot so be made afraid:
Kings will command and bear the sway;

Kings will inquire and find the way,
How all of you may easily pay;
Which they'll lay out as they think best,
In earnest sometimes and in jest.
What counsels would be overthrown,
If all were to the people known?
Then to no use were council tables,
If state affairs were public babbles.
I make no doubt all wise men know
This were the way to all our woe,
For ignorance of causes makes
So many gross and foul mistakes:
The model of our princely match,
You cannot make but mar or patch.
Alas how weak would prove your care;
Wish you only his best welfare.
Your reasons cannot weigh the ends,
So mixed they are twixt foes and friends.
Wherefore again mere seeing people,
Strive not to see so high a steeple;
Like to the ground whereon you go,
High aspects will bring you woe.
Take heed your paces be all true,
And do not discontents renew;
Meddle not with your prince's cares,
For who so doth, too much he dares.
I do desire no more of you,
But to know me as I know you.
So shall I love, and you obey,
And you love me in a right way.
                    [. . .]
Come counsel me when I shall call;
Before, beware what may befall.
Kings will hardly take advice;
Of counsel they are wondrous nice.
Love and wisdom leads them still,
Their counsel tables up to fill.
They need no helpers in their choice;
Their best advice is their own voice.
And be assured such are kings,
As they unto their counsel brings,

Which always so compounded are,
As some would make and some would mar.
If I once bend my angry brow,
Your ruin comes, though not as now:
For slow I am revenge to take,
And your amendments, wrath will slake.
Then hold your prattling, spare your pen,
Be honest and obedient men.
Urge not your justice; I am slow
To give you your deserved woe.
If proclamations will not serve,
I must do more, peace to preserve;
To keep all in obedience,
And drive such busy-bodies hence.

7 From Michel de Montaigne, 'Of the Cannibals', translated from the French by John Florio (1603)

I have had long time dwelling with me a man who for the space of ten or twelve years had dwelt in that other world which in our age was lately discovered in those parts where Villegaignon first landed and surnamed Antarctic France ... This servant I had was a simple and rough-hewn fellow, a condition fit to yield a true testimony. For subtle people may indeed mark more curiously and observe things more exactly, but they amplify and gloss them, and the better to persuade and make their interpretations of more validity, they cannot choose but somewhat alter the story. They never represent things truly, but fashion and mask them according to the visage they saw them in, and to purchase credit to their judgement and to draw you on to believe them they commonly adorn, enlarge, yea, and hyperbolize the matter. Wherein is required either a most sincere reporter or a man so simple that he may have no invention to build upon and to give a true likelihood unto false devices, and be not wedded to his own will. Such a one was my man, who besides his own report hath many times showed me divers mariners and merchants whom he had known in that voyage. So am I pleased with his information that I never enquire what cosmographers say of it. We had need of topographers to make us particular narrations of the places they have been in. For some of them, if they have the advantage of us that they have seen Palestine, will challenge a privilege to tell us news of all the world besides. I would have every man write what he knows and no more – not only in that, but in all other subjects. For one may have particular knowledge of the nature of one river and experience of the quality of one fountain that in other things knows no more than another man, who nevertheless to publish this little scantling will undertake to write of all the physics. From which vice proceed divers great inconveniences. Now (to return to my purpose) I find, as far as I have been informed, there is nothing in that nation that is either barbarous or savage, unless men call that barbarism which is not common to them. As indeed we have no other aim of truth and reason than the example and idea of the opinions and customs of the country we live in. Where is ever perfect religion, perfect policy, perfect and complete use of all things. They are even savage as we call those fruits wild which nature of herself and of her ordinary progress hath produced, whereas indeed they are those which ourselves have altered by our artificial devices and diverted from their common order we should rather term savage. In those are the true and most profitable virtues and natural proprieties most lively and vigorous which in these we have bastardized, applying them to the pleasure of our corrupted taste. And if, notwithstanding, in divers fruits of those countries that were never tilled we shall find that in respect of ours they are most excellent and as delicate unto our taste, there is no reason art should gain the point of honour of our great and puissant mother Nature. We have so much by our inventions surcharged the beauties and riches of her works that we have altogether over-choked her; yet wherever her purity shineth, she makes our vain and frivolous enterprises wonderfully ashamed . . .

All our endeavours or wit cannot so much as reach to represent the nest of the least birdlet, its contexture, beauty, profit, and use, no, nor the web of a silly spider. 'All things,' saith Plato, 'are produced either by nature, by fortune, or by art. The greatest and fairest by one or other of the two first, the least and imperfect by the last.' Those nations seem therefore so barbarous unto me because they have received very little fashion from human wit, and are yet near their original naturality. The laws of nature do yet command them, which are but little bastardized by ours. And that with such purity as I am sometimes grieved the knowledge of it came no sooner to light at what time there were men that better than we could have judged of it. I am sorry Lycurgus and Plato had it not, for meseemeth that what in those nations we see by experience doth not only exceed all the pictures wherewith licentious poetry hath proudly embellished the golden age and all her quaint inventions to feign a happy condition of man, but also the conception and desire of philosophy. They could not imagine a genuity so pure and simple as we see it by experience, nor ever believe our society might be maintained with so little art and human combination. It is a nation, would I answer Plato,

that hath no kind of traffic, no knowledge of letters, no intelligence of numbers, no name of magistrate nor of politic superiority, no use of service, of
riches or of poverty, no contracts, no successions, no dividences, no occupation but idle, no respect of kindred but common, no apparel but natural,
no manuring of lands, no use of wine, corn or metal. The very words that
import lying, falsehood, treason, dissimulation, covetousness, envy, detraction, and pardon were never heard of amongst them. How dissonant would
he find his imaginary commonwealth from this perfection?

1576–1642
Timeline of key events, publications and theatrical productions[1]

1576   James Burbage's Theatre built
1577   Francis Drake begins his voyage around the world
       Curtain and first Blackfriars built
       Raphael Holinshed, *Chronicles of England, Scotland and Ireland*
1579   John Stubbs loses his right hand for criticizing marriage negotia-
       tions between Elizabeth and the Duke of Anjou
       Christopher Saxton publishes the first atlas of England and Wales
1580   Drake returns
       Jesuit missionaries arrive in England
1581   Parliament introduces fines of £20 for 'popish recusants' not
       attending church
       Seneca, *Ten Tragedies*
1582   Legislation makes any Catholic clergyman in England liable to exe-
       cution
1583   Irish Rebellion defeated
       Throckmorton Plot to assassinate Elizabeth
       Queen's Men established
1584   Munster plantation established

---

1 The dates of plays are those of the first performance, as listed in the appendix in
   Andrew Gurr, *The Shakespearean Stage 1574–1642*, 3rd edn (Cambridge,
   1992). Uncertainties over dating are indicated by question marks.

1585	Beginning of English military intervention in the Netherlands
	Unsuccessful English settlement established at Roanoke, Virginia
	Francis Drake's West Indies voyage
1586	Trial of Mary Queen of Scots
	Babington Plot against Elizabeth
	Death of Philip Sidney
	William Camden, *Britannia*
1587	Execution of Mary Queen of Scots
	Rose Theatre built
	Kyd, *The Spanish Tragedy* (?)
1588	Defeat of the Spanish Armada
	First Marprelate tracts, agitating for Church reform
	Marlowe, *Doctor Faustus* (?)
1589	George Puttenham, *The Art of English Poesie*
	Marlowe, *The Jew of Malta* (?)
1590	Spenser, *The Faerie Queene*, Books I–III
	Shakespeare, *1–3 Henry VI* (?)
1591	Laws against recusants tightened
	Tacitus, *Histories*, Books I–IV
1592	Plague closes London theatres for 2 years
	Rose Theatre opens
	Marlowe, *Edward II*
1593	Death of Marlowe
	Shakespeare, *Richard III*
1594	First of 4 years of bad harvests
	Swan Theatre built
	Shakespeare, *A Midsummer Night's Dream*, *Romeo and Juliet* (?)
1595	Shakespeare, *Richard II* (?)
1596	Harvest failures push wheat prices to record levels
	England's population reaches 4 million
	Oxfordshire Rising
	Spenser, *The Faerie Queene*, Books IV–VI
	Shakespeare, *1–2 Henry IV* (?)
1597	Statutes for relief of poor and punishment of vagrants
	Second Blackfriars built
	Jonson imprisoned for co-authorship of *The Isle of Dogs*
	Francis Bacon, *Essays*
1598	Tacitus, *Annals*
	Shakespeare, *Much Ado About Nothing* (?)

1599   Globe opened
         Dekker, *The Shoemaker's Holiday*
         Shakespeare, *As You Like It*
1600   London's population reaches 200,000
         Fortune built
         Shakespeare, *Hamlet, Twelfth Night*
1601   Rebellion and execution of the Earl of Essex
         Poor Law extended and consolidated
         Royal proclamation expels blacks from England
1602   Shakespeare, *Troilus and Cressida* (?)
1603   Death of Elizabeth I; accession of James I
         Plague
         Montaigne, *Essays*
         Jonson, *Sejanus*
         Shakespeare, *Measure for Measure, Othello* (?)
1604   Hampton Court Conference: James rejects puritan proposals for
         Church reform
         Chapman, *Bussy D'Ambois*
         Marston, *The Malcontent*
1605   Gunpowder Plot
         Chapman, Jonson and Marston, *Eastward Ho!*
         Marston, *The Fawn*
1606   Blasphemy Act restricts references to religion in plays
         New laws against Catholics
         Dekker, *The Whore of Babylon*
         Jonson, *Volpone*
         Shakespeare, *King Lear, Macbeth*
1607   Settlers land in Virginia
         Midlands Rising
         Shakespeare, *Antony and Cleopatra* (?)
1608   Dekker and Middleton, *The Roaring Girl* (?)
1609   Ulster plantation established
         Cockpit built
         Jonson, *Epicene*
1610   Parliament: negotiations fail for a Great Contract to regulate royal
         financial affairs
         Jonson, *The Alchemist*
         Shakespeare, *The Winter's Tale* (?)
1611   Authorized Version of the Bible
         Middleton, *A Chaste Maid in Cheapside*

1612	Death of Prince Henry leaves Charles as heir to the throne
	Shakespeare, *The Tempest* (?)
	Webster, *The White Devil*
1613	Frances Howard obtains divorce and marries James's favourite, Robert Carr
	Poisoning of Thomas Overbury
	Globe burns
1614	Addled Parliament dissolved by James before passing laws
	Second Globe built
	Jonson, *Bartholomew Fair*
	Webster, *The Duchess of Malfi*
1616	Trial and conviction of Carr and Howard for murder of Overbury
	Death of Shakespeare
	Jonson, *Works*
1617	George Villiers, James's court favourite, becomes Earl of Buckingham
	Walter Raleigh's Guiana voyage
	King James I, *Works*
1618	Start of Thirty Years' War
	Execution of Walter Raleigh
1619	William Harvey discovers the circulation of blood
1620	The *Mayflower* lands in New England
1621	Parliament attacks monopolies and impeaches Francis Bacon
	Dekker, Ford and Rowley, *The Witch of Edmonton*
	Massinger, *A New Way to Pay Old Debts*
1622	Completion of the Banqueting House at Whitehall, designed by Inigo Jones
	Middleton and Rowley, *The Changeling*
1623	Prince Charles and Buckingham make an unsuccessful voyage to Spain to woo the Spanish princess
	Shakespeare, First Folio published
1624	Parliament passes Statute against Monopolies
	Tensions between Calvinists and Arminians become apparent in the Church
	Middleton, *A Game at Chess*
1625	Death of James I; accession of Charles I
	Plague epidemic
	Death of Webster

1626   Charles introduces a Forced Loan to fund intervention in Thirty Years' War
        Charles dissolves parliament after House of Commons tries to impeach Buckingham
        Death of Bacon
1627   Buckingham leads unsuccessful voyage to aid French Protestants at La Rochelle
        Death of Middleton
1628   Tumultuous parliament produces the Petition of Right
        Assassination of Buckingham
1629   Last parliament until 1640 ends in violence and disorder
        Ford, *'Tis Pity She's a Whore* (?)
1630   Dearth: wheat prices reach record levels
        Peace treaties with France and Spain
        Birth of future Charles II
1631   Death of John Donne
1632   Massinger, *The City Madam* (?)
1633   Charles visits Scotland
        William Laud appointed Archbishop of Canterbury
        Donne, *Poems*
1634   Ship Money introduced
        Performance of Milton's *Masque (Comus)*
        William Prynne has his ears cropped for the anti-theatrical tract, *Histrio-Mastix*
1635   Ship Money extended
1636   England's population reaches 5 million
1637   Puritan writers John Bastwick, Henry Burton and William Prynne branded, mutilated and fined for their attacks on the Laudian Church
        Death of Jonson
1638   Judges endorse the king's right to levy Ship Money
        Brome, *The Antipodes*
1639   First Bishops War against Scotland
1640   Short Parliament dissolved
        Long Parliament convenes
1641   Execution of the Earl of Strafford
        Parliament passes Grand Remonstrance, attacking Charles's Personal Rule
1642   Theatres closed by London government
        Civil War begins

Bibliography of dramatic texts

This is a list of the editions I have used for references to dramatic texts. Shakespeare texts are not listed, since I have used throughout *The Norton Shakespeare*, ed. Stephen Greenblatt *et al.* (New York and London, 1997). For many texts by other playwrights, I have used *English Renaissance Drama: A Norton Anthology*, ed. David Bevington *et al.* (New York and London, 2002); in such cases, I use below the abbreviation *ERD*. I have not listed plays to which I have referred without quoting, since the choice of edition in such cases is not significant.

Francis Beaumont and John Fletcher, *The Island Princess*, in *The Dramatic Works in the Beaumont and Fletcher Canon*, ed. Fredson Bowers (Cambridge, 1966-96).

Richard Brome, *The Antipodes*, in *Three Renaissance Travel Plays*, ed. Anthony Parr (Manchester and New York, 1995).

Elizabeth Cary, *The Tragedy of Mariam*, *ERD*.

George Chapman, *Bussy D'Ambois*, ed. Nicholas Brooke (Manchester, 1969).

George Chapman, Ben Jonson and John Marston, *Eastward Ho*, in 'The Roaring Girl' and Other City Comedies, ed. James Knowles (Oxford, 2001).

Common Conditions, ed. C. F. Tucker Brooke (New Haven, 1915).

John Day *et al.*, *The Travels of the Three English Brothers*, in *Three Renaissance Travel Plays*, ed. Anthony Parr (Manchester and New York, 1995).

Thomas Dekker, *The Shoemaker's Holiday*, *ERD*.

Thomas Dekker, *The Whore of Babylon*, in *Thomas Dekker: Dramatic Works*, ed. Fredson Bowers 4 vols (Cambridge, 1953-61).

John Heywood (?), *Gentylnes and Nobylyte*, in *Three Rastell Plays*, ed. Richard Axton (Cambridge, 1979).

Thomas Heywood, *If You Know Not Me, You Know Nobody, Part I*, ed. Madeleine Doran (Oxford, 1935).

Thomas Heywood, *A Woman Killed with Kindness*, ed. Brian Scobie (London and New York, 1985).

Ben Jonson, *Bartholomew Fair*, *ERD*.

Ben Jonson, *The Devil is an Ass*, in *Ben Jonson: 'The Devil is an Ass' and Other Plays*, ed. Margaret Jane Kidnie (Oxford, 2000).

Ben Jonson, *Epicene*, *ERD*.

Ben Jonson, *Sejanus His Fall*, ed. Philip J. Ayres (Manchester, 1990).

Ben Jonson, *Volpone*, *ERD*.

King Leir, ed. Sidney Lee (London, 1909).

A Knacke to Knowe a Knave, ed. G. R. Proudfoot (Oxford, 1963).

Thomas Kyd, *The Spanish Tragedy*, *ERD*.

John Lyly, *Endymion*, *ERD*.

Christopher Marlowe, *Doctor Faustus*, *ERD*.

Christopher Marlowe, *Edward II*, *ERD*.

Christopher Marlowe, *The Jew of Malta*, *ERD*.

John Marston, *The Fawn*, ed. Gerald A. Smith (Lincoln, Nebr., 1965).

John Marston, *The Malcontent*, *ERD*.

Philip Massinger, *The City Madam*, in *The Plays and Poems of Philip Massinger*, ed. Philip Edwards and Colin Gibson, 5 vols (Oxford, 1976).

Philip Massinger, *A New Way to Pay Old Debts*, *ERD*.

Thomas Middleton, *A Chaste Maid in Cheapside*, *ERD*.

Thomas Middleton (?), *The Revenger's Tragedy*, *ERD*.

Thomas Middleton, *Women Beware Women*, *ERD*.

Thomas Middleton and Thomas Dekker, *The Roaring Girl*, *ERD*.

Thomas Middleton and William Rowley, *The Changeling*, *ERD*.

George Peele, *The Battle of Alcazar*, in *The Dramatic Works of George Peele*, ed. George Tyler Prouty, 3 vols (New Haven, 1961–70).

William Rowley, Thomas Dekker and John Ford, *The Witch of Edmonton*, ed. Peter Corbin and Douglas Sedge (Manchester, 1999).

Mary Sidney, *The Tragedy of Antonie*, in *Renaissance Drama by Women: Texts and Documents*, ed. S. P. Cerasano and Marion Wynne-Davies (London and New York, 1996).

Thomas of Woodstock, ed. Peter Corbin and Douglas Sedge (Manchester, 2002).

Cyril Tourneur, *The Atheist's Tragedy*, ed. Irving Ribner (London, 1964).

William Wager, *Enough is as Good as a Feast*, in *'The Longer Thou Livest' and 'Enough is as Good as a Feast'*, ed. R. Mark Benbow (London, 1967).

John Webster, *The Devil's Law-Case*, ed. Elizabeth M. Brennan (London and Tonbridge, 1975).
John Webster, *The Duchess of Malfi*, ERD.
John Webster, *The White Devil*, ERD.

Suggestions for further reading

1 The Renaissance theatre

David M. Bevington, *From 'Mankind' to Marlowe: Growth of Structure in the Popular Drama of Tudor England* (Cambridge, Mass., 1962).

A. R. Braunmuller and Michael Hattaway, eds, *The Cambridge Companion to English Renaissance Drama* (Cambridge, 1990).

Stephen Greenblatt, *Shakespearean Negotiations: The Circulation of Social Energy in Renaissance England* (Oxford, 1988).

Andrew Gurr, *Playgoing in Shakespeare's London*, 2nd edn (Cambridge, 1987).

Andrew Gurr, *The Shakespearean Stage, 1574–1642*, 3rd edn (Cambridge, 1992).

Jean E. Howard, *The Stage and Social Struggle in Early Modern England* (London and New York, 1994).

G. K. Hunter, *English Drama, 1586–1642: The Age of Shakespeare* (Oxford, 1997).

David Scott Kastan and Peter Stallybrass, eds, *Staging the Renaissance: Reinterpretations of Elizabethan and Jacobean Drama* (London, 1991).

Laura Levine, *Men in Women's Clothing: Anti-theatricality and Effeminization, 1579–1642* (Cambridge, 1994).

Louis A. Montrose, *The Purpose of Playing: Shakespeare and the Cultural Politics of the Elizabethan Theatre* (Chicago, 1996).

Steven Mullaney, *The Place of the Stage: License, Play, and Power in Renaissance England* (Chicago, 1988).

2 Identity and gender

Francis Barker, *The Tremulous Private Body: Essays on Subjection* (Ann Arbor, 1995).

Catherine Belsey, *The Subject of Tragedy: Identity and Difference in Renaissance Drama* (London and New York, 1985).

Mark Breitenberg, *Anxious Masculinity in Early Modern England* (Cambridge, 1996).

Marjorie Garber, *Coming of Age in Shakespeare* (London and New York, 1981).

Stephen Greenblatt, *Renaissance Self-Fashioning: From More to Shakespeare* (Chicago and London, 1980).

Lisa Jardine, *Still Harping on Daughters: Women and Drama in the Age of Shakespeare* (New York, 1983).

Coppélia Kahn, *Man's Estate: Masculine Identity in Shakespeare* (Berkeley, 1981).

Carolyn Lenz *et al.*, eds, *The Woman's Part: Feminist Criticism of Shakespeare* (Urbana, 1980).

Katharine Eisaman Maus, *Inwardness and Theater in the English Renaissance* (Chicago and London, 1995).

Sara Mendelson and Patricia Crawford, *Women in Early Modern England, 1550–1720* (Oxford, 1998).

Michael Neill, *Issues of Death: Mortality and Identity in English Renaissance Tragedy* (Oxford, 1997).

Karen Newman, *Fashioning Femininity and English Renaissance Drama* (Chicago and London, 1991).

Stephen Orgel, *Impersonations: The Performance of Gender in Shakespeare's England* (Cambridge, 1996).

Gail Kern Paster, *The Body Embarrassed: Drama and the Disciplines of Shame in Early Modern England* (Ithaca, 1993).

Bruce R. Smith, *Shakespeare and Masculinity* (Oxford, 2000).

Frank Whigham, *Seizures of the Will in Early Modern English Drama* (Cambridge, 1996).

3 Desire and domesticity

Janet Adelman, *Suffocating Mothers: Fantasies of Maternal Origin in Shakespeare's Plays, 'Hamlet' to 'The Tempest'* (New York and London, 1992).

Celia Daileader, *Eroticism on the Renaissance Stage* (Cambridge, 1998).

Mario DiGangi, *The Homoerotics of Early Modern Drama* (Cambridge, 1997).

Heather Dubrow, *Shakespeare and Domestic Loss: Forms of Deprivation, Mourning and Recuperation* (Cambridge, 1999).

Peter Erickson, *Patriarchal Structures in Shakespeare's Drama* (Berkeley, 1985).

Jonathan Goldberg, *Sodometries: Renaissance Texts, Modern Sexualities* (Stanford, 1992).

Jeffrey Masten, *Textual Intercourse: Collaboration, Authorship, and Sexualities in Renaissance Drama* (Cambridge, 1997).

Carol Thomas Neely, *Broken Nuptials in Shakespeare's Plays* (New Haven and London, 1985).

Marianne Novy, *Love's Argument: Gender Relations in Shakespeare* (Chapel Hill, 1984).

Mary Beth Rose, *The Expense of Spirit: Love and Sexuality in English Renaissance Drama* (Ithaca, 1988).

Bruce R. Smith, *Homosexual Desire in Shakespeare's England: A Cultural Poetics* (Chicago and London, 1991).

Lawrence Stone, *The Family, Sex and Marriage in England 1500–1800* (London, 1979).

Valerie Traub, *Desire and Anxiety: Circulations of Sexuality in Shakespearean Drama* (London, 1992).

Valerie Traub, *The Renaissance of Lesbianism in Early Modern England* (Cambridge, 2002).

Susan Zimmerman, ed., *Erotic Politics: Desire on the Renaissance Stage* (New York and London, 1992).

4 Society

Jean-Christophe Agnew, *Worlds Apart: The Market and the Theater in Anglo-American Thought, 1550–1750* (Cambridge, 1986).

Michael D. Bristol, *Carnival and Theater: Plebeian Culture and the Structure of Authority in Renaissance England* (New York and London, 1985).

Douglas Bruster, *Drama and the Market in the Age of Shakespeare* (Cambridge, 1992).

Jonathan Haynes, *The Social Relations of Jonson's Theatre* (Cambridge, 1992).

Richard Helgerson, *Forms of Nationhood: The Elizabethan Writing of England* (Chicago and London, 1992).

Jean E. Howard and Phyllis Rackin, *Engendering a Nation: A Feminist Account of Shakespeare's English Histories* (London and New York, 1997).

Ronald Knowles, ed., *Shakespeare and Carnival: After Bakhtin* (Basingstoke, 1998).

Lawrence Manley, *Literature and Culture in Early Modern London* (Cambridge, 1995).

Annabel Patterson, *Shakespeare and the Popular Voice* (London, 1989).

J. A. Sharpe, *Early Modern England, A Social History 1550–1760* (London, 1987).

David L. Smith *et al.*, eds, *The Theatrical City: Culture, Theatre and Politics in London, 1579–1649* (Cambridge, 1995).

Robert Weimann, *Shakespeare and the Popular Tradition in the Theatre* (Baltimore, 1978).

Keith Wrightson, *English Society 1580–1680* (London, 1982).

5 Religion

Patrick Collinson, *The Birthpangs of Protestant England: Religious and Cultural Change in the Sixteenth and Seventeenth Centuries* (Basingstoke, 1988).

Donna Hamilton and Richard Strier, eds, *Religion, Literature and Politics in Post-Reformation England, 1540–1688* (Cambridge, 1996).

John Knott, *Discourses of Martyrdom in English Literature, 1563–1694* (Cambridge, 1993).

Claire McEachern and Debora Shuger, eds, *Religion and Culture in Renaissance England* (Cambridge, 1997).

Kristen Poole, *Radical Religion from Shakespeare to Milton: Figures of Nonconformity in Early Modern England* (Cambridge, 2000).

Marsha S. Robinson, *Writing the Reformation: 'Actes and Monuments' and the Jacobean History Play* (Aldershot, 2002).

Debora Shuger, *Habits of Thought in the English Renaissance: Religion, Politics, and the Dominant Culture* (Berkeley, 1990).

Alan Sinfield, *Literature in Protestant England 1560–1660* (London and Canberra, 1983).

John Stachniewski, *The Persecutory Imagination: English Puritanism and the Literature of Religious Despair* (Oxford, 1991).

Alexandra Walsham, *Providence in Early Modern England* (Oxford, 1999).

6 Politics and the court

Rebecca Bushnell, *Tragedies of Tyrants: Political Thought and Theater in the English Renaissance* (Ithaca, 1990).

Martin Butler, *Theatre and Crisis 1632–1642* (Cambridge, 1984).

Jonathan Dollimore, *Radical Tragedy: Religion, Ideology and Power in the Drama of Shakespeare and his Contemporaries*, 2nd edn (New York, 1989).

Jonathan Dollimore and Alan Sinfield, *Political Shakespeare: Essays in Cultural Materialism*, 2nd edn (Manchester, 1994).

Jonathan Goldberg, *James I and the Politics of Literature: Jonson, Shakespeare, Donne, and their Contemporaries* (Baltimore and London, 1983).

Margot Heinemann, *Puritanism and Theatre: Thomas Middleton and Opposition Drama under the Early Stuarts* (Cambridge, 1980).

J. W. Lever, *The Tragedy of State* (London, 1971).

Stephen Orgel, *The Illusion of Power: Political Theatre in the English Renaissance* (Berkeley, 1975).

J. P. Sommerville, *Royalists and Patriots: Politics and Ideology in England 1603–1640* (London and New York, 1999).

Leonard Tennenhouse, *Power on Display: The Politics of Shakespeare's Genres* (New York and London, 1986).

Albert Tricomi, *Anti-Court Drama in England 1603–1642* (Charlottesville, 1989).

7 Race and colonialism

Catherine Alexander and Stanley Wells, eds, *Shakespeare and Race* (Cambridge, 2000).

Anthony Barthelemy, *Black Face, Maligned Race: The Representation of Blacks in English Drama from Shakespeare to Southerne* (Baton Rouge, 1987).

Jack D'Amico, *The Moor in English Renaissance Drama* (Tampa, 1991).

Stephen Greenblatt, *Marvelous Possessions: The Wonder of the New World* (Oxford, 1991).

Andrew Hadfield, *Literature, Travel, and Colonial Writing in the English Renaissance 1545–1625* (Oxford, 1998).

Kim F. Hall, *Things of Darkness: Economies of Race and Gender in Early Modern England* (Ithaca, 1995).

Margo Hendricks and Patricia Parker, eds, *Women, 'Race,' and Writing in the Early Modern Period* (London, 1994).

Ania Loomba, *Gender, Race, Renaissance Drama* (Manchester, 1989).

Ania Loomba and Martin Orkin, eds, *Post-Colonial Shakespeares* (London and New York, 1998).

Joyce Green MacDonald, *Race, Ethnicity, and Power in the Renaissance* (Madison, NJ, 1997).

Joyce Green MacDonald, *Women and Race in Early Modern Texts* (Cambridge, 2002).

James Shapiro, *Shakespeare and the Jews* (New York, 1996).

Index